An American Stand

An American Stand

Senator Margaret Chase Smith and the Communist Menace, 1948–1972

Eric R. Crouse

LEXINGTON BOOKS
A division of

ROWMAN & LITTLEFIELD PUBLISHERS, INC.
Lanham • Boulder • New York • Toronto • Plymouth, UK

Published by Lexington Books
A division of Rowman & Littlefield Publishers, Inc.
A wholly owned subsidiary of The Rowman & Littlefield Publishing Group, Inc.
4501 Forbes Boulevard, Suite 200, Lanham, Maryland 20706
http://www.lexingtonbooks.com

Estover Road, Plymouth PL6 7PY, United Kingdom

Copyright © 2010 by Lexington Books
First paperback edition 2013

British Library Cataloguing in Publication Information Available

Library of Congress Cataloging-in-Publication Data

The harback edition of this book was previously cataloged by the Library of Congress as
follows:

Crouse, Eric Robert, 1960-
  An American stand : Senator Margaret Chase Smith and the communist menace, 1948-
1972 / Eric R. Crouse.
    p. cm.
  Includes bibliographical references and index.
  1. Smith, Margaret Chase, 1897-1995. 2. Anti-communist movements—United States—
History. 3. Women legislators—United States—Biography. 4. United States. Congress.
Senate—Biography. 5. United States—Politics and government—1945-1989. 6. Maine—
Politics and government—1865-1950. 7. Maine—Politics and government—1951- I. Title.
  E748.S667C76 2010
  328.73'092—dc22
  [B]   2010013831

ISBN: 978-0-7391-4442-8 (cloth : alk. paper)
ISBN: 978-0-7391-8184-3 (pbk. : alk. paper)
ISBN: 978-0-7391-4444-2 (electronic)

Printed in the United States of America

Table of Contents

Acknowledgments

Writing a book that covers the big topics of McCarthyism, the Korean War, nuclear arms, the Vietnam War, popular opinion, and a successful female politician was an enjoyable process made even better by the assistance and support that I received along the way from many people. I lost count of those who shared stories of Margaret Chase Smith.

Collection specialist Angela Stockwell of the Margaret Chase Smith Library was a great help, always responding promptly to my many requests. One of my best purchases was a book I bought at the Margaret Chase Smith Library years ago. I would have been lost without Janann Sherman's *No Place for a Woman: A Life of Senator Margaret Chase Smith* (2000). I am thankful for the support of the Ada E. Leeke Research Fellowship for *An American Stand* and for *Dear Senator Smith: Small-Town Maine Writes to Senator Margaret Chase Smith about the Vietnam War, 1967–1971* (2008).

I am grateful for Joseph Parry of Lexington Books in supporting both *Dear Senator Smith* and *An American Stand*. I really appreciate the impressive speed and quality of work of Lexington Books. Comments from anonymous readers provided invaluable feedback. Some material of this book can be found in "Senator Margaret Chase Smith Against McCarthyism: The Methodist Influence," *Methodist History* 46, no. 3 (April 2008): 167–78. I thank this journal for granting permission to republish some sections in revised form.

The support of Tyndale University College is wonderful. There are only a few Christian universities in Canada and I am fortunate to be in an environment where there are high standards for academic scholarship and religious faith. Daniel Scott, dean of the university, always granted my requests for help in pushing this project forward. The Tyndale Faculty Research Fund was also essential. I am grateful to Ian Gentles, an accomplished historian in another field, for directing my attention to *The Black Book of Communism* and for his advice and support. I am also thankful for the support of Helen Noh, Sujin Yang, Daniel Wong, and Brad Faught. The Tyndale library staff of Norma Stuckless, Jennifer Spencer, and Hugh Rendle assisted me on many occasions. Michelyne Goulet, Will Kinchlea, and Ruth Whitt were helpful with formatting, and Victor Degtiarev and other members of the IT Department solved any computer problems that I experienced.

My wife Ann-Marie is the great woman in my life, and I am blessed beyond words.

Finally, hearing stories from missionaries and others who experienced unbelievable suffering in communist-controlled countries opened my eyes to a side of communist leadership that usually receives little attention in American foreign policy history books. My hope is that I have been fair in my assessment of how various Americans responded to the threat of communism, a danger that appeared very real to many but less so to others.

Introduction

For one and one half hours on the steps of a college library in May 1970, Senator Margaret Chase Smith stood before the angry and curious faces of mostly college students in the manner she knew and had exercised in her twenty plus years as a senator. Her character exemplified moral absolutism or misguided self-righteousness; she would stay as long as the students wanted to challenge her support for Richard Nixon's Vietnam War policy, notably the American troop "incursion" in Cambodia.

The college audience mattered because the Vietnam War had touched the lives of students in graphic or subtle ways, because she herself had no college education, and because she believed that the students could learn from older Americans, particularly from a woman who in a man's world had taken a stand on many major Cold War issues. And why should they not listen to the first woman in American history to be elected in both the House of Representatives and the Senate, the first politician to take a public stand against Senator Joseph McCarthy's wild accusations, the first woman seriously considered as a vice president, the first woman of a major political party to run for president of the United States, and the only woman to serve a long term on the powerful Senate Armed Services Committee? Had she not proven herself in the eyes of the "greatest generation," those men and women who "were participants in and witness to sacrifices of the highest order" in the Great Depression and World War II years?[1] Should not young people also trust her for choosing the best path for America?

This study is not a biography and there is no attempt to offer a fuller treatment of Smith's relations with Republican leadership and her links to constituents concerned with many issues beyond national security.[2] The focus is on the major anticommunist episodes of her years in the Senate, especially her rhetoric and beliefs and the coast-to-coast response of mostly ordinary Americans, many of whom defined the Cold War as mainly a fight between good and evil. The book's central argument is that America's confrontation with global communism, at great sacrifice of lives and money, continued to make sense to Smith and other like-minded people because they never lost their belief that communism was a sinister system that did not properly respect human life and the freedoms and values held dear by Americans. Many appeared to embrace the notion of the grand narrative of American exceptionalism which assumed the United States was "a divinely favored nation with unique freedoms." Protection of "the blessings of liberty" was paramount and what unfolded in the minds of some was a theology of anticommunism that saw evil behind the actions of communist leaders.[3]

For those inclined to view communism as evil or even the Cold War as a "spiritual war," there were abundant stories of communist repression and terror in newspapers and magazines throughout the 1950s and 1960s. Recent scholarship on the crimes of communism claims that communist regimes were "criminal enterprises in their very essence" carrying out the planned killing of at least 85 million people in the twentieth century. The argument goes that communism was not a benign system that took a mythical "wrong turn" under the direction of any particularly brutal leader. Rather, its goal from start to finish was to crush all "class enemies."[4]

Given that she was one of few women in Congress and that she earned the reputation as a moderate on most issues, her position on national security makes for an especially interesting case. If she did not fully embrace an "inherently evil" argument, she came close. A recent study on foreign policy and religion claims that many American political leaders of the early Cold War years "perceived communism to be evil" because of its "dogmatic atheism"; America's mission was to oppose communism and the feared spread of "godless materialism around the world."[5] Discussing the power of communist governments in her newspaper column "Washington and You," Smith wrote that communism "defends violence and evil force as a means of grabbing and keeping such ownership and control by dictators. It is anti-religious and a relentless foe of the church" and anyone could see "the evil of it and to reject it vigorously." On many occasions, she publicly stated that communist leaders were "evil men."[6] Singling out the Soviet Union, she wrote that its "leaders may change but they all continue the same policy of hate and dreams of world conquest."[7] With communism "human life is worth nothing" and even the lives of earlier communist leaders such as Vladimir Lenin and Joseph Stalin "meant nothing," since "they are now merely names which their evil followers use only" to ensure enslavement of the people.[8] As she saw it, "the very creed of communism is to ruthlessly kill anything that stands in its path toward world domination and slavery."[9]

To be sure, such rhetoric voiced in the early 1950s with America at war in Korea was not unusual for the times, but Smith did offer similar statements throughout the 1960s and her zealous opposition to the "extreme Leftists" in the United States, in her final years in the Senate, reveals a broadened fear that communist forces were successful in inciting civil disorder at home. She had always been aware of the potential danger of communism within America, but it was late in her political career before she saw left radicalism as a threat approaching the seriousness of any external communist threat.[10] Her focus was mainly on elite communist leadership abroad. The important point for her was that the main driving force behind communism was a heinous ideology rather than geopolitics or the flawed character of a particular communist leader.[11] Simply put, communist leaders were sinister because communism was sinister.

From the late 1940s to the early 1970s, Smith faced the challenges of a woman, with ordinary and modest beginnings, placed in the center of political power. Recent scholarship exploring gender in foreign policymaking identifies a brotherhood of warrior intellectuals who upheld an ideology of masculinity and conformed to Cold War orthodoxy that had no room for talk of appeasement. Establishment males who entered national security circles (politicians and bureaucrats) drew on the "masculine code of strength, loyalty, stoic service, and engagement in struggle" modeled in elite boarding schools, Ivy League fraternities, and the military.[12] This was not Smith's world, but she did embrace the manly traits of toughness and courage in the fight against communism no less so than the male brotherhood of elite anticommunists. As a woman often employing a masculine disposition, she stands out as one of the more captivating anticommunists of the Cold War years. If Harry S. Truman was the first Cold Warrior who saw the Cold War "as nothing less than a religious war," Smith was the first female Cold Warrior.[13] In addition to gender considerations, her stand on communism offers a particularly fascinating view on the importance of ideas and beliefs in motivating people to fight communism.[14]

She first gained intense nationwide attention after June 1, 1950, when she confronted McCarthy for his irresponsible methods of attacking communism in the United States and the government's complacency in fighting the red menace. Twelve days later she was on the cover of *Newsweek* with the story line, "Senator Smith: A Woman Vice President?" Moderate Republicans, Democrats, and other progressive Americans responded to her "heroic" confrontation with appreciation and praise, believing she represented a more appropriate and honorable anticommunism devoid of selfish political opportunism. However, it is important to note that she shared many of the goals of the most fervent anticommunists, a confusing fact in light of her opposition to McCarthy's methods.

Delighted that Smith visited "Free China" at a volatile time in 1955, Madame Chiang Kai-shek acknowledged the senator's "courageous and gallant stand" against communism as many Americans likewise did throughout her Senate career.[15] Further evidence of her intense anticommunism is clear in her position on the Korean War, the nuclear arms race, and America's involvement in Southeast Asia. When a growing number of Americans could not comprehend America's commitment in Vietnam, where young men were dying and where the government was spending billions of dollars, Smith and her supporters maintained that the United States could not choose "appeasement" to the forces of Ho Chi Minh. For her, it was simple: the communists desired to control the world and the United States had to stop them. If antiwar Americans found government arguments for the domino theory nonsense, there were others unwilling to take any chances with a sinister force.

In Cold War rhetoric, the communist "menace" was more than a manufactured concept brimming with emotional sway.[16] The reality and examples of communist repression were ubiquitous and Smith wanted America to hit back hard to stop communists' violent plan to destroy the free world. Stalin did abandon Lenin's prediction of revolutions arising in advanced industrial countries, but he did not discard the goal of world revolution in favor of "socialism in one country."[17] Unconvinced that the Soviet Union desired "peaceful coexistence," Smith believed that the Soviet leaders expected and worked toward the destruction of capitalism. The arguments of critics who opposed hard-line Cold War views rang hollow to others greatly troubled by the repressiveness of atheistic communism. In her final years in Washington, she found the Vietnam War frustrating and longed for its completion, but she had little sympathy for the position that highlighted the injustices of American society, that viewed the nuclear arms race as immoral, and that understood America's involvement in Vietnam as an injudicious venture that prevented the self-determination of the Vietnamese people. If her worldview was too simplistic, it was, nevertheless, commanding in its clarity. Repeatedly taking a "stand," Smith embodied the degree of power and purpose that some thought was necessary to combat communist "slavery."

Communist leaders were willing to sacrifice the lives of massive numbers of citizens and soldiers to realize their military and political goals. For North Vietnam's foremost military figure (Vo Nguyen Giap), the war was not a tragedy but "a noble sacrifice."[18] In wars, there are evil acts committed on all sides. The antiwar movement viewed the devastation caused by American bombing as immoral and there were incidents of American ground troops perpetrating horrific criminal acts in Southeast Asia.[19] Still, only a small number of Americans saw the United States as an evil and lawless nation that had no interest in bringing to justice those identified as committing a crime. In contrast, the record for human justice in twentieth century communist regimes is a catastrophic one.

There were Americans in communist circles with sincere and noble ideals who were unaware of the horrific murders and evil acts carried out by the communist leadership in the Soviet Union.[20] The exodus of communists breaking from the Party after Nikita Khrushchev's famous February 1956 speech that exposed the murderous crimes of Stalin bears this out. But as the sixties unfolded, leftists and some liberals increasingly challenged Cold War thinking and lost to them was the belief that violence was the defining characteristic of communism. Their focus was on a war conducted by deceitful politicians, a war they described as categorically meaningless.

The major arguments put forward by opponents of the Vietnam War were good ones: the United States was culturally ignorant of Vietnamese society and history; American policymakers incorrectly viewed Vietnam as "a Cold War crucible" or, in other words, a front in the conflict between communist powerhouses and the United States; Southeast Asia did not warrant being central in American strategic and economic thinking; it was wrong to claim that American credibility would suffer if the communists prevailed; other options beyond American military intervention existed; and the United States should have allowed Vietnamese nationalism to take its natural course along communist revolutionary lines.[21] For a small number of radical antiwar activists, the Vietnam War did the most in casting communism as a system that offered a better option than the capitalistic imperialism that they argued was the practice of the United States. In their eyes, it certainly was not the malignant system that some estimate had murdered approximately 70 million Asians, mostly by the "deliberate policy" of using famine as a weapon.[22]

As influential as various antiwar arguments were for a significant number of Americans in the late 1960s, they had far less resonance with conservative Christians fixated on the belief that communism was an atheistic and aggressive system that had no or few redeeming qualities. America's surprisingly high level of religiosity made it an oddity among other modern-industrial Western nations; church membership from the years 1950 to 1970 ranged between 55 and 69 percent of the population.[23] In particular, there were the evangelicals composing as much as one third of the population, who grew up hearing stories of pious missionaries donating most of their lives in Asia in the nineteenth and twentieth centuries.[24] Nelson Bell, Billy Graham's father-in-law, was a passionate Cold Warrior who drew on his many years in Asia as a missionary in arguing for greater military action to defeat communism. Were not the experiences and knowledge of missionaries of Southeast Asia as valid as that of other voices, including those Asian experts removed from the State Department during the McCarthy hysteria?[25] In their view of communism, conservative Catholics and Protestants had an intense awareness of Original Sin and spiritual darkness, a worldview that mystified some secular humanists. In literature, radio, film, and revival campaigns, Billy Graham warned Americans that communism "is master-minded by Satan."[26] Cardinal Francis Spellman of New York spoke for countless Catholics when he declared that "Christ-hating communists" pledged their allegiance to Satan.[27] Popular books by Catholics such as Thomas Dooley's _Deliver Us From Evil: The Story of Viet Nam's Flight to Freedom_ (1956) revealed the evils of "Communist terror."[28] _Our Sunday Visitor_, _The Brooklyn Tablet_, and _The Tidings_ were among the Catholic publications filled with heroic tales of martyrs who opposed communist evil.[29] There are always exceptions, but conservative Catholic and Protestant leaders were less likely to question America's conflict with aggressive communism, be it in Korea, Southeast Asia, or anywhere else in the world. They recognized evil when they saw it, and their message reached far beyond their church constituents.

Actually, most Americans did not require churches to instruct them on the ways of communist leaders. There were the events of the Hungarian Revolution (1956), the construction of the Berlin Wall (1961), and the Soviet invasion of Czechoslovakia (1968), to name only three. Americans without any consistent adherence to formal religious traditions were vigilant foes of communism. In newspaper and magazine reports, rhetorical texts laden with powerful images and symbols concerning Cold War conflicts enlisted the sympathies of ordinary Americans for the defeat of the evil "other." In the early Cold War years, there were numerous Americans quick to challenge any force seeking to destroy their cherished freedoms and, in fact, missed by strident McCarthyites was the breadth of the anticommunist movement. There were liberal anticommunists no less committed to fighting communism than McCarthyites; even most American socialists had no love for revolutionary communism.[30]

Smith's understanding was better than some and she viewed a communist as "a black-sheep cousin of a Socialist."[31] Although not a religious leader she appeared to be a woman of integrity for those seeking leaders they could trust to protect Americanism from communist assaults. She did believe that "an extremely strong factor in meeting the communist challenge is religion," yet she kept spiritual language general and to a minimum and thus she did not offend broader America.[32] She was more a toned-down Moses guiding the people on what she believed was the right path.[33] As one biographer argues, "Cold War morality, not raw meat, motivated Smith."[34]

One study of anticommunism in America mistakenly claims that "anticommunism at the populist level is an ideology of unhappiness. It is not, in this sense, the voice of the 'real' America."[35] But if understood as an "orientational metaphor," a "stand" is positive and representative of something that is inspiring.[36] Upholding duty and action against forces that might weaken American values, Smith was one who took a "stand" against global communism in a manner that attracted praise from the press and ordinary people in every region of the nation. Of course, she had weaknesses. For example, usually quiet in the Senate, her political visibility was spotty and when she did go on record a parochial and impatient tone occasionally surfaced. Nonetheless, she remained a credible source to a wide spectrum of "real" Americans, even if they did not always agree with her. There were liberals who appreciated her stand against McCarthy and conservatives who supported her consistent anticommunist hard-line stand on foreign policy. Smith encouraged newspaper mythmaking that portrayed her as a consistent and principled Cold Warrior who appealed to grassroots Americans. In the long run, her opposition to communism was an enduring theme that garnered a high degree of attention, for better or worse, coast to coast. Rarely using explicit spiritual rhetoric, but getting a Manichean-type message out nonetheless, she made it clear that communism was a dangerous force that threatened goodness.

How Smith rose to political standing is the focus of chapter 1. From a working-class family and with no college education, she reached high and won a Senate seat in 1948. Making the cover of *U.S. News and World Report*, she was a bright spot for the Republican Party that witnessed the defeat of Thomas Dewey to Harry S. Truman and the loss of seventy-four seats in the House and nine seats in the Senate.[37] What is striking is her emergence as a Cold Warrior who concentrated on the serious and "masculine" issue of national security in the wake of the red menace. Her credibility as one who was not soft on communism is the main theme covered in chapter 2. How did she survive her stand against McCarthyism when almost all of her male colleagues ducked for cover? Certainly, the reaction to her "Declaration of Conscience" speech, which sought to protect the freedoms dear to the American people, underscored the contested terrain of what was an appropriate response to communism. Many liberals took the communist threat seriously, but the excesses of McCarthy were unacceptable. Chapter 3 centers on Smith's assessments of the Korean War published in her syndicated column "Washington and You." Clarifying her Cold War credentials, she voiced hard-line rhetoric and stimulating views that generated good discussion at a time when there was an information vacuum from the White House. Chapter 4 examines why leaders such as Nikita Khrushchev described her as "the devil in a disguise of a woman" and why many Americans supported her views on the nuclear arms race. For her, the credibility of a massive nuclear response to any attacks was essential. Given the rarity of female senators, it is ironic and revealing that there were few male politicians as rigid as Smith on articulating a clear message of deterrence. Chapter 5 pays particular attention to the divide among Americans on the nation's involvement in Southeast Asia. In response to the antiwar movement, she repeatedly argued that the United States was in Vietnam "to stop the communists from conquering the world." Difficult to comprehend for some, she continued to believe that war against the communist menace was a righteous cause. In her eyes, the communist system had not softened to the point that American and communist leaders could sit down and reconcile their differences. Smith did lose political ground when she failed to offer a judicious response to those opposing the war and when Nixon's visits to Beijing and Moscow in early 1972 appeared to undercut her long-standing position on "evil" communist leaders.

All in all, Smith's anticommunist beliefs were not irrational notions based mainly on ignorance. Even if she and other supporters embraced a different position from that of intellectuals and pundits opposed to the war, they still used their minds for a critical examination of what they perceived was ultimately of greater importance in defending America. In such thinking, there were traces of a just war theory that justified a level of destruction if it prevented greater evil.[38] Smith would have supported much of revisionist scholarship that views America's involvement in Southeast Asia as a noble cause.[39] She wanted the military to do whatever it took to finish the job of defeating the communists, meaning more bombs and no half measures, so that the American troops could return home sooner rather than later. Praised or condemned, she remained true to a clear stand against communist expansion by aggression. However, this apparently winning formula that had served her well in the past was not enough to secure her victory in 1972.

And yet Smith's Cold Warrior stand was not the main reason for her political loss. Even as Nixon carried out détente with communist leaders, the perceived brutal nature of communism allowed a long shelf life for Cold Warriors.[40] After the experiences of the sixties, America in the 1970s and beyond was more conservative than many thought possible. As one sixties radical put it, "The Right took over the government, the Left took over the English department."[41] Smith lost due to a number of mistakes, including a failure to offer constituents a vision or plan to justify her place in Washington for six more years. Rather than forward-looking and inspiring, her memoirs released at the beginning of the campaign had an angry and defensive tone which seemed to substantiate accusations that she easily took offense with those who allegedly slighted her. An unfavorable assessor of the memoirs, wrote of "a world sharply divided into friends, traitors and enemies, with the lady senator always vindicated (occasionally vindictive) and triumphant."[42] This certainly hurt her case. But even more significant, Smith simply lacked the energy to stand forcefully in a stirring manner, as she had in key moments throughout her political career, in order to remain credible in the male domain of Washington politics. While she and executive assistant William C. Lewis pondered the devastating loss in November 1972, Nixon, another earlier Cold Warrior (who scored high marks with his visits to China and the Soviet Union), basked in the glory of an overwhelming victory over George McGovern, who represented the hope of antiwar liberals and others on the left.

The position of Smith's public statements and her correspondence with ordinary Americans is unmistakable. On the issue of communism, she rarely unmasked any political calculations, subtleties, or contradictions that probably existed behind her Cold War thinking. By opposing communism forcefully, she believed she could help protect the United States for all present and future Americans. Her consistent masculine Cold War stand against the apparent evil nature of communism, stark in its simplicity, was consistent with the ideal that great sacrifices sprung from moral duty. She did her part by rejecting any elusion or sanitization of the ruthless and murderous actions of communists, but her anticommunist stand that worked in the 1950s and early 1960s received greater scrutiny after 1965 when Americans responded to the battles being fought both in Southeast Asia and on the home front.

NOTES

1. Tom Brokaw, *The Greatest Generation* (New York: Random House, 1998), 11.

2. For a full biographical treatment of Smith, see Janann Sherman, *No Place for a Woman: A Life of Senator Margaret Chase Smith* (New Brunswick, N.J.: Rutgers University Press, 2000).

3. On exceptionalism, see Frank Costigliola and Thomas G. Paterson, "Defining and Doing the History of United States Foreign Relations: A Primer," in *Explaining the History of American Foreign Relations*, 2nd ed., ed. Michael J. Hogan and Thomas G. Paterson (Cambridge: Cambridge University Press, 2004), 11–13. My use of the term "theology" is from Ernest R. May's comments on Robert McNamara's Vietnam War book. May writes: "There was a theology at the time, or at least a set of beliefs, that the book does not capture." See Robert S. McNamara, *In Retrospect: The Tragedy and Lessons of Vietnam* (New York: Vintage Books, 1996), 422. Also, see "'Cold War' Termed a Spiritual Clash," *New York Times*, 16 June 1952 and "World Seen Split by Two Ideologies," *New York Times*, 18 July 1949. For a discussion on the communist threat to American values in the early twentieth century, see Melvyn P. Leffler, *The Specter of Communism: The United States and the Origins of the Cold War, 1917–1953* (New York: Hill and Wang, 1994), 14–15. For a study that focuses on the core values of policymakers as they relate to economic and technological superiority, see Melvyn P. Leffler, *A Preponderance of Power: National Security, the Truman Administration, and the Cold War* (Stanford: Stanford University Press, 1992).

4. Séphance Courtois, et al., *The Black Book of Communism: Crimes, Terror, Repression*, trans. Jonathan Murphy and Mark Kramer (Cambridge, Mass.: Harvard University Press, 1999), x, xvii–xviii, 4.

5. William Inboden, *Religion and American Foreign Policy, 1945–1960* (Cambridge University Press, 2008), 4.

6. "Important to Know What Communism Is," "Washington and You" (W&Y), 28 January 1953, Margaret Chase Smith Library (MCSL). The best source for Smith's usage of the term "evil" is her newspaper column, particularly the years 1950–1953.

7. World Trip Report, 18 April 1955, World Trip 1954–1955 Folder, MCSL.

8. "We Should Use Stalin's Death as a Weapon," W&Y, 17 March 1953, MCSL.

9. W&Y, 26 January 1953, MCSL.

10. Elaine Tyler May argues that many Americans believed that "the real dangers to America were internal ones" and one could find refuge in the family and home. See May, *Homeward Bound: American Families in the Cold War Era*, 2nd ed. (New York: Basic Books, 2008), 9.

11. Cold War historian John Lewis Gaddis writes that it was not clear whether any other Soviet would have implemented collectivization of agriculture and industrialization "with the brutality Stalin relied upon, or that they would have followed them with massive purges against mostly imaginary enemies." See John Lewis Gaddis, *We Now Know: Rethinking Cold War History* (Oxford: Oxford University Press, 1997), 8. Gaddis cites that Stalin's policies before World War II resulted in at least 17 million deaths.

12. Robert D. Dean, *Imperial Brotherhood: Gender and the Making of Cold War Foreign Policy* (Amherst: University of Massachusetts Press, 2001), 4–5, 19.

13. On Truman, see Elizabeth Edwards Spalding, *The First Cold Warrior: Harry Truman, Containment, and the Remaking of Liberal Internationalism* (Lexington: University Press of Kentucky, 2006); and on Truman and "religious war," see Inboden, *Religion and American Foreign Policy, 1945–1960*, 1. On Smith, see Patricia Ward Wallace, *Politics of Conscience: A Biography of Margaret Chase Smith* (Westport, Conn.: Praeger, 1995), 131. Wallace writes, "In her long-nurtured role as military expert she decided to confront the evil of world communism and became the nation's first female cold warrior."

14. In *We Now Know*, Gaddis writes that "historians of the Cold War need to look quite carefully at what those who *saw* distinctions between good and evil *thought and did* about them." As historians, "we have to take seriously what *they at the time believed*" (287). Helpful is Melvyn P. Leffler, "The Cold War: What Do 'We Now Know'?" *The American Historical Review* 104, no. 2 (April 1999): 501–24.

15. Madame Chiang Kai-shek to MCS, 9 May 1955, World Trip Folder, MCSL.

16. For more on language and emotion, see Frank Costigliola, "The Creation of Memory and Myth," in *Critical Reflections on the Cold War: Linking Rhetoric and History*, ed. Martin J. Medhurst and H. W. Brands (College Station: Texas A & M University Press, 2000), 38–54.

17. Gaddis, *We Now Know*, 13–14.

18. Christian G. Appy, *Patriots: The Vietnam War Remembered from All Sides* (New York: Viking, 2003), 43.

19. In 1970, a Citizens Commission of Inquiry into U.S. War Crimes began hearings. See Charles DeBenedetti and Charles Chatfield, *An American Ordeal: The Antiwar Movement of the Vietnam Era* (Syracuse: Syracuse University Press, 1990), 307.

20. Like virtually every human being, the leftist Americans of these years wanted their lives to have meaning. Many communists and others on the left did do good works for the working class, African Americans, and others exploited in an often harsh urban-industrial environment; left-wing social action in the United States improved the lot of a considerable number of Americans.

21. These themes are discussed in Andrew J. Rotter, "Chronicle of a War Foretold: The United States and Vietnam, 1945–1954," in *The First Vietnam War: Colonial Conflict and Cold War Crisis*, ed. Mark Atwood Lawrence and Fredrik Logevall (Cambridge, Mass.: Harvard University Press, 2007), 282–306.

22. Courtois, et al., *The Black Book of Communism*, xviii, 4.

23. Stephen J. Whitfield, *The Culture of the Cold War*, 2nd ed. (Baltimore: The Johns Hopkins University Press, 1996), 83.

24. For example, see Wayne Flynt and Gerald W. Berkley, *Taking Christianity to China: Alabama Missionaries in the Middle Kingdom, 1850–1950* (Tuscaloosa: The University of Alabama Press, 1997).

25. McNamara, *In Retrospect*, 33.

26. Whitfield, *The Culture of the Cold War*, 81. In the fifties, Graham referred to the evil of communism in many of his sermons. In one of his popular books, he warned: "Motivated by such a fanatical, burning desire to win, the Communists find no sacrifice too great to make for their cause." See Billy Graham, *World Aflame* (New York: Doubleday & Company, Inc., 1965), 7.

27. Seth Jacobs, *America's Miracle Man in Vietnam: Ngo Dinh Diem, Religion, Race, and U.S. Intervention in Southeast Asia* (Durham, N.C.: Duke University Press, 2004), 82–83.

28. Thomas A. Dooley, *Deliver Us from Evil: The Story of Viet Nam's Flight to Freedom* (New York: Signet Books, 1962), 118. For the opinion of another Catholic who had viewed the Vietnam struggle as between good and evil, but who was critical of *Deliver Us from Evil*, see, Appy, *Patriots*, 47–50.

29. Rick Perlstein, *Before the Storm: Barry Goldwater and the Unmaking of the American Consensus* (New York: Hill and Wang, 2001), 104–5.

30. For an overview of the various categories of anticommunists, see Richard Gid Powers, *Not Without Honor: The History of American Anticommunism* (New York: The Free Press, 1995).

31. W&Y, 28 January 1953, MCSL.

32. Senator Margaret Chase Smith Public Speech, 25 July 1960, MCSL.

33. One critic in 1950 referred to her as "a Moses in nylons." See "Senator Smith! How Could You?" Scrapbook, vol. 88, 41, MCSL.

34. Wallace, *Politics of Conscience*, 142.

35. Joel Kovel, *Red Hunting in the Promised Land: Anticommunism and the Making of America* (London: Cassell, 1997), 118.

36. George Lakoff and Mark Johnson, *Metaphors We Live By* (Chicago: The University of Chicago Press, 1980), 14–21.

37. Sherman, *No Place for a Woman*, 88–89.

38. Professor of religion at Princeton University, Paul Ramsey was one who articulated such thinking in the 1960s. See Paul Ramsey, *The Just War: Force and Political Responsibility* (Lanham, Md.: Rowman & Littlefield Publishers, Inc. 2002).

39. The most recent and forceful revisionist study is Mark Moyar, *Triumph Forsaken: The Vietnam War, 1954–1965* (Cambridge: Cambridge University Press, 2006). On Vietnam War historiography, see David Anderson, "The Vietnam War," in *A Companion to American Foreign Relations*, ed. Robert D. Schulzinger (Malden, Mass.: Blackwell Publishing, 2003), 309–29. A helpful review of earlier scholarship is Gary R. Hess, "The Unending Debate: Historians and the Vietnam War," *Diplomatic History* 18, Issue 2 (1994): 239–64. Critical of a revisionist perspective is Mark Philip Bradley and Marilyn B. Young, eds., *Making Sense of the Vietnam Wars: Local, National, and Transnational Perspectives* (Oxford: Oxford University Press, 2008), 7. Also of significance is the rift in how academics perceive communism. See John Earl Haynes and Harvey Klehr, *In Denial: Historians, Communism & Espionage* (San Francisco: Encounter Books, 2003).

40. One historian writes: "There is no reason to believe that the American people as a whole ever changed their ideas about communism or, indeed (judging by Nixon's victories in 1968 and 1972), ever turned en masse against the war." See Powers, *Not Without Honor*, 319.

41. Todd Gitlin quoted in Kenneth J. Heineman, *God is a Conservative: Religion, Politics, and Morality in Contemporary America* (New York: New York University Press 1998), 5. Also, see John Micklethwait and Adrian Wooldridge, *The Right Nation: Conservative Power in America* (New York: The Penguin Press, 2004); Leo Ribuffo, "Why Is There So Much Conservatism in the United States and Why Do So Few Historians Know Anything about it?" *The American Historical Review* 99, no. 2 (April 1994), 438–49, and Jerome L. Himmelstein, *To the Right: The Transformation of American Conservatism* (Berkeley: University of California Press, 1992). On the rise of intellectual conservatism from the lonely days of the 1940s to the more promising 1970s, see George H. Nash, *The Conservative Intellectual Movement in America Since 1945* (New York: Basic Books, Inc., 1979).

42. Sherman, *No Place for a Woman*, 216.

1

Rise to Political Standing

The two women having lunch at the House restaurant on Capitol Hill, in 1946, were Representative Margaret Chase Smith and her friend May Craig, the Washington correspondent for the Guy Gannett newspapers of Maine. Speaking frankly, Craig informed Smith: "you have reached your peak—you can go no further—so you must adjust yourself to going downhill from now on."[1]

Given the push for women to put their wartime employment behind them and return to their "rightful" place in the home and the almost total male dominance of mid-century Washington politics, such blunt advice seemed prudent. But Smith had no interest in confining herself to the domestic sphere or coasting politically. She reached high and scored a Senate seat in 1948, thus becoming the first woman in American history to be elected in both the House of Representatives and the Senate. No less striking was her emergence as a Cold Warrior who concentrated on the serious and "masculine" issue of national security in the wake of communist threats. She was ready to make her mark in Cold War America; it did not matter that she had little in common with the upper-class and educational background of major Washington policymakers who—pressured to conform "to dominant ideologies of masculinity"—exercised a "brotherhood" of privilege and power or that she did not fit the model of "domestic containment" which discouraged women from political activism.[2] That she was a working-class small-town girl with no college education did not stop her from creating her masculine Cold Warrior image that proved her worthiness to fight the communist menace.

Margaret Chase's birthplace was in Skowhegan, Maine, a small mill town of approximately five thousand located on the Kennebec River thirty-seven miles north of Augusta. Born in 1897, Chase saw her community blossom before its manufacturing declined after the late 1920s. In the "good" years, her parents remained poor working-class people as had been the case of their parents. Margaret's paternal grandfather was a Methodist Episcopal Church minister, who died at age forty, leaving his family in financial difficulty, and her maternal grandfather was a carpenter who had come to Skowhegan as a child of poverty from St. Georges, Quebec.[3] Margaret's father worked as a hotel waiter and later as a barber, and her mother took on menial jobs at local businesses while she reared six children. As the oldest child, Margaret brought in additional money with various jobs including delivering milk from the family cow to a neighbour, working as a temporary domestic, and finding employment during the Christmas rush at town stores. At age thirteen, she earned her first "real" job at a 5-and-10-cent store. From her teenage years to early adulthood, her jobs included dishwasher, textile mill employee, store clerk, telephone operator, office worker, and rural school teacher. The Chase family had warm clothes and adequate food, but, according to Margaret, "none of the frills that a lot of families had."[4]

From her home life, Chase learned the importance of hard work, thrift, and self-sacrifice, and from her community she acquired the Mainer traits of contrariness, pragmatism, and "a stern morality" associated with hard times. In addition, there were the powerful influences of Yankee straightforwardness, self-discipline, moderation, and integrity. Recent biographer Janann Sherman sees Chase as a "simple, rural, New England conservative" who trusted her Yankee values for courage, moral authority, and order.[5] Patricia L. Schmidt refers to Chase's moral center and "Yankee Protestantism," a legacy of her Puritan forebears that directed her to identify right and wrong within herself.[6] Her passion for playing high school basketball also enhanced her moral, social, and physical development. In her senior year she captained her team to victory at the state championship.[7] Her nickname "Marcus" hints of "the dominance of a confident, masculine persona."[8] Margaret's mother was the financial backbone; her father became dependent on alcohol, an experience that would lead her to question notions of patriarchy.[9]

High school graduation was in 1916, a year of uncertainty with the raging war in Europe that gave witness of the horrors of trench warfare and shocking new weapons created by advanced technologies. President Woodrow Wilson had kept the United States out of the war even as Germany's unrestricted submarine warfare and sinking of American ships raised the stakes. The final straw centered on national security; in early 1917 there was the disclosure of Germans secretly seeking an alliance with Mexico that would help the Mexicans regain lost territory from the United States. Wilson asked Congress to declare war on Germany and on April 4 and 6, the Senate and House endorsed the war resolution. The only dissenting vote came from Jeannette Rankin, the first female elected to the United States House of Representatives.

Within a month, the initial group of Skowhegan young males gathered for duty and the *Independent-Reporter* wrote that "[M]any a silent prayer was offered for the welfare and safety of the boys who were going forth through unknown ordeals and hazards to fight under the Stars and Stripes." The armed forces increased from 200,000 to over 4 million with close to 1.4 million troops fighting on the Western Front. Almost 50,000 Americans died in battle and another 60,000 succumbed to disease and noncombat causes. Among those not returning were seventeen Skowhegan boys including Harry St. Ledger, Margaret's friend who often took her to the movies. The painful experience of the war profoundly and permanently influenced her attitudes toward peace and national security; she came to the conclusion that a strong military was the way to peace.[10]

Despite Chase's energy and drive, the positive influences that arose from her town, and the character development that came with struggle and perseverance, she did not realize her dream of attending college. With her parents unable to pay for further education, her plan to become a gym teacher was not viable; her immediate and more realistic path was full-time employment. Fortunately, her varied talents blossomed, particularly her genius for organization when she was the circulation manager of Skowhegan's weekly newspaper, the *Independent-Reporter*. During her tenure, no other New England weekly had a higher circulation.[11] Her desire of reaching college eventually disappeared when she began earning more money and status.

In the Progressive Era of the mid-1890s through the First World War there was an acceleration of political activity by women, including the formation and impressive growth of various national women's organizations. The most notable evidence of change was the Nineteenth Amendment that gave women the right to vote in 1920. In the same year, Chase joined the Skowhegan Sorosis, a branch of a national women-only club that attracted ambitious women interested in civic and community projects; she became president two years later. An ambitious young working-class lady, she made additional connections with business and professional career women of the newly formed Maine Federation of Business and Professional Women's Club (BPW.) Chase began her political education, including lessons on how to master the art of pressure-group politics and how to gain political office. The *Independent Woman*, the official voice of the BPW, empowered women to break down gender barriers in business and politics. Chase became president of the Skowhegan BPW and later president of the Maine State Federation BPW.[12]

Chase's relationship with Republican politician Clyde Smith, an older man by twenty-one years who she had met in her late high school years, drew her further into the world of politics. The personable Smith had an impressive business and political resume. Beginning in 1915, he was first selectman of Skowhegan (comparable to mayor) for over fifteen years. Together the couple often attended meetings, luncheons, and dinners with other political leaders and Margaret's reputation grew as a dynamic and serious young woman with political connections, talents, and competency. Adding to her list of impressive accomplishments, Chase was secretary of the Skowhegan Republican Committee in 1926 and four years later Maine State Republican Committeewoman, the latter mainly due to the support of Willard H. Cumming who hired her as the office manager of Cummings Shoddy Mill and encouraged her greater involvement in Republican politics.[13]

Clyde Smith longed to be governor and he took an important step in this direction when he exchanged wedding vows with Margaret in May 1930 inside the tiny family parlor of the Chase home. Demonstrating some independence, Margaret kept her maiden name to go with her married name; within a year, however, she did yield to her husband's request and quit working for Cummings. Given Smith's penchant to invite guests home for dinner and longer visits without notice and Margaret's refusal to hire servants, there was no end of work to keep their large mansion in order.[14]

Throughout the Great Depression years, political activity consumed the Smiths. "Mrs. Margaret Chase Smith" was in the news as often as her husband. She was active in the Women's Republican Club and remained Republican State committeewoman for six years. In 1932, the Republican National Committee appointed her to campaign support for President Herbert Hoover, who won Maine and one other state. Clyde's gifts of distinguished oratory, good judgment, and compassion for working people took him further than selectman of Skowhegan; he served terms in the Maine House and the Maine Senate before his victory as U.S. Representative from the Second Congressional District and member of Congress in 1937. Concerning Margaret's role in Washington, he was sensitive about nepotism and he vetoed appointing his wife officially to his staff. Constituents disagreed and he relented when faced with a petition signed by thousands who "stated that they had voted for Margaret as much as for Clyde when they cast their ballots."[15] Consequently, Margaret acted as Clyde's manager, driving the car, handling the correspondence, and watching over other political duties. In reflecting on her marriage to the much older man, Margaret stated, "It was not a great love, not that kind. It was more a business arrangement."[16] Certainly, she was a great political asset to her husband; two years before their departure to Washington, the *Lewiston Evening Journal* proclaimed her "very popular" and "one of the cleverest women political workers of Maine."[17]

There were considerable adjustments when the Smiths went to Washington so that Clyde could begin his work in Congress. Missing her associations with women's groups in Maine, Margaret joined the Congressional Club, composed of the wives of Washington leaders. Her working-class background and the self-perception of being "country folk" made her uncomfortable at various formal gatherings where the social trappings contrasted sharply with her origins. According to Sherman, Margaret was more at ease with her reputation as a "working girl." Viewing Washington society as frivolous and unaware of the political benefits of social gatherings, Clyde avoided "going socially" as much as possible. A more serious issue was his health when he suffered a heart attack in 1938 that left him inactive for six weeks. To make matters worse, he detested Washington political life and the lack of power he had as a small player in a minor party; he longed to return to Maine and cap his political life with the governorship.[18]

One important consequence of Clyde's fragile health was Margaret's more active political role such as substituting for him at meetings with party officials and constituents. What set her apart politically from him was her support for increased military preparedness. In October 1938, she gave a speech to the Kennebec County Women's Republican Club entitled "The Experiences of a Congressman's Wife in Washington." But Margaret, without the assistance and knowledge of Clyde, spoke of serious issues and argued that additional money should go to the Navy, a position at odds with her husband, who strongly opposed military expansion. Approximately three years before the Japanese assault on Pearl Harbor, she predicted: "Those who oppose naval protection fail to perceive that the real attack, if any, will be by way of the sea."[19] Likely a number of Maine constituents closely following Hitler's successes in Europe (including the meetings in Munich one month earlier that saw the British and French concede the German annexation of Czechoslovakian land) pondered Margaret's Navy Day message for a strong military.

When he became seriously ill, Clyde encouraged Margaret to file primary petitions in her own name to carry on his unfinished work.[20] After his death in early April 1940, she finished his term and campaigned for the following regular term, adopting an aggressive position of war preparation. The *Portland Press Herald* reported her concerns: "Utilizing every lesson that we can from the European conflict, we must rebuild our defenses on the land and sea and in the air."[21] Her warnings received the approval of many. In a letter to the *Lewiston Daily Sun* editor, a Mrs. O. E. Johnson praised Smith's "active and aggressive" manner in demanding the War Department improve coastal defense.[22] American women had been voting for only twenty years, the odds were heavy against women entering politics, and common attitudes were that campaigning "was too arduous and politically too dirty for women."[23] But Smith pre-empted her political opponents on the defense issue; without a record they could assail, they were mostly confused on how to tarnish her campaign. When her opponents resorted to declarations about the weaker sex, her supporters responded with strength-affirming rhetoric: "The comely but firm-jawed lady from Skowhegan . . . will boldly champion and espouse the rights of her people with absolute courage and fearlessness."[24] Smith won the Republican primary by a large margin and defeated her Democrat opponent in September.

There were seven women in the Seventy-seventh Congress. Smith listed House Labor Committee and Military Affairs as her two preferences for committee work, stating in her initial weekly column "Washington and You," in early 1941, that the Labor Committee was "integral to national defense, and therefore a place on Military Affairs would give me an opportunity of watching labor and national defense both."[25] Instead of Labor and Military Affairs, however, her assignments were more in line with gender stereotypes: Education, Invalid Pensions, and Post Offices and Roads. Still, she maintained her interest in national security and the bolstering of the army, and she cast her support for a large increase in defense spending and the first peacetime draft in American history. Going against the expectations of the Republican Party, the freshman congresswoman voted for the Selective Training and Service Act. Unconvinced that isolationism was the best strategy for achieving peace, she supported President Franklin Roosevelt's foreign policy. She was the only Maine representative who supported the Lend-Lease Act of 1941.[26] She explained to her constituents that "even though there is only a chance of attack, I dare not risk the menace." America needed to be strong in the face of dictators and the world they could shape.[27] Her forceful and independent thinking for military preparedness was a political coup, especially in light of the surprise Japanese attack on Pearl Harbor in December 1941. One newspaper columnist boasted that Smith "voted consistently for preparedness, putting aside party prejudice and placing the National good above politics, not an easy road to choose. Hats off to Margaret Smith!"[28] In 1942, she received almost 70 percent of the election vote. Of course, the Maine shipyards and economy stood to benefit as the defense industry awarded contracts for the building of merchant ships for Britain, minesweepers, and other projects.

It was also favorable for Smith that many voters found the novelty of a female leader fascinating. As Sherman explains, in the eyes of the public her sex often placed her "outside, and frequently above, politics as usual," due to the perception of women being more moral and selfless than men.[29] Still, the barriers that came with her sex likely outweighed the advantages. From the beginning of her political rise, she feared being viewed as "a feminist concentrating on legislation for women."[30] Understanding that "feminism" was a political liability in her day, she presented herself as a politician first. To be sure, she desired to be taken seriously by both voters and her male colleagues in Washington, and an effective strategy was to promote individual achievement without gender considerations.

Image making was essential and Smith took a major step forward in January 1943, when she joined the House Naval Affairs Committee, a powerful committee chaired by Democrat Carl Vinson. In a tactical move she requested Appropriations as her first choice understanding that Republican leaders would prevent her from joining this prominent committee. To her delight, she received their approval to go on the important Naval Affairs Committee and the essential endorsement of Vinson, who read her Navy Day speech of 1938 with interest.[31] In recognition of her early achievements on the Naval Affairs Committee, Colby College in late 1943 awarded her a Master of Arts, a college degree that had eluded her. Colby was an institution that favored the children of prominent families, but she now had her honorary degree.

Much of Smith's initial committee work was the investigation of vice and prostitution near naval ports, a response to fears stated in newspapers that "a diseased prostitute, receiving upwards of three dozen men in a night, could do far more damage than a 500-pound bomb dropped squarely in the middle of an Army Camp."[32] Scholars examining the dynamics of gender in World War II note the association between sexy women and aggressive power, clearly seen in the iconography of erotic paintings of women on fighter planes and bombs. But what if there was an unleashing of this erotic force within the nation? A rising fear, Elaine May Tyler argues, was that any such thing would spell disaster.[33] It is interesting that the independent Smith played a major role in investigating the serious consequences of "female sexuality on the loose," another example of women exercising independence. Her work on this issue was one of many cases when she defied gender constraints of what she could or could not do. If the issue was national security her gender was not going to stop her from defending the nation.

Robert Dean argues that participation in war has "been a basic constituent of ideologies of elite masculinity and of male citizenship and political power," thus war veterans seeking a place in politics found it advantageous to construct "a narrative of heroic wartime service."[34] War provided opportunities for men to be real men. Dean claims that while in battle during the Korean War Joseph Alsop "discarded a feminized bodily cowardice for the tested masculine courage demanded by the manhood script of his class."[35] Smith could not participate in war like a good number of her male colleagues did, but she could show evidence of heroism. For example, before Christmas 1944, she took a 24,000-mile tour of the Pacific war theater, where she observed carrier battle exercises on the USS *Saratoga* and dodged sniper bullets in Saipan, thus challenging the perception of women being weak.

One could believe that Smith would have done more to serve her country if allowed. In fact, her best known achievement in the war years was her fight for women to have a greater military role, specifically to be a regular part of the army except combat duty. She found it an injustice that Women Accepted for Voluntary Emergency Service (WAVES) and Women's Army Corps were set up as reserves without the option of regular military personnel which had better pay and privileges. A bill passed in June 1943 made the women's auxiliaries a regular branch of the military services, though Smith judged the bill inadequate since it did not permit the WAVES to serve overseas.[36] In 1944, she introduced a bill to rectify this shortcoming, and a revised bill passed allowing women to serve in the Americas, Alaska, Hawaii, and the Caribbean. After a prolonged fight for women to have permanent regular status in the military, she witnessed victory in 1948.[37] The path to victory was clearer with the realization that there was a need for military women now that the United States faced a Cold War. With these battles, Smith made significant steps in the art of politics, especially how to "play hardball."[38]

When the war ended in Europe on May 8, 1945, Smith remained serious about the unfinished work of defeating the enemy and was against Americans celebrating too soon. Instead, "everybody should work a few hours longer and make these few added work hours on this V-E Day a symbol of our determination to carry on to the end in the Pacific. . . . Let's wait until we can all take time off for V-J Day—Victory over Japan."[39] This example of steady focus on victory over the enemy was the model she applied to the Cold War. Adding to her own sense that military strength was vital for American well-being was the military influence of William (Bill) Lewis, who was her personal secretary and confidant for almost all of her years in political leadership. Almost fifteen years younger than Smith, Lewis was a West Point cadet before earning a degree at the University of Oklahoma followed by a master's degree in Business Administration at Harvard. When he met Smith in 1943, he was a lieutenant in the Naval Reserve and in 1947 he resigned his naval commission and became a full colonel in the Air Reserve. Smith herself received the commission of lieutenant colonel from the Air Force Reserve in 1949 for her support of a separate Air Force; she continued to make her name known in "the male domain of conquest and courage."[40]

After World War II, the United States could not return to isolationism, particularly since Americans like Smith wondered if the Soviets had inherited Nazism's aggression. Former British Prime Minister Winston Churchill warned of the Soviet threat and the "Iron Curtain" splitting Europe, George Kennan presented compelling analysis of Soviet expansionist policies in his "Long Telegram" sent to the State Department from Moscow, and President Harry Truman fired Secretary of Commerce Henry A. Wallace for his opposition to the administration's emerging anti-Soviet policy, all events of 1946. The following year saw the creation of the Truman Doctrine that promised American support of free peoples under threat, the Marshall Plan that guaranteed financial aid for a weak European economy ripe for communist intrusion, and the National Security Act that established the Department of Defense, the National Security Council, and the Central Intelligence Agency. Washington planned to counter any Soviet assaults on liberty, justice, and a liberal market economy.

Smith was fully supportive of Truman's plan to aid the Greek government with its war against communist rebels and Turkey in its confrontation with the Soviet Union over the control of the Dardanelles. Moreover, she was against any money from the Marshall Plan going to the Soviets, explaining that such assistance "would merely be interpreted by Russia as appeasement and weakness."[41] For most Americans, trepidation went beyond alarm of the USSR alone. The enduring perception among Americans was that communists throughout the world, controlled by the USSR, represented a monolithic identity.[42] Off the map was any interpretation that Joseph Stalin's "postwar goals were security for himself, his regime, his country, and his ideology, in precisely that order."[43] Behind Stalin's aggressiveness, Americans like Smith believed, was the criminal character of communist ideology that sought to dominate the world. The fall of Czechoslovakia to communism in February 1948 deeply affected Smith and her interpretation that the coup represented another Munich appeasement of 1938 matched Truman's assessment. For her, the Soviet blockade of all surface traffic between West Germany and the communist-encircled West Berlin in 1948 and 1949, was another step of communist domination of Europe and then the world.[44]

Smith gained important publicity when she was the only female politician belonging to a special subcommittee of the House committees on Armed Services and Appropriation that took a five-week trip to Europe and the Middle East. She demonstrated her heroism when she remained calm during a potentially deadly episode of airplane trouble during the return flight to the United States. After a frightening return to the Azores and a safe landing, Rep. Dewey Short (R-MO) stated that Smith was "the best soldier—and sailor of us all." The *Washington Post* reported that she "showed remarkable poise and cheerfulness" and the *Evening Star* (Washington) quoted one military aide on the flight explaining that she was so calm "that the rest of us would have been ashamed to show our fear openly." To Maine journalists she proved her mettle: "It is a real test of courage to remain poised and at least outwardly cheerful when deadly peril threatens . . . but courage and strength of character . . . enabled Maine's Rep. Smith to show, during four long hours of the touch-and-go race between life and death last Friday, the poise, the cheerfulness and calmness . . . [that gave lie to] the bigoted phrase . . . 'no place for a woman.'"[45]

The few females who had made it to the Senate did so from an appointment rather than on their own, but with the encouragement of Bill Lewis Smith made plans to make a run in 1948. Months later, when a fractured elbow while campaigning failed to stop her from her appointments, the press focused on her "unwomanly" courage. Such stories were good copy for the press and they helped Smith with image making that challenged gender stereotypes of weak and fearful women. If she felt the weight of those believing that self-supporting women who failed to conform to the domestic ideal were suspect and perhaps even un-American, she plunged ahead regardless.[46] Her victory in the primary over formidable candidates Governor Horace Hildreth and former Governor Sumner Sewall, both supported by powerful machine politics, and her landslide triumph against her Democratic opponent in September 1948 made her the first woman in American history elected in both the House of Representatives and the Senate. This was an impressive achievement in the immediate post–World War period when it was paramount to preserve jobs for men. An increasing number of women did find employment outside the home, but few of them ever came close to the wage or status of their male peers in male-dominated fields, and, certainly, it was rare for a woman to win political contests.

Smith's political rise generated national discussion of her suitability for the vice presidency and others wrote about her potential as the president of the United States.[47] Was it possible for Americans to take seriously the idea of a female vice president or president, particularly one who had no college education? Aware of the importance of a higher education, she regretted her weak academic experience in high school. Asked years later in an ABC television interview what she would have done differently as a young girl, she stated: "In school I would have placed more emphasis on History. I didn't do much with History in those days and I have missed it in this [Senate] position."[48]

In mid-twentieth century, it seems clear that one way for a woman in Washington politics to enhance her status in the Senate was to pursue serious "manly" issues, and Smith's focus on military defense fit the bill. Desiring committee work on the Senate Armed Services, she immediately made hard-line speeches that the United States had no option but to rearm itself to meet Soviet challenges: "We should make it crystal clear to the Politburo that we will back up our firm talk. . . . We should extend the olive branch with an eagle, instead of a dove carrying it to the bear."[49] In a letter to one female constituent, she wrote of her "unbroken record of voting for defense measures" in the face of bitter attacks of "economy-at-any-price advocates," and how she was one of only several senators who supported a 70-Group Air

Force in August 1949. She claimed "that no one has more persistently fought for national preparedness than I."[50] To one young lady, she wrote: "My record will show that I have supported every measure submitted to Congress during my service in the House and Senate for the military preparedness and national security of our country."[51]

Believing the Soviets sought global domination as expressed in Marxist rhetoric, Senator Smith soon established her fierce anticommunism.[52] It is revealing that her "Washington and You" columns, written in simple and straightforward language and printed five days a week in over 30 newspapers across the nation, covered national defense more than any other topic. In her very first column of April 5, 1949, which began her five-day run that would last until 1954, she warned her readers of "the men of the Kremlin."[53] Her next column explained that the "ruthless men of the Politburo" had utter disregard and contempt for human life and thus they were willing to sacrifice the lives of millions of Russians to reach their goals.[54] In fact, any Soviet who dared to question the policies of the Communist Party "is promptly liquidated by a firing squad or exiled to tortuous labor in Siberia."[55] When the communists behind the Iron Curtain celebrated Stalin's birthday, the "fear-inspired homage" demonstrated "fear, enslaved obedience, [and] sinister power."[56] In light of such an atmosphere, Smith shared with her readers the possibility that Stalin's successor might "successfully liquidate his rivals."[57] For the United States it was no time for complacency especially since the Soviet Union had the advantage of "slave labor" in building up its military.[58] With the communists there could be no compromise with America's security.[59] Being more specific with her concerns, she warned readers that the Soviets could drop a bomb on any American city or invade Alaska and sweep across an unfortified Canada "to our border."[60]

But some Americans, Smith thought, failed to realize the extent of the communist menace and foolishly believed that communist leaders wanted peace, resulting in the United States making "great mistakes" in demobilizing the military forces too fast.[61] She also found that the American government was so eager to support Yugoslavian leader Josip Tito and widen the breach between Tito and Stalin that it gave inadequate attention to the possibility of American aid to Yugoslavia being "a super double-cross to throw us off guard"; the common enemy was not merely a nation but a totalitarian ideology and Tito was "just as much a Communist as Stalin."[62] Smith's support of the North Atlantic Treaty Organization and the United Nations put her at odds with the isolationist leanings of Republican heavyweight Senator Robert Taft, who viewed the Cold War, in the words of Walter LaFeber, "as a crusade against the Antichrist."[63] But in favoring NATO, she was careful not to appear weak as were "pseudo-liberals" who favored "unabated compromise" and were too accommodating "to all men at all times."[64] Clarifying the seriousness of communist aggression, Smith also told her readers that the Cold War "is the same as that of World War II—a struggle between democracy and totalitarianism."[65]

However, an important point was not to take the same path of the communists and deny freedom of expression, a theme central in her critical statements on Senator Joseph McCarthy the following year. Commenting on the attendance of communist representatives at the Cultural and Scientific Conference for World Peace held in New York, Smith wrote there must be a guarantee for the communist representatives in New York to speak freely. If some thought her position was too accommodating on this issue, she also forcefully warned of the dangers of communism to national security: "We must stop and destroy Communism" without curtailing freedom of speech. The best methods to fight communism were infiltration and exposure because it, "like germs of disease, withers and dies under the rays of truth."[66] It is striking that her commonsense discussion of world peace concludes with her linking disease and communism. At the very beginning of her Senate term, she shared the view of other American politicians who saw communism as the contaminated "Other" that sought to infect America with deadly subversive ideas.[67] Throughout her senatorial career, the Soviet Union and communism became "obsessions."[68]

How does one account for the intense anticommunism of a woman born and raised in a small New England town? Smith's early World War II warnings of Maine's vulnerability as the closest American territory to Nazi aggression, revealed her fear of external attack. In addition, Maine had a large shipbuilding industry and there were benefits for a Maine politician to support the buildup of national defense. National security was an important issue that demanded her attention and from the very beginning of her political career she embraced core values of defending liberal capitalism, political institutions, and America's "physical base or territorial integrity."[69] Connected to this, in the case of Smith, were gender and religious considerations. The threat of communism was "menacingly real to the domestic and foreign policymakers of the early 1950s" and Rhodri Jeffreys-Jones claims there was considerable pressure on Smith to conform to a masculine Cold War stereotype in order to gain the acceptance of male senators.[70] It is not clear how much this pressure motivated her to become a Cold Warrior, since she had demonstrated her strength and independence to take bold stands not always acceptable in the eyes of key senators. There appeared to be something more substantial behind her persistent opposition to communism than local politics and gender insecurities. William Inboden notes the Truman administration's secret policy directive NSC-68, that articulated the strategic and ideological direction of American Cold War policy, "reads in parts more like a sermon than a policy blueprint." For example, the document alerted that the USSR "is animated by a new fanatic faith, antithetical to our own, and seeks to impose its absolute authority over the rest of the world."[71] Historians are beginning to trace the role that religion played among American policymakers in defining the seriousness of the communist threat.[72] In fact, beyond religious leaders some of the most vigilant foes of communism were politicians with church connections who expressed their concerns from the press box.[73]

Smith's foundation to oppose communism may be attributable, in large part, to her Christian beliefs and the value of a moral perspective in judging the actions of atheistic communists. Like all astute politicians of the Cold War years, she identified herself with a specific church in an age when religious identification was important to most constituents.[74] She counted herself as a Methodist in a manner similar to Robert Bellah's "civil religion," meaning religion that is not "any specific sense Christian," but represents a "collection of beliefs, symbols, and rituals with respect to sacred things" and serves "as a genuine vehicle of national religious self-understanding."[75] Perhaps the strong Roman Catholic background of her mother's people also prepared Smith to be sympathetic to Catholicism, including its fervent anticommunism.

She kept her faith mainly private and biographies give no information on whether she attended church often or had any connections with conservative Christian leaders. She did, however, on occasion publicly express the importance of religion. She had no issue with a politician being informed by a religious framework; indeed, she wrote that "we need more religion and less politics in our country."[76] To a church congregation, she stated that, "Surely our first armament must be spiritual for victories are never won by people of little faith."[77] Encouraged that more Americans were turning to "divine guidance," Smith told audiences that the Golden Rule must win in "the struggle of good and evil—of moral force against physical force."[78] She thought that American foreign policy was amiss in sending an ambassador to atheistic Russia but not having one for Christian Spain, an inconsistency she believed "many Americans" resented.[79] She embraced the notion that the United States and Christianity were under constant threat of attack by the Soviets "because the one thing the Communists fear the most is the Church."[80] As was the case with other Americans at mid-century, she believed that religion was "the most formidable barrier to communist world domination."[81] Cognitive psychology states that individuals "are reluctant to discard or even qualify" highly valued beliefs.[82] If not in the exact words of a fiery anticommunist minister, Smith held a Christian worldview that shared common ground with those who viewed the power of communism as a dark spiritual force. New evidence that was inconsistent with her interpretation or otherwise ambiguous received little of her attention, something she could get away with in the 1950s but less so after 1965.

In her "Washington and You" newspaper column of February 7, 1950, Smith wrote that she might discontinue her monthly "brickbats and bouquets" reports because her column mail was "so heavy with bouquets." Coming three days before Joseph McCarthy's initial speech on communists working in the government, her disclosure that "there are only a rare few strong letters of criticism" spoke well of her approval rating during her first year in the Senate.[83] Of course, this Senate honeymoon period could not last and after an episode with McCarthy she would be pushed to take an even more pronounced anticommunist stand.

Given the scarcity of female politicians, Smith's rise to political standing and subsequent approval were impressive. Her specific attention to national defense issues allowed her to participate in the male sphere of politics, beyond the expectations that many had for the working-class girl from a small town without the benefits of college education and machine politics. If male "establishment" Cold Warriors learned of the importance of "service" and "sacrifice" in boarding schools, Ivy League fraternities, and other elite circles, she found them in more modest settings. Drawing on her independent character, New England conservative values, and sense of moral authority, she forged ahead understanding that a woman in politics required "unlimited courage and perseverance."[84] To enhance her place in politics overwhelmingly dominated by males, her boldness against the red menace was fundamental if she was to survive the bruising political battles of the Cold War.

NOTES

1. Margaret Chase Smith, *Declaration of Conscience*, ed. William C. Lewis (Garden City, New York: Doubleday & Company, 1972), 4. Recent biographies include Sherman, *No Place for a Woman*, Patricia L. Schmidt, *Margaret Chase Smith: Beyond Convention* (Orono, Maine: University of Maine Press, 1996), and Wallace, *Politics of Conscience*. On the employment opportunities of women immediately after the war, see May, *Homeward Bound*, 74–76.

2. Dean, *Imperial Brotherhood*, 6, 13. On the domestic version of containment (American focus on the home for security) as it related to the Cold War, see May, *Homeward Bound*.

3. Sherman, *No Place for a Woman*, 8–10; Schmidt, *Beyond Convention*, 10–13.

4. Sherman, *No Place for a Woman*, 10–12. Also see, Schmidt, *Beyond Convention*, 23–26, 31, 47–49; Frank Graham, Jr., *Margaret Chase Smith: Woman of Courage* (New York: The John Day Company, 1964), 18–23; Alice Fleming, *The Senator from Maine: Margaret Chase Smith* (New York: Thomas Y. Crowell Company, 1969), 3, 7, 12, 20–22.

5. Sherman, *No Place for a Woman*, 5, 10.

6. Schmidt, *Margaret Chase Smith*, xxi.

7. Fifty years later, Mainers continued to refer to her basketball feats. See G. D. to MCS, 20 April 1967, Vietnam War Correspondence, MCSL.

8. Schmidt, *Margaret Chase Smith*, 30.

9. Schmidt, *Margaret Chase Smith*, xiv.

10. Sherman, *No Place for a Woman*, 15, 45.

11. Sherman, *No Place for a Woman*, 18; Schmidt, *Margaret Chase Smith*, 57–58; Fleming, *The Senator from Maine*, 26.

12. Sherman, *No Place for a Woman*, 19–21; Schmidt, *Margaret Chase Smith*, 62–63; Fleming, *The Senator from Maine*, 26–27.

13. Sherman, *No Place for a Woman*, 26–27; Graham, Jr., *Margaret Chase Smith*, 27; Schmidt, *Margaret Chase Smith*, 86.

14. Sherman, *No Place for a Woman*, 29; Schmidt, *Margaret Chase Smith*, 87.

15. Smith, *Declaration of Conscience*, 65.

16. Quoted in Sherman, *No Place for a Woman*, 31.

17. "GOP Nationally is Interested in '36 Campaign in Maine," *Lewiston Evening Journal*, 7 March 1935, 9.

18. Sherman, *No Place for a Woman*, 37–8; Schmidt, *Margaret Chase Smith*, 105–6; Graham, Jr., *Margaret Chase Smith*, 28.

19. Smith, *Declaration of Conscience*, 65–66.

20. "Special Election to Fill Vacancy by Smith's Death," *Lewiston Daily Sun*, 9 April 1940, 5.

21. "Mrs. Smith Urges Defense Preparations Immediately," *Portland Press Herald*, 25 May 1940.

22. *Lewiston Daily Sun*, 10 June 1940.

23. Graham, Jr., *Margaret Chase Smith*, 29–33.

24. Sherman, *No Place for a Woman*, 46.

25. W&Y, 1 January 1941, MCSL.

26. Fleming, *The Senator from Maine*, 38–39.

27. Quoted in Schmidt, *Margaret Chase Smith*, 122.

28. Quoted in Schmidt, *Margaret Chase Smith*, 127.

29. Sherman, *No Place for a Woman*, 51.

30. Smith, *Declaration of Conscience*, 85. Writing in the early 1970s, she stressed, "And if there is any one thing I have attempted to avoid it is being a feminist. I definitely resent being called a feminist."

31. Smith, *Declaration of Conscience*, 67; Fleming, *Margaret Chase Smith*, 43.

32. Quoted in Sherman, *No Place for a Woman*, 59.

33. May, *Homeward Bound*, 68.

34. Dean, *Imperial Brotherhood*, 38.

35. Dean, *Imperial Brotherhood*, 43.

36. Sherman, *No Place for a Woman*, 68. Fleming, *The Senator from Maine*, 48–49.

37. Smith, *Declaration of Conscience*, 97.

38. Sherman, *No Place for a Woman*, 72.

39. Quoted in Schmidt, *Margaret Chase Smith*, 142–43.

40. Schmidt, *Margaret Chase Smith*, 173.

41. Gregory Peter Gallant, "Margaret Chase Smith, McCarthyism and the Drive for Political Purification," Ph.D. Dissertation, University of Maine, 1992, 28–30.

42. Fraser J. Harbutt, *The Cold War Era* (Malden, Mass.: Blackwell Publishers Inc., 2002), 68.

43. John Lewis Gaddis, *The Cold War: A New History* (New York: The Penguin Press, 2005), 11. For a concise overview of "shaping the postwar world order," see Harbutt, *The Cold War Era*, 14–37.

44. Gallant, "Margaret Chase Smith, McCarthyism and the Drive for Political Purification," 35, 37, 42. Gallant writes, "By the end of 1948, Smith had adopted completely what has been termed the anti-communist persuasion and with it a belief in 'Red Fascism' and the continual application of the Munich Analogy to the formulation of United States foreign policy" (43).

45. "Congressmen Have a Narrow Escape at Sea," *Washington Post*, 18 October 1947, Scrapbook, vol. 50, 124, MCSL; The *Evening Star*, 18 October 1947, Scrapbook, vol. 50, 128, MCSL; Sherman, *No Place for a Woman*, 78.

46. On such suspicion toward women active outside the home, see May, *Homeward Bound*, 22.

47. One California man wrote to her that he was ready to get on a soapbox and see her election as president. See W&Y, 3 October 1949, MCSL.

48. Senator Margaret Chase Smith Interview, ABC-TV, 13 August 1963, MCSL.

49. Quoted in Sherman, *No Place for a Woman*, 101.

50. MCS to Virginia Dagget, 19 July 1950, Declaration of Conscience Correspondence, MCSL.

51. MCS to Abbie Harvey, 24 August 1950, Korean War Correspondence, MCSL.

52. Over the years there has been a lively historiographical debate on who is more the villain: the communist or anticommunist. For recent assessments of the "revisionists" and "traditionalists," see Haynes and Klehr, *In Denial*, and Ellen Schrecker, ed., *Cold War Triumphalism: The Misuse of History After the Fall of Communism* (New York: The New Press, 2004).

53. W&Y, 5 April 1949, MCSL.

54. W&Y, 6 April 1949, MCSL.

55. W&Y, 5 October 1949, MCSL.

56. W&Y, 29 December 1949, MCSL.

57. W&Y, 2 January 1950, MCSL.

58. W&Y, 29 September 1949, MCSL.

59. W&Y, 13 April 1949, MCSL.

60. W&Y, 9 December 1949, MCSL.

61. W&Y, 26 August 1949, MCSL.

62. W&Y, 20 and 22 September 1949, MCSL.

63. Walter LaFeber, *America, Russia, and the Cold War, 1945–1996*, 8th ed. (New York: McGraw Hill, 1997), 130.

64. W&Y, 13 April 1949, MCSL.

65. W&Y, 2 September 1949, MCSL.

66. W&Y, 12 April 1949, MCSL.

67. Geoffrey S. Smith, "National Security and Personal Isolation: Sex, Gender, and Disease in the Cold-War United States," *The International History Review* XIV, no. 2 (May 1992), 308–12.

68. Gallant, "Margaret Chase Smith, McCarthyism and the Drive for Political Purification," 25.

69. Melvyn P. Leffler, "National Security," in *Explaining the History of American Foreign Relations*, 2nd ed., ed. Michael J. Hogan and Thomas G. Paterson (Cambridge: Cambridge University Press, 2004), 126.

70. Paul G. Pierpaoli, Jr., *Truman and Korea: The Political Culture of the Early Cold War* (Columbia: University of Missouri Press, 1999), 159; Rhodri Jeffreys-Jones, *Changing Differences: Women and the Shaping of American Foreign Policy, 1917–1994* (New Brunswick, N.J.: Rutgers University Press, 1997), 105.

71. Inboden, *Religion and American Foreign Policy, 1945–1960*, 2.

72. In recent years, there has been considerable discussion on the place of religion in American foreign policy. A growing number of historians who claim that religion plays an integral role in the construction and justification of foreign policy find it troubling that skeptics judge religious belief to be inconsequential in explaining the motivation behind various decisions and actions in political circles. See Andrew Preston, "Bridging the Gap between the Sacred and the Secular in the History of American Foreign Relations," *Diplomatic History* 30, no. 5 (November 2006): 783–812. For a critique on the use of religion to explain foreign relations, see Robert Buzzanco, "Where's the Beef? Culture without Power in the Study of U.S. Foreign Relations," *Diplomatic History* 24, no. 4 (Fall 2000), 628–29.

73. Eric R. Crouse, "Popular Cold Warriors: Conservative Protestants, Communism, and Culture in Early Cold War America," *Journal of Religion and Popular Culture* II (Fall 2002): 1–16. Put another way, the Cold War "represented the latest battle in humanity's constant fight against the forces of darkness and the essential selfishness of human nature." See Mary E. Stuckey, *Defining Americans: The Presidency and National Security* (Lawrence: The University Press of Kansas, 2004), 246.

74. For further discussion, see Eric Crouse, "Senator Margaret Chase Smith Against McCarthyism: The Methodist Influence," *Methodist History* 46, no. 3 (April 2008): 167–78.

75. Robert Bellah, "Religion in America," *Dædalus* 96, no. 1 (Winter 1967): 1–21. Margaret's mother had Catholic and French-Canadian ancestry and her parents were married in a Catholic church (Sherman, *No Place for a Woman*, 10–11).

76. General Speeches in Maine, October–November, 1951, 391, MCSL.

77. Speech at Old Alna Church, 17 August 1952, 40. Even in the late 1960s, she held that "the woes that plague the world today stem from Godlessness." For example, see MCS to Reverend Ralph E. Peterson, 31 July 1967, Religion Correspondence, MCSL.

78. See General Speeches in Maine, October–November 1951, 390, MCSL.

79. W&Y, 22 June 1949, MCSL.

80. Speech at Centenary Methodist Church, Skowhegan, Maine, 30 May 1954, 163, MCSL.

81. Scrapbook, vol. 138, 69, MCSL.

82. Richard Immerman, "Psychology," in *Explaining the History of American Foreign Relations*, 2nd ed., ed. Michael J. Hogan and Thomas G. Paterson (Cambridge: Cambridge University Press, 2004), 116. Immerman writes: "We may tend, for example, to overestimate the influence of personal dispositions on behavior and to underestimate the influence of situational influences (commonly referred to as the Fundamental Attribution Error, FAE)."

83. W&Y, 7 February 1950, MCSL.

84. Dean, *Imperial Brotherhood*, 4. Statements and Speeches, 117, 15 April 1953, MCSL.

2

Red Menace

On June 1, 1950, Senator Margaret Chase Smith met Senator Joseph Mc-Carthy on the underground Senate subway tram, an awkward encounter for both. "'Margaret,' he said, 'you look very serious. Are you going to make a speech?'" When she admitted that he would not like her speech, he ended the brief verbal exchange with a threatening reminder of the political power he wielded.[1] On the Senate floor, with McCarthy sitting two rows behind, Smith, who was no great orator, nervously presented her fifteen-minute "Declaration of Conscience" speech; her main critique was the detestable manner of politicians playing politics with the issue of national security at the expense of individual freedom.[2] She had earlier gone on record that communism must be destroyed, but it was a political gamble to challenge the hard-hitting tactics of McCarthy. Her stand generated nationwide attention in public and private space that underscored the contested terrain of what was the appropriate response to the red menace.

The Soviet's acquisition of the atomic bomb, the spreading of communism in Europe, the communists taking control of China, and the charge that government official Alger Hiss shared military secrets with the Soviets, and other sensational reports of communist spies were worrisome news that had a profound impact on American society in the late 1940s and beyond.[3] In 1950 before the communist invasion of South Korea, one political scientist wrote that even if communism did not precipitate armed conflict "nothing worthy of the name of peace can be achieved as long as Communism seeks to absorb other states by threat and ruse, refuses to respect the basic rules of good faith in its dealings with other states, and violates men's rights."[4] Recent scholarship claims that the accompanying anxieties and feelings of distrust and hostility toward communist foes was a primary agent of social cohesion and America stood ready but wary to confront the latest threat.[5] One study argues that 1950 was the pivotal year of transformation for Main Street America when trauma, pessimism, and anguish over Cold War developments subdued an optimistic American public. While this interpretation of trauma and pessimism suffers from evidentiary shortcomings—notably a lack of evidence on what ordinary Americans believed—there was at mid-century a growing and powerful force of anticommunist thinking throughout the United States.[6] A national survey in the early fifties, for example, showed that 91 percent of Americans held that high school teachers who were communists should be fired and 77 percent approved having their American citizenship taken away.[7] Americans did not stop pursuing and experiencing the richness of post–World War II life that the Depression and the war had denied. At the same time, the perception grew stronger that communism was a violent and brutal ideology with little respect for human life and freedoms.

Fear of the communist "other" had been part of the American experience before the rise of McCarthy and surely the Wisconsin senator represented a blazing light of anticommunism on the national scene that highlighted the path that political figures had been traveling.[8] In fact, one scholar clarifies the common mistake of seeing the term "McCarthyism" as a "synonym for the anticommunist political repression of the early Cold War."[9] Years before McCarthy's famous speech, President Harry S. Truman and many other politicians on both sides of the aisle valued the political capital gained by scaring Americans with ominous scenarios of increased communist power. Making reference to the Truman Doctrine, Fred O. Seibel's 1947 cartoon shows Truman offering "we the people" a scary dose of "RUSSIAN AGGRESSION" medicine.[10] Fuelling fear of communist strength within the borders of the United States were Truman's Executive Order 9835 that established a federal loyalty program and the actions of the House Committee on Un-American Activities against communists or those in sympathy. Across the nation, seventeen states excluded communists from the ballot.[11]

Movies, novels, comic books, and other popular cultural products increasingly embraced anticommunist themes.[12] The common message in some Hollywood films of the late 1940s and early 1950s, such as "The Red Menace," "The Red Nightmare," "I Was a Communist for the FBI," was for Americans to do their patriotic duty and report those with communist sympathies.[13] There was ample rhetoric in newspapers throughout the nation that painted a frightening picture of the communist threat. In 1949, the *Los Angeles Times* warned of the collapse of capitalism and the emergence of a communist America—"the United Soviet States of the American Republic (USSAR)." In his letter to the *Washington Herald-Times*, Robert Palmer urged parents to drill the letters "D.B.A.C. (don't be a communist), in every child's mind."[14] When commercial pilot and skywriter Jack Tatum tested his equipment in the moonlight above Chicago's North Side, the Civil Aeronautic Administration's Midway office received hundreds of telephone calls from concerned citizens. Responding to Tatum's solo flight in the *Chicago Tribune*, the same day Smith's "Declaration of Conscience" received coverage, one man declared: "We heard the roaring and we woke up. We got frightened because we saw the smoke making sickles in the sky. How were we to know the communists weren't coming?"[15] That hundreds allegedly responded to this Russian "invasion" is significant in a large metropolitan center such as Chicago, but even small newspapers in the deep south like the *Anniston Star* in Alabama declared in early June that politicians had "so lost their balance and sense of values in recent months that the whole American people is about to become psychopathic in fear of the Russian menace."[16] McCarthy's methods were ruthless in the eyes of his detractors, but his crusade against communism reflected the anticommunist popular culture and climate of American society.

Recent scholarship using newly released archival documents confirms that mid-century Americans were correct in believing that there was significant communist infiltration of American government.[17] High-profile figures such as Alger Hiss, Julius and Ethel Rosenberg, and others were not innocent victims of anticommunist paranoia, but guilty communist spies.[18] And yet the high point of communist penetration in government fell soon after the end of World War II and by the late 1940s the communists were on the run. Some found it difficult to hold public addresses, as was the case in Trenton, New Jersey in 1947, when communist leaders faced an anticommunist mob determined to defend "The American Way" from "Commies," "rats," "bastards," and "Stalin-lovers."[19] Frequently perceived as communists during the red scare era, a number of progressives and those on the left acquiesced to the forces of anticommunism, understanding that to do otherwise could result in painful consequences. The label "communist" was the typical label for anyone viewed as a radical or "un-American" and some paid a penalty for such identification.

A psychological fear spread through the government with people dreading ruined careers as a result of McCarthyite "guilt-by-association and guilt-by-accusation tactics."[20] There is the common claim that the broader red scare of the immediate post–World War II period was a witch-hunt driven by anticommunist hysteria.[21] The numbers vary widely with one study claiming that the red scare "ruined the lives of hundreds of thousands of Americans" and another study suggesting that 2,000 government employees lost their jobs of which McCarthy was responsible for no more than 40 cases.[22] Even if there is little evidence of the red scare having much of an effect on the employment status of Main Street Americans or causing widespread "ruined" lives, a number of real communists had their lives turned upside down. There is no question that the web of McCarthyism was frightening for those on the left. Many sensible Americans saw McCarthyism as dangerous.[23] Of course, no American experienced the Soviet-style "justice" that resulted in ruthless executions of the "Great Terror" or the long horrifying sentences to isolated labor camps of so-called enemies of the state.[24] Shocking too are the Soviet state-induced famines that caused the murder of millions in the 1930s. Often ignored in history books is that the number of Americans adversely affected by the red scare is minuscule compared to the millions of Soviet people who had suffered since the Bolshevik Revolution of 1917.

The birth of McCarthyism occurred on February 9, 1950, in a Wheeling, West Virginia, speech to the Women's Republican Club. Considerable confusion clouds the motive for McCarthy's actions and the content of his speech. No recording of the speech survived and he later denied uttering the words "a list of 205" communists in the State Department.[25] Spiced with Christian rhetoric, his Lincoln Day address did warn of the threat of communism in America: "Today we are engaged in a final, all-out battle between Communistic aetheism [sic] and Christianity."[26] This Christian element itself was not controversial in America; many politicians and a large segment of the population agreed. The major controversy concerned McCarthy's subsequent mudslinging, his baseless defamation of a varying number (205, 81, or 57) of communists in the State Department, and his usurping of executive and judicial authority, all of which became known as "McCarthyism," a term coined by newspaper cartoonist Herbert Block barely a month after the Wheeling speech.[27] For Smith and others, his effective use of Senate immunity to make reckless charges on a person's character without fear of legal reprisal, his inconsistent statements, and his bullying tactics were inexcusable.

In the late 1950s, journalist Richard Rovere stated that McCarthy "was in many ways the most gifted demagogue ever bred on these shores. No bolder seditionist ever moved among us—nor any politician with a surer, swifter access to the dark places of the American mind."[28] And yet Rovere's words and subsequent condemnation of McCarthy had not been the dominant position of ordinary Americans. Citing a January 1954 Gallup Poll, Rovere acknowledged that 50 percent of Americans had a "favorable opinion" of McCarthy compared to 29 percent holding an "unfavorable opinion."[29] Even among Democrats he was a hero; a large number of grassroots Catholics, who typically voted for the Democratic Party, had embraced the Wisconsin senator. Complicating the predicament for the Democratic Party in the early Cold War years was that Democrats represented a "mutually antagonistic amalgam" of left-liberals in the North, labor and ethnics in the cities, and conservatives in the South.[30] Republican leaders made political gains at the expense of Democratic Party leaders who were on the defensive as a result of McCarthy's attacks on Truman's administration. Moreover, newspaper editors took greater note that old party labels were losing much of their force since the political demarcation was more between liberal and conservative factions.[31] Consequently, it is no surprise that a significant number of Democrats supported McCarthy.

As for McCarthy and Senator Smith, their relations as Republican colleagues in the Senate were good when he launched his campaign to expose card-carrying communists in the State Department. They were both Cold Warriors, but there were significant differences between the two. McCarthy had a college degree; Smith had no college education. He was loud and flamboyant; she was quiet and restrained. He was a Catholic who attended mass regularly; she was a Methodist who rarely attended church services. He was a heavy drinker and smoker; she neither drank nor smoked. He enjoyed women of the night life; she was a lady. He had support from the conservative Republican hierarchy; key conservative Republican leaders viewed her as a liberal New Deal Republican. His Senate activities were inconsistent; she took all Senate responsibilities very seriously. His anticommunism was less effective and perhaps less sincere than hers.[32]

Smith sought to understand McCarthy's "disturbing and frightening" information of red infiltration. No shrinking violet on the issue of communism, she had already expressed her desire to see its destruction. Initially impressed by his "photostatic copies" of evidence, she began to doubt that he could substantiate his serious charges against targeted individuals. Was it her lack of college education, law training, and expertise that prevented her from appreciating the evidence behind McCarthy's claims? She told McCarthy, "Perhaps I'm stupid, Joe. But they [photostatic copies] don't prove a thing to me that backs up your charges."[33]

McCarthy's lack of proof that a person was a communist or "fellow red" did not deter him and more people realized his power. As many opponents understood it, judge and jury fused into one and the legal safeguards dear to the American experience, particularly the presumption of innocence until proven guilty, appeared to evaporate. The potential damage from McCarthy's abusive tactics on innocent individuals and on American democracy was disconcerting, no less so for anticommunist liberal intellectuals. And for those who had some real connection with left-wing activism in an earlier era, there was no appreciation for historical context; accusers searched for the sins of communist affiliation committed by people grinded by the gloomy and starving years of the Great Depression or those lured by the romanticism of communism expressed in college leftist circles.

While McCarthy gained power in Washington, Professor W. A. McConagha of Lawrence College, Wisconsin, warned that the day "politics becomes an enterprise in chicanery, dishonesty, and cunning, the most dishonest and the most cunning must ultimately rise to the top." When those with power utilize a campaign of smear against those who are innocent, repeating vile accusations to the point that the public accepts on the basis that where there is smoke there must be fire, the accused are often left broken. As McConagha explained, "It is a tragic truth that he who filches from me my good name takes that with which in comparison money is trash. He robs me not merely of what I live by, he robs me of what I live for—which leaves me desperately poor."[34] In April 1950, one opponent of McCarthy wrote, "must we, at Easter time, when our own greatest of Christian nations worships and professes the Master of self-sacrifice, demonstrate to the world from the hallowed halls of our government a major absorption in puny self-seeking and wrangling and fear."[35] Having experienced the anticommunist hysteria and "scandals" of the Attorney General A. Mitchell Palmer raids that took place in 1919–1920, a Newton, Massachusetts man had contempt for McCarthy's use of "rabble-rousing tactics" that communists themselves employed. He warned that, "Inflamed prejudice is not an atmosphere in which either justice or democracy can flourish."[36] Acknowledging the fear tactics of McCarthyism, H. H. Fisher, chairman of the Hoover Institute and Library On War, Revolution, and Peace, Stanford University, explained that there were Republicans upset to see party leaders finding profit in the irresponsible behavior of McCarthy—behavior that damaged national morale and gave aid and comfort to enemies of the American way.[37] For various critics of McCarthyism, communism was more a threat *to* America than a threat *in* America.

There were senators on both sides of the floor who disagreed with McCarthy's methods, but they feared the political consequences of challenging him. To be sure, there were many Republicans, frustrated with the political longevity of the Democrats in the White House, supportive of McCarthy's work to weaken the Democratic Party. The dilemma that Republican senators faced was weighing their sense of human dignity and fair play against party loyalty and hatred for communism at a time when the memory of high-ranking State Department official and Soviet spy Alger Hiss was still fresh.[38] Although Hiss did elude the charge of treason for his spying in the 1930s, his conviction of perjury and five-year prison sentence in early 1950 profoundly affected many Americans. In addition to the Hiss episode, there were several important cases in the public eye creating wide distrust of the government: State Department China expert John Stewart Service gave the pro-communist publication *Amerasia* classified government reports, yet Service, the editor of *Amerasia*, and three others dodged prison sentences because the Office of

Strategic Services (forerunner of the Central Intelligence Agency) gathered evidence illegally; Judith Coplon, a Justice Department employee convicted of supplying Soviets with confidential FBI reports, eluded prison time as a result of a technicality; and the exposure of Harry Gold, the American communist who received secret atomic information from British Klaus Fuchs of the Manhattan Project.[39]

The only woman among ninety-five males in the Senate, Smith acted because no one else, Democrat or Republican, was willing to speak out publicly. In one of her March newspaper columns, she had reiterated her revulsion for the political trick of smearing an opponent with the communist label.[40] By June she wanted to take a bolder stand, but she had to be cautious and only a small number of people knew of her plans to confront McCarthyism, because secrecy was necessary in order to prevent the Republican hierarchy from silencing her. Republican National Chairman Guy Gabrielson supported McCarthy, believing that the "average person" was not "close enough to know or care about the methods" of attacking communism.[41] Members of old guard, conservative Republicanism, guided by the powerful leadership of Senator Robert Taft of Ohio, were suspicious of the moderate and independent-thinking Smith, who some believed was a New Dealer under the skin because of her voting record.[42] Forgotten was her clear opposition to communism stated in her newspaper columns and numerous public statements. After all, not once did Smith ever claim to be a liberal.[43]

On June 1, before packed galleries in the Senate, Smith began her dramatic speech declaring that those who shouted the loudest about "Americanism" while attacking a person's character are those who are ignoring basic principles of Americanism: "The right to criticize; The right to hold unpopular beliefs; The right to protest; The right of independent thought." There was no mistaking her disgust for McCarthy and the impact he was having on the Senate that had "long enjoyed worldwide respect as the greatest deliberative body in the world." Sadly the Senate's deliberate character was being "debased to the level of a forum of hate and character assassination sheltered by the shield of congressional immunity."[44] Her additional criticism spared neither the Democratic Party nor the Republican Party. She spoke of the government's whitewashing tactics and ineffectiveness in confronting the communist menace, particularly "its complacency to the threats of communism here at home and the leak of vital secrets to Russia through key officials of the Democratic Administration." Citing the proven cases of Amerasia, Hiss, Coplon, and Gold, she understood Americans' "distrust and strong suspicion that there may be something to the unproved, sensational accusations." Still, she spoke of the disgrace of a Republican "witch hunt" and leaders who lacked political integrity and intellectual honesty and who were willing to "ride to political victory on the Four Horsemen of Calumny—Fear, Ignorance, Bigotry, and Smear." Republicans too eager to win jeopardized the stability of the two-party system that protected American liberties from a dictatorship. She found it shocking that both Democrats and Republicans played "directly into the Communist design of 'confuse, divide, and conquer.'" Smith ended her speech with a call for unity to fight "the enemy instead of ourselves." Although six moderate Republicans signed their support for the declaration, they took no part in its development.[45] Given that her speech was critical of both the Democrats and the Republicans and showed alarm for both McCarthyism and the government's poor record in fighting communism, there were very different interpretations and versions of her stand in the media.

Since press editors often saw themselves as moral guardians of society seeking to shape and reflect the voice of the people, their response to the "Declaration of Conscience" provides a guideline to the various moods of the nation on the state of communism in America. Embedded in some press coverage was a spiritual theme. The *Washington Post* claimed that Smith's address provided desperately needed words for "the salvation of the country," the *Chicago Sun-Times* stated that "it has in it the ring of Lexington and Valley Forge, of the Gettysburg address, of the American classroom, of the American home, the American Sunday school and the American church," and the *Syracuse Herald-American* argued that "it should be studied in every school and commented on from every pulpit."[46] Coast to coast, editors had "broken into hallelujahs," wrote an Oregon editor.[47]

In their assessments of her stand, some editors used unhealthy air as a metaphor for McCarthyism. A Hartford, Connecticut, editor wrote of a "cool breeze of honesty from Maine"; a Huntsville, Alabama, editorial welcomed the "draft of clean, wholesome air, turned upon the national capital"; the *Lewiston Daily Sun* spoke of the speech as "a fresh breeze in the fear-ridden atmosphere" of McCarthyism; and the *Washington Star* echoed that Smith's words came "as a much-needed breath of fresh air in the fetid and essentially un-American atmosphere" caused "by irresponsible people galloping around in the Senate."[48] There had been a hunger to see a politician take action against McCarthyites polluting the nation with a brand of anticommunism which many people found deplorable. Newspapers found the Declaration of Conscience good copy and liberal editors apprehensive about the rise of right-wing anticommunism were eager to embrace a Republican critique of McCarthy.

Various newspapers were somewhat clumsy with the theme of Smith's sex and some attempted to undermine her with chauvinist comments or confine her to the domestic sphere. In Massachusetts, the *Fitchburg Sentinel* was extremely critical of her statement and the newspaper suggested that all the earlier attention paid to her political achievements seemed "to have gone to her pretty head."[49] One critic referred to her as "a Moses in nylons."[50] One major supporter of McCarthy was Colonel Robert McCormick's *Chicago Tribune*, which downplayed her speech while making sexist references to the woman from Maine with "pink cheeks and silver hair."[51] The juxtaposition of beauty and the beast is evident in an issue of the *St. Petersburg Times*; presenting an attractive and smiling photograph of Smith, the paper compared the "beauty" to the "wild man from Wisconsin."[52] In their celebration of her speech, the *Boston Post* wrote that all Americans "can rejoice that a woman had tied on her dust cap, seized a broom, and launched a housecleaning." From the West, the *Montana Standard* suggested a reappraisal of the habit of men accusing women of talking idly and favoring "intuition instead of intellect."[53]

A number of titles of newspaper articles portrayed her as a stern mother figure, including the following sample: "Lady Senator Tongue-Lashes Mc-Carthy & Co." (*New York News*), "Mrs. Smith, Only Woman Senator, Flays Republican Leadership" (*Burlington Labor News*, Iowa), "Margaret Chase Smith Calls to Order 'Little Wanton Boys' of U.S. Senate" (*The Washington Evening Star*).[54] The *Detroit Free Press* appeared to commend her ability to provide "sharp expression" to the feelings of the American people tired with the recent political circus, but, nonetheless, the newspaper made the sexist comment that the "logic of her 'plague-on-both-your-houses' castigation sounds typically feminine."[55]

As for political cartoons of Smith, which offered valuable commentary, many highlighted gender themes. The *Chicago Sun* presented a cartoon of a little girl identified as Smith pulling on the arm of her father, identified as the G.O.P., who sat on the street curb outside a saloon inebriated after consuming bottles of bigotry, calumny, smear, and fear. The accompanying title is "Father, Dear Father, Come Home With Me Now."[56] A Sidney L. Maxwell cartoon for the Guy Gannett Publishing Company showed Smith after having dumped a large pail of "SMEAR MATERIAL" on McCarthy's head. Walking away, she has a determined look on her face, smacking her hands together, while McCarthy stands with the pail on his head and face covered in black that had run down on his coat and pants.[57] It was one more victory for women daring to take a stand. In "Two Wrong Approaches to Communist Charges," Silvey Jackson Ray of the *Kansas City Star* has Smith standing on the steps of the Capitol building pointing with each arm to a large pail of "SMEAR" and "WHITE-WASH," symbolizing her disgust with the deeds of both Republican and Democrat males. When Westwood Pegler, columnist of the *Washington Times-Herald*, wrote that Smith took advantage of the "special privilege" of her gender to selfishly attack the Republican Party, the *Nashville Tennessean* responded to Pegler's "unjustified" comments with a cartoon entitled "Pegler Doesn't Approve of Me!" The cartoon showed a vulnerable and weak Smith sitting down slumped forward with her head and arms buried on her desk. In his more accurate portrayal of her character, Herbert L. Block of the *Washington Post* has a stern-looking Smith standing in the kitchen ordering a guilty-looking boy with elephant head, who is filthy from McCarthyism, upstairs to his bedroom for punishment.[58]

There were also cartoons with ambiguous messages and whose interpretations were left up to the individual reader. For example, the *Washington Star's* Gib Crockett portrayed a beaten and bruised elephant youngster, representing the G.O.P, met at the door by a sympathetic and comforting mother, representing Republican National Chairman Guy George Gabrielson. He asks, "THOSE NASTY OL' DEMOCRATS AGAIN?" To which the G.O.P. replies, "N-N-NO MAMA . . . IT WAS MY GIRL FRIEND FROM MAINE!" Then there were the disparaging cartoonists who had little love for the senator from Maine. Viewing her as a harmful liberal Republican senator, Joseph Parrish of the conservative *Chicago Tribune* was especially derogatory toward Smith. One Parrish cartoon entitled "Hit'em Again, Maggie" has Smith, as a bully with a smug smile, holding a brick to be thrown at a defenseless elephant, with the label "The Party," chained to a post, while other "New Deal" and eastern Republicans encourage her.[59] Interestingly, there were critics who attempted to demean her by portraying her as representing manly strength.

Negative editorials were often more abrasive than unfavorable cartoons of Smith, especially those written by some conservative editors who saw her as a traitorous liberal in the wrong party, suggesting she was soft on communism. The *Omaha Evening World-Herald* presented fearful warnings of a "world-wide conspiracy" and "aggressive Soviet despotism" directed against America that demanded more vigilant action than Smith's "feather dusters." Given the whitewashing of Alger Hiss, the Amerasia plot, and the communist spying of American atomic secrets, particularly the free access of Dr. Klaus Fuchs to top secret information, the midwestern newspaper found it strange that the government was reluctant "to act vigorously in defense of our Republic."[60] Other press supportive of McCarthy argued that he, at the risk of his career, was faithfully arousing America to the real danger of communism, stopping the conspiracy of silence in the government, and forcing politicians to take action and clean up the rotten mess of treasonous acts and sabotage that had been shaping policies. Some argued that instead of being beguiled by the Democrats, Smith could have been of real service to her country had she aided McCarthy in his effort to halt the betrayal of Americans.[61] The *Indianapolis Star* wrote that her outburst will provide "aid and comfort to Reds and Red-lovers. With appropriate deletions, it will be gleefully picked up by the Commie and pinko press everywhere."[62] The language was less hostile, but an editorial from the *New Bedford Standard-Times*, Massachusetts, claimed that Smith misconceived the issue; it judged that President Truman's dismissing of loyalty probes as a red herring and the government's lack of action toward those suspected of being threats to the national security was at fault for any cases which saw innocent people charged by McCarthy.[63]

Viewing communist conspiracy as "a clear and present danger" to national security, the *Brooklyn Tablet*, a Catholic weekly newspaper, wrote that Smith and others who opposed McCarthy should "put up or shut up." These Catholics stated that there was nothing wrong with a political party or a politician gaining political capital from the successful prosecution of communist activity within the government: "Such political capital is earned by genuine patriotic service in defense of the security of the United States. Why should it not be eagerly sought rather than scorned?"[64]

Others used her speech as a springboard to criticize Republican "self-appointed liberals" and the liberal New Deal administration. When Smith questioned the fairness of an editorial by Frederic Nelson of the *Saturday Evening Post*, he reiterated his argument that her speech's focus was on the "supposed unfairness of the investigators rather than on the danger to the country from the presence of spies and fellow travelers in the government." He argued that he did not mistake the point of the speech, especially given the joyful response of "so-called liberal columnists" who "thought they got the point" of her condemnation of McCarthy tactics. Nelson added that he admired Smith for her good intentions, but their exchange does demonstrate liberal and conservative forces at work.[65] Somewhat surprising, because Smith's criticism of McCarthy attracted the most attention, practically missed by both liberals and conservatives was her call for greater opposition to the communist menace.

Statements from newspaper editors require careful attention since their approach depended on their political leanings and target audience. Privileging certain voices, the *New York Times,* for example, targeted a more educated, secular, and urbane audience and was less likely to connect with many average Americans who cared more about providing bread and butter for their families than the McCarthyite smearing of individuals. Newspapers such as the *Omaha Evening World-Herald* appealed to the conservative base of middle America when it argued that most Americans found the whitewashing of the guilty more rampant than any smearing of the innocent. Precisely because the Declaration of Conscience criticized both Republicans and Democrats, newspapers had considerable freedom to offer their own positive interpretation or misrepresent what Smith said with derogatory innuendoes, knowing that few readers would have read the text in full. Given the clear political affiliation of many newspapers, one had to question any claims of objectivity and nonpartisanship by liberal, conservative, large metropolitan, small local,

It never Keld
BUT she was
prepared to
face the consequences,
had it not worked

30   Chapter 2

or even centrist newspapers. Some editors outside Maine claimed they knew the desires of the people of Maine better than Smith: the *Boston Daily Record* asserted that the people in Maine "were deeply disappointed" that her Senate speech suited "a radical New Deal gathering" and, in a similar vein, the *Bridgeport Post* of Connecticut suggested that her declaration did not find favor with "the rock-ribbed" people of Maine.[66] Examined carefully, however, most newspapers and magazines revealed a serious concern for communism; where they differed was on the methodology of fighting communism.

Many Americans at the grassroots level voiced their approval of Smith in letters to the editor. For example, in the *Portland Press Herald*, Curtis Gerry wrote that Smith's presentation "should go down in history, for certainly it is as stirring and timely a message as the Gettysburg Address."[67] Writing to the *Boston Herald*, a staunch Republican newspaper, George W. Harrington suggested the substitution of a few women of Smith's caliber in place of a dozen run-of-the-mill senators would save the country from ruin.[68] William B. Grant of Cambridge, Massachusetts, stated that Smith effectively articulated the danger of McCarthy's intellectually insulting methods.[69] Such assessments were high praise for someone with a modest education, a junior senator representing a small state, the only woman in virtually an exclusive men's club dominated by males with advanced educations and social connections.

Letters to the editor critical of Smith gave evidence of a religious component of a right-wing movement opposed to big government and apparently unconcerned with the methods used by McCarthy. Wishing that she would "get on the Lord's side" and be more supportive of McCarthy and her Republican Party, H. C. Kennedy of Somerset, Kentucky declared: "Senator McCarthy is rendering a great service to the people of the United States, and in doing so he is having to go up against the world, the flesh and the devil."[70] Identifying "the State Department as the epicenter of conspiratorial subversion and perversion," right-wing Democrats could be as critical of the State Department as were Republicans.[71] The slurs against McCarthy upset C. J. Nolan, a registered Democrat from Seymour, Indiana. He believed that the government fell for the same trick that Delilah carried out on Samson, namely Russia acquiring Uncle Sam's secrets without the government understanding the consequences. Nolan found it disgusting that there were spies in the State Department when he bought war bonds and when one of his 12 children fought in Europe with millions of other Americans. He was hopeful that McCarthy, the good marine, would "bomb out these pussyfooters who have fooled the people."[72]

Others argued that the Democrats were hardly innocent of aggressive politics since they effectively used fear tactics for political gain. E. C. Blake of Franklin, New Hampshire, found it "astonishing" that Smith and her six co-signing colleagues attacked McCarthy so "bitterly." Asking when did they embrace a "holier-than-thou attitude," he pointed out that the Democrats had maintained power for eighteen years by promoting fear that "terrible Republican reactionaries" in power would result in hunger, lost jobs, homes, and farms, no unemployment insurance, no social security, and no labor union activity. It was time to recognize these tactics favored by the New Dealers and Fair Dealers and support McCarthy and "good plain American commonsense."[73]

The stir that the Declaration of Conscience created in editorials, political cartoons, and letters to the editor was no less so in private correspondence sent to Smith. While it is difficult to accurately discern what a commentator sincerely thought on important issues debated in the public forum, private letters offer good indicators on how Americans felt about Smith and the threat of communism in the United States in general. Assessments in public and private space carry different weight. For example, to journalists President Truman publicly ridiculed the speech with one brief comment, but privately he told Smith that it "was one of the finest things that has happened here in Washington in all my years in the Senate and the White House."[74]

Even allowing that letters cannot represent the views of all Americans, letters and telegrams sent to Smith do shed light on the major opinions in circulation. Congratulating Smith for her speech, Jackson J. Holtz, National Commander of the Jewish War Veterans of the United States of America, wrote that her timely and "forthright statement on traditional, fundamental Americanism desperately needed to be said. It expressed the sincere convictions of the overwhelming, though often inarticulate, majority of our fellow citizens."[75] The Rev. Robert W. Olewiler of Grace Reformed Church in Washington, D.C., sent Smith a letter and copy of his radio sermon that praised the religious element within the Declaration of Conscience, an act that she greatly appreciated.[76] Representative Walter A. Lynch of New York City, who sat on the Ways and Means Committee, judged her statement as "the best 'I am an American' speech of the century."[77] Raymond A. Robinson, director of research at the Crowell-Collier Publishing Company, had been a loyal Republican for decades until the contemptible performances of McCarthy. Smith's declaration, however, had a profound impact on him: "I cannot recall anything since the war that has made me want to stand up and cheer as those honest, noble and patriotic sentiments you expressed."[78]

A significant number of letters sent to Smith were from press elites, delighted that someone finally had the moral courage to voice opposition against the shameful methods of McCarthy. Although Julius Frandsen as news editor of the Washington Bureau, United Press Associations could not say so publicly, he did write to Smith privately commending her Senate presentation.[79] Likewise, Philip L. Graham, publisher of the *Washington Post*, sent his "heartiest congratulations."[80] Virginia Marmaduke, a *Chicago Sun Times* reporter, wrote, "your honest, forthright stand on the current McCarthy witch hunt makes me want to break my silence and tell you plainly how very proud I am of you."[81] "Your splendid speech melts my reportorial objectivity," admitted Rose McKee of the International News Service.[82] Llewllyn White, national editor of the *Reporter*, stated: "In all my fifty years, I cannot remember being more stirred or heartened by such an example of the living faith of a public official."[83] Mc-Carthyism was clearly difficult for many of the press, and they were hungry for someone to give them hope, someone they could rally behind.

For many American women who looked for a source of inspiration in the media, Smith fit the bill. With the return of war veterans and additional expectations for women to stay home and have children, women lost some ground they had gained during the war years. Smith represented a success story of what an apparently independent woman could achieve. Ten Republican women from New Hampshire commended her for her courageous stand.[84] Filled with "bursting pride," a woman from the small coastal community of Bar Harbor, Maine, praised Smith for speaking for the common people and restoring faith in democracy, and another wrote from nearby Blue Hill that she was a disgusted Republican who found Smith's stand heartening.[85] Smith's "one hundred percent American speech" gave a Waterville, Maine, woman greater hope for the future than anything else she had experienced in sixteen years.[86] Another from Portland, Maine, observed that there was now pride in the faces of some who initially questioned Smith's place in the Senate.[87] Of the women who wrote letters, many gave some evidence of having a college education or being involved in professional activity.[88]

Letters to Smith also offered important insights on political life at the grass roots. Thankful for the Declaration of Conscience but discouraged by the antics of politicians, a Bideford, Maine, woman made the point that if there was no practice of dignity and integrity in Washington, the voting public would have few choices beyond charlatans and opportunists.[89] Describing herself as an old Republican, a Greenville Junction, Maine, woman made the observation that older Republicans in Maine tended to deplore McCarthy whereas young G.O.P leaders endorsed McCarthy without the support of the general rank and file of young Republicans. She noted that confusion in the minds and hearts of countless Americans overshadowed any good accomplished by McCarthy.[90] A male constituent used his congratulatory letter to Smith as a forum to express his disgust for the wrangling occurring in Washington. He had been a member of the Republican Party since voting age, but the party had reached an all-time low. He wanted to see more planning and mobilization for war, reduction of government waste, and lower taxes. He suggested the creation of the "American Party," a party led by someone like "Senator

Bird" with the backing of conservative Southern Democrats and astute Republicans.[91] Before one man moved from Maine to Florida, his aunt advised him that a vote for Smith was the smart choice. Smith's commonsense speech vindicated his aunt's judgement completely, and he noted that in the St. Petersburg, Florida, area both young Democrats and Republicans found her speech uplifting. As had been the case when he was at Boston University, he wrote that the Democrats of his acquaintance would support a Wilkie type of Republican but never Taft and "old-guard Republicans."[92]

Progressive women's groups such as the Women's International League for Peace and Freedom expressed appreciation for Smith's analysis of the political exploitation of fear and ignorance. Alarmed that the widespread support for bills designed to target subversive activities were instead threats to individual freedom and democracy, President Annalee Stewart wrote: "Whatever the dangers may be from fifth columns the greatest danger lies, we believe, in our lack of vigorous faith in our own democratic institutions."[93] Actually, cases of anticommunist persecution were rare in correspondence to Smith. One case took place in Clinton, Maine, where a schoolteacher, according to his wife, was victim of an unfair attack on his character and reputation by a student's parents. Not members of the Republican Party, the couple believed that McCarthyism provided the model for such "guerrilla" tactics.[94]

A Gallup Poll found McCarthy's support was strong among manual workers while weak among business and professional people.[95] Those under suspicion were more apt to be well-educated people with liberal sensibilities, and thus McCarthyism was less a threat to working-class people. Of the many letters sent to Smith by professionals, more were praising than critical of Smith's opposition to McCarthy. Lawyers and others in the field of law and justice were particularly quick to applaud her and political affiliation did not appear to be an important issue. James Lawrence-Fly, a Democrat and New York lawyer, thanked Smith for her example of statesmanship rarely seen in political circles, and Augustus W. Bennet, a Republican and New York lawyer, shared his high regard for her ability and integrity.[96] Writing from Harvard Law School, Lewis Pickett congratulated her for representing the best traditions of Republicanism and Americanism.[97] Harry J. Freebourn of the Montana Supreme Court sent his congratulations, as did a retired District Court Judge of Minneapolis who explained that he was a hereditary and lifelong Republican, whose loyalty was wavering because of McCarthyism.[98] In his praise of the Declaration of Conscience, Associate Justice Jesse W. Carter of the Supreme Court of California, and a self-proclaimed Democrat, wrote that no one political party had a corner on virtue, honesty, and political sagacity and, thus, it was time for politicians to focus on constructive measures and let the Department of Justice handle criminal investigation and law enforcement.[99]

The reaction to the Declaration of Conscience from college professors and other educators was overwhelmingly positive. H. B. Kirshen, the head of the Department of Economics and Sociology, University of Maine, Orono, wrote that the fear generated by McCarthy was a serious distraction to genuine efforts of identifying real communists. Heartened that it was Smith who spoke for the cause of civil liberties, he stated that she deserved every conceivable amount of acclaim.[100] Reporting on his several months in Europe, Arthur Deering, Dean of the College of Agriculture, University of Maine, Orono, stated that Europeans found McCarthy's tactics shocking. He understood the seriousness of rooting out communists, but improper tactics hurt the innocent and assisted the guilty.[101] Thomas S. Hayes, professor of English at Biblioteca de la Universidad, Puerto Rico, wrote that Smith's words had reached all good and thinking people and that her lesson in patriotism had elicited the acclaim of his university colleagues.[102] A similar message came from W. H. Howells, anthropology professor at the University of Wisconsin.[103] Richard Swift, instructor of government at New York University, requested copies of her "courageous" speech.[104] Writing that the South desperately needed the two-party system, Ralph Purcell, a political science professor at Emory University, believed that if the Republicans campaigned on the platform and record similar to Smith's they would receive surprising support in the South.[105] College students likewise indicated their endorsement of Smith including the Young Republican Club of the University of Michigan, Ann Arbor.[106]

Many letters offered impressive analysis. One Democrat claiming he wanted to assist Smith discussed historiography, bureaucracy theory, and ideological polarization. He predicted that in future historical accounts of the early post–World War II period, "many of the alleged cases of treason will turn out to be something almost worse." Referring to how government bureaucrats kept problems hidden in order to protect their promotions, he wrote of "the protective tropism to Protect the Organization." He offered criticism of both conservatives and liberals. He described McCarthy as "an incipient Fascist or GPU agent" who unfortunately missed his true calling by not being born in Russia where he could have fashioned a beautiful stage trial. As for the "professional liberals," they had much explaining to do regarding their "courtship and deification of a dictatorship like the Soviet Union." Finally, he claimed that numerous Americans who voted for the Truman government were weary over its conduct, but they were also fearful that the Republican Party represented only well-off, white, Protestant Americans. These voters expected that the Republicans would seek to restore the status quo of the pre-Depression years and thus decimate New Deal accomplishments.[107]

There were also many letter writers who were quite hostile to Smith's performance in the Senate and they defended McCarthy with passion. One man wrote that at a community gathering in Freeport, Maine, people debated whether Smith was a Republican or Democrat of the Truman school. He questioned whether Washington had a different standard of decency than Maine. He wanted to know what she was doing "to clean out the cesspools of vile depravity in our government," asking, "is 'smear' worse than degeneracy and treason?" The constituent failed to see how her "'bipartisan' approach" would have uncovered Hiss; he believed that voters were more supportive of McCarthy's methods than the alternative of using "kid gloves and soft soap."[108] The implication here was that the Democrats did not adopt a manly approach.

Writing that he had traveled extensively enough in four states that he understood the pulse of average Americans, a West Virginian declared that McCarthy was not on trial and questioned Smith's latest outburst and why she had been on the Republican side of the house for years without "stirring up the animals or attempting to clean house in government."[109] This was a good point, because Smith normally carried out her political duties quietly, rarely speaking in the Senate. A Brooklyn, New York, telegram from one woman stated: "YOUR SPEECH WAS A DISGRACE TO THE REPUBLICAN PARTY IT STINKS ON ICE SENATOR MCCARTHY IS A TRUE LOYAL AMERICAN AND A CREDIT TO HIS COUNTRY AND NOT AFRAID TO SHOW UP THE CROOKS."[110] A Houston, Texas woman declared, "I think we should all get down on our knees and thank the good Lord for what Senator McCarthy has done for the American people."[111] Arguing that Smith fell into the Soviet trap of aiding and comforting communists, John Chapple, managing editor of the *Ashland Daily Press*, lamented her failure to recognize the criminal conspiracy of communism that sought to destroy family life, religious freedom, and America's existence as a free nation.[112] Basil Brewer, publisher of the *Standard-Times* (New Bedford, Massachusetts), voiced his anger that she was easy on the Democratic administration, but hard on Republicans, to the point that the Democrats could use her statement to bolster their election prospects.[113]

Alfred Kohlberg, a McCarthyite from New York City, used satire to defend the work of McCarthy. In a letter with letterhead "National Committee to Stop McCarthy in '52 (not inc.), Kohlberg wrote of the consequences of evil McCarthyism sweeping America: "In his mad advance McCarthy threatens the safety of every Red in the government. If McCarthy succeeds, the Rockefeller, Carnegie and other tax-free Foundations will lose their Fellow Traveler privileges. Schools will be forced to speak well of America; worship of Stalin will be ended." Ignoring or not understanding the satire, Smith responded stating, "You obviously are extremely confused."[114]

Many Republicans in western states had few good things to say to Smith. A Colorado Springs man assailed Smith for her attack on McCarthy, who had the guts to confront communist movements, and her "liberal" and "socialistic" voting record. Frustrated that she failed to understand the impact that "Kremlinites" had in the government, he wrote: "To me your actions have been of the insurgent and renegade type against the best interests of the citizens of our Country in many instances."[115] The gulf between eastern Republicans and midwestern Republicans existed and people of the Midwest generally were more supportive of McCarthy. A member of the Federated Women's Republican Clubs of Missouri sent a blistering letter explaining that Smith's left-wing outburst received "universal and emphatic condemnation" of the Republican Club. She gave a brief lesson on the prevailing political climate in Missouri: "We are not socialistically minded in the Midwest, not even the Democrats for the most part, though some go along for sake of tradition and hatred of the party that freed the slaves. We are concerned about Communist infiltration in government, and everybody knows the Roosevelts played along with them for sake of their votes, and betrayed our country to help Stalin." She concluded that she supported more women in government, but judged Smith to be a very poor representative of women, the Republican Party, and American heritage.[116] A Chicago resident explained that the Midwest was very suspicious of the State Department and thus most people there judged McCarthy as one "performing a great and patriotic service."[117] The Republican Women's Federation of Oakland County, Michigan, unanimously adopted a resolution of support for McCarthy and his work to safeguard the nation.[118] Smith could not escape the belief of midwest Republicans that she was an eastern liberal; many of them who viewed communism as a sinister force had yet to learn of or appreciate her vigorous stand against it.

Throughout the twentieth century, those in religious quarters often presented the most fervent attacks against communism. A significant number of letters to Smith contained religious rhetoric, including a Flushing, New York, resident who wrote: "Communism, to many of us old-fashioned Americans, is a heinous crime against God, the United States Republic, and suffering humanity!"[119] Certainly, McCarthy's Roman Catholicism was an important issue with many Americans. In the 1950s, Richard Rovere suggested that Irish Roman Catholics saw McCarthy as "the flaming avenger of their own humiliations of the past and who could not believe that the criticism he provoked was based on anything but hatred of his Church and his name."[120] Some scholars see much of the support for McCarthyism based less on Catholic or Protestant identifications and more on liberal or conservative affinities: "McCarthy appealed to conservatives, whether Catholic or Protestant."[121]

Protestant fundamentalist literature indicates that there were fundamentalists who ignored his Catholicism and openly supported his efforts, mainly because they shared a common distaste for the United Nations, the New

Deal, and the State Department. Separatist fundamentalists, who typically were unwilling to have close relations with "people having the 'wrong theology,' were willing to overlook a politician's 'wrong theology' in deference to his 'right politics.'"[122] Fundamentalist preacher John R. Rice, who often warned of the dangers of the "Romanists," nonetheless, wrote, "We are for the work Senator McCarthy is doing in exposing Communists infiltrating our government."[123] Referring to the "powers of darkness" that were rampant, one Pennsylvania Presbyterian minister made it clear to Smith that it was unwise for the Senate to oppose the work of McCarthy in revealing the links between the State Department and communism.[124]

It is true that those who identified themselves more with fundamentalism tended to accept an assault on communism even if that meant compromising civil liberties. However, such moral absolutism had limitations. Most evangelical Protestants understood communism to be locked in a battle with Christianity, but their attitude toward McCarthyism was often ambivalent. Characterized by the *Chicago Daily News* as "Communism's Public Enemy Number One," evangelist Billy Graham admired those who hounded alleged communist subversives in government, yet he was reluctant to publicly endorse McCarthy: "I have never met McCarthy, corresponded with him, exchanged telegrams or telephoned him. I have no comments to make on the Senator."[125]

While it is difficult to accurately gauge the response of Christian churches, some were clearly more vocal in their criticism of McCarthyism. A recent study on McCarthyism and Presbyterians in the three major denominations (Presbyterian Church, U.S.A; Presbyterian Church, U.S.; and United Presbyterian Church of North America) demonstrates that while there was support for McCarthy, far more Presbyterians found his investigative tactics inappropriate.[126]

Letters from more liberal churches were especially supportive of Smith's message on protecting civil liberties. Harper Sibley, president of the United Council of Church Women, wrote that thousands of churchwomen were ready to help her in any way they could.[127] Representing the Maine Methodist Conference Board of Education and Missions, the Rev. G. Duncan Moore expressed relief that a senator with courage finally took a stand against McCarthyism.[128] There was support from Congregationalist clergy, including the Rev. Kingsley W. Hawthorne who rejoiced that Smith had the courage and decency to speak the truth.[129] The Rev. Ralph Edward Kyper, a Unitarian minister, likewise commended Smith on her words of sanity in days of mass hysteria.[130] Offering a similar message was the Rev. Theodore A. Webb, a Universalist clergyman who was more favorable to the logical approach of former vice president Henry A. Wallace and the Progressives, writing that few people realized and understood the restrictions placed on thinkers and those on the left.[131] This type of support for Smith ran the risk of being more harmful than beneficial, but these liberal churches devoid of an orthodox biblical message represented a declining number of church people. To be sure, it is highly unlikely that she sought close relations with leftist clergy.

Right-wing Republicans critical of her voting record, that placed her in with the eastern and liberal Republican "Me Too" bloc that allegedly supported Democrat policies, failed to brand her unworthy of the party.[132] They were unhappy with her stand against McCarthy, but by mid-June she reported that correspondence sent across the nation was approximately eight to one in favor of her position.[133] A political boost was her place on the June 12 cover of *Newsweek* with the title "Senator Smith: A Woman Vice President?" Americans coast to coast saw her as a legitimate Republican vice presidential nomination in 1952 and some even talked about the presidency.[134] Most people accorded her with respect, seeing her as a "spokesman" for the people.[135] Change came slowly for acceptance of women in politics, yet there were encouraging signs; recent scholarship shows that the ideology of domesticity was not as dominant in postwar mass culture as Betty Friedan had argued.[136] When the press attempted to connect Smith to the domestic sphere, her character usually represented leadership rather than submission and vulnerability.

A McCarthyite tactic was to question the masculinity of an opponent. One man writing from California declared that it was unfortunate that a "schoolmarm" prepared the Declaration of Conscience and thus left-wingers interpreted it as censure of McCarthy and approval of Truman. McCarthy had no choice but ram his way into the fight against communism since the government was only espousing "double-talk." Making a reference to the suspect masculinity of liberal politicians, the man dismissed the "old-maidish senators from the New England states, as they never were two-fisted."[137] This could be an effective tactic given that a significant number of Americans who were supportive of McCarthy voiced their disapproval of "timid" politicians.[138]

However, a woman and a hard worker with working-class origins, Smith did not fit McCarthy's category of a "sissified" eastern establishment figure that allegedly allowed communist infiltration. He was unsure how to control the forceful Smith—a highly principled, no-nonsense woman—who had proven herself as a strong personality capable of holding her own. Her quiet approach in the Senate did not give her the visibility of more dynamic politicians, but silence and composure also hinted of strength of character. Uncommon for McCarthy, he sat white-faced during her speech, offered no rebuttal, and gave no official comment to the press. He allegedly revealed to his friends that he would not respond to "the spanking" Smith gave him.[139]

Even before the rise of McCarthyism, a Colorado man noted Smith's role in the Senate to "watch over that aggregation of boys in their second childhood and now and then lay a restraining hand and voice on their impulsive, inane legislative acts."[140] This was wishful thinking; she had the respect of her colleagues, particularly those who knew of her impressive attentiveness and comprehensive groundwork in committees, but there is little evidence that her influence on other senators was of any lasting significance. For example, she made no effort to bolster the unity of the six Republican senators who signed the declaration and within a few short weeks all but one retracted their support.

Aware that the Declaration of Conscience had no effect in reducing McCarthy's power, Smith needed the support of her constituents and the press to survive the rough political waters. The liberal press stood by Smith because she offered a better brand of anticommunism that respected civil liberties. Here was a Cold Warrior they could support, someone who upheld both anticommunist vigilance and also the freedoms that Americans held dear. As for the Republican Party, the more moderate East Coast establishment controlled much of the money and media influence.[141] If she remained a star in the eyes of her constituents and the press, most Republicans had little to gain in attacking her. Actually, it was difficult for conservative Republicans to effectively brand her a leftist and "godless" politician soft on communism.

When managing editor Jack Lait and columnist Lee Mortimer, both of the *New York Daily Mirror*, characterized Smith as a left-wing apologist in their 1952 book *USA Confidential*,[142] she filed a million-dollar libel suit and she and her executive assistant Bill Lewis presented a deeper analysis of the Declaration of Conscience which concluded that she *approved* of McCarthy's objectives. She also wanted to get "the subversives out of government and out of the country," but without "smearing innocent people to do it."[143] Although her Declaration of Conscience lacked specifics, she believed that Truman was guilty of whitewashing Alger Hiss and that the Department of Justice and Millard Tydings Committee were guilty of whitewashing those involved in the Amerasia Case.[144] Eventually wining her suit against Mortimer, Smith proved she was not under the influence of the left wing.[145]

Smith was a Cold Warrior who saw communism as a sinister force and if a number of McCarthyites were unaware that she also sought the destruction of communism, she found strength in her own moral position on the best way to fight the red menace. No surprise to those who read her Declaration of Conscience carefully, she had the temperament to "out-McCarthy McCarthy." To an Arizonan man, she clarified her support of the Internal Security Subcommittee, led by Senator Pat McCarran (D-NV), a fervent anticommunist who believed that communists had infiltrated the United Nations, the press, churches, colleges, and labor unions. Passed in 1950 over Truman's veto, the Internal Security Act (McCarran Act) required the federal registration of "Communist organizations."[146]

She spoke out against communism many times in the press and in one of her newspaper columns she asked Americans to respond to her position on banning the Communist Party. Readers overwhelmingly supported such action and she became one of the first politician of the Eighty-third Congress to introduce bills to outlaw the Communist Party.[147] When her bill failed to get strong support from various national organizations, she began to sound more like a McCarthyite: "I have been quite puzzled about the indifference and negative attitude of some leaders and groups who do a great deal of talking about the menace of communism. . . . Yet, for some reason they will take no action to make communism illegal."[148] Many years later in retirement, she dismissed the claim that McCarthy had damaged the American image in the world and the ability for the United States to pursue foreign policy objectives.[149] Although this was a rather curious statement, perhaps she believed that the image of American anticommunist hysteria offered more benefits than shortcomings in the sense that it was a statement to outsiders of Americans being on guard and not completely sidetracked by the charms of prosperity and consumerism. In any event, Smith took a stand that some judged to be a mindless reactionary one, even though she was a moderate on most issues outside national security. In 1954, I. F. Stone, a leftist intellectual, wrote that Smith's "outdoing McCarthy" and her desire to deprive "Communist conspirators" of citizenship represented a betrayal of American democracy.[150] There is merit to such criticism; her bills did reveal hypocrisy in the sense that they denied the individual rights that her Declaration of Conscience appeared to cherish.[151] In light of the conflicting critiques of Mortimer and Stone, Smith had work to do in communicating her exact position on communism, especially since she was up for reelection in 1954.

After Smith delivered her Declaration of Conscience many Americans responded positively, delighted that someone finally had the moral courage to voice strong opposition against the methods of Joseph McCarthy. That others faulted her and continued to support McCarthy reveals that Americans did not agree on the best method of defeating communism. As the sole female senator, she did well in the short term, but with the tough demands of Washington politics and the coming of the Korean War, she believed it would be more pressing for her to prove she was a stalwart Cold Warrior prepared to fight the red menace.

NOTES

1. Smith, *Declaration of Conscience*, 11–12.
2. Smith, *Declaration of Conscience*, 13.

3. On Hiss, see G. Edward White, *Alger Hiss's Looking-Glass Wars: The Covert Life of a Soviet Spy* (Oxford: Oxford University Press, 2004). A recent study that focuses on Russian World War II espionage and dates the roots of the Cold War in the late years of World War II is Katherine A.S. Sibley, *Red Spies in America: Stolen Secrets and the Dawn of the Cold War* (Lawrence: University Press of Kansas, 2004). Sibley notes that the number of American communists engaged in spying was much higher than what earlier academics believed (5).

4. William B. Prendergast, "State Legislatures and Communism: The Current Scene," *American Political Science Review* XLIV, no. 3 (September 1950), 574, Communism Folder, MCSL.

5. Harbutt, *The Cold War*, states that this social cohesion did not survive "the shattering experience of the Vietnam War" (ix).

6. Lisle A. Rose, *The Cold War Comes to Main Street: America in 1950* (Lawrence: University Press of Kansas, 1999).

7. Samuel A. Stouffer, *Communism, Conformity, and Civil Liberties: A Cross-section of the Nation Speaks Its Mind* (Garden City, N.Y.: Doubleday & Company, Inc., 1955), 40, 43, 86–87.

8. Studies that survey American anticommunism throughout the twentieth century include: Ted Morgan, *Reds: McCarthyism in Twentieth-Century America* (New York: Random House 2003); Kovel, *Red Hunting in the Promised Land*; Powers, *Not Without Honor*; and M. J. Heale, *American Anticommunism: Combating the Enemy Within, 1830–1970* (Baltimore, Md.: Johns Hopkins University Press, 1990).

9. Ellen Schrecker, "McCarthyism: Political Repression and the Fear of Communism," *Social Research* 71, no. 4 (Winter 2004), 1042–43. Others also designate McCarthyism as a "political phenomenon that extended well beyond the antics of Senator McCarthy." See Richard M. Fried, *Nightmare in Red: The McCarthy Era in Perspective* (New York: Oxford University Press, 1990), 9. Also, Morgan, *Reds*.

10. See cartoon in Walter LaFeber, *America, Russia, and the Cold War, 1945–2002*, updated 9th ed. (McGraw-Hill 2002), 54.

11. Prendergast, "State Legislatures and Communism," 557.

12. For an introduction of the red menace in popular culture, see Michael Baron and Steven Heller, *Red Scared! The Commie Menace in Propaganda and Popular Culture* (San Francisco: Chronicle Books 2001). In *Dictators, Democracy, and American Public Culture: Envisioning the Totalitarian Enemy, 1920s–1950s* (Chapel Hill: University of North Carolina Press 2003), Benjamin L. Apers applies the term "cultural producers" in a broader sense to include "professors, policymakers, speechwriters, presidents, filmmakers, novelists, and business leaders" whose impact on society was hegemonic (8).

13. Margot A. Henriksen, *Dr. Strangelove's America: Society and Culture in the Atomic Age* (Berkeley: University of California Press 1997), 69–70.

14. Eric R. Crouse, "Responding to the Reds: Conservative Protestants, Anti-Communism, and the Shaping of American Culture, 1945–1965," in *Historical Papers 2002: Canadian Society of Church History*, ed. Bruce Reimer, 100.

15. Quoted in Anne Sheck, "Margaret Chase Smith's 'Declaration of Conscience,'" 4, Declaration of Conscience Folder, MCSL.

16. "Speech That May Make History," *Anniston Star*, 4 June 1950, Scrapbook, vol. 88, 8, MCSL.

17. John Earl Haynes and Harvey Klehr, *Early Cold War Spies: The Espionage Trials That Shaped American Politics* (Cambridge: Cambridge University Press, 2006), 2–3. For a sampling of archival documents, see Harvey Klehr, John Earl Haynes and Kyrill M. Anderson, *The Soviet World of American Communism* (New Haven, Conn.: Yale University Press, 1998).

18. On the Rosenbergs, see Ronald Radosh and Joyce Milton, *The Rosenberg File: A Search for the Truth*, 2nd ed. (New Haven, Conn.: Yale University Press, 1997).

19. Robert Myers, "Anti-Communist Mob Action: A Case Study," in *Readings in Collective Behavior*, 2nd ed., ed. Robert R. Evans (Chicago: Rand McNally 1975), 152–61.

20. Smith, *Declaration of Conscience*, 9.

21. One representative study that sees the era as one of mass hysteria is David Caute, *The Great Fear: The Anti-Communist Purge under Truman and Eisenhower* (New York: Simon and Schuster, 1977).

22. Melvin Small, *Democracy & Diplomacy: The Impact of Domestic Politics on U.S. Foreign Policy, 1789–1994* (Baltimore: Johns Hopkins University Press, 1996), 82. Arthur Herman, *Joseph McCarthy: Reexamining the Life and Legacy of America's Most Hated Senator* (New York: The Free Press, 2000), 4. Herman writes: "The best and most generous estimate is that during the entire decade of the red scare, ten thousand Americans lost their jobs because of their past or present affiliation with the Communist Party or one of its auxiliary organizations."

23. Powers, *Not Without Honor*, 254–56.

24. Anne Applebaum, *Gulag: A History* (New York: Anchor Books, 2003).

25. Herman, *Joseph McCarthy*, 98–100. Herman argues that McCarthy made "a good point badly."

26. Joseph R. McCarthy Speech at Wheeling, McCarthy, Joseph R. Folder, MCSL.

27. Richard H. Rovere, *Senator Joe McCarthy* (New York: Harper Torchbooks, 1959), 5–7.

28. Rovere, *Senator Joe McCarthy*, 3.

29. Rovere, *Senator Joe McCarthy*, 23.

30. Harbutt, *The Cold War*, 6. The Republicans had their own "tense marriage" between East Coast internationalists and the agrarians in the Midwest and west.

31. "Pegler Says," Scrapbook, vol. 88, 66, MCSL.

32. Sherman, *No Place for a Woman*; Schmidt, *Margaret Chase Smith*; Wallace, *Politics of Conscience*; Herman, *Joseph McCarthy*; David Oshinsky, *A Conspiracy So Immense: The World of Joe McCarthy* (New York: The Free Press, 1983); Thomas C. Reeves, *The Life and Times of Joe McCarthy* (New York: Stein and Day, 1982).

33. Smith, *Declaration of Conscience*, 7. Even Robert Kennedy had been supportive of McCarthy. See Arthur M. Schlesinger, Jr., *Robert Kennedy and His Times* (Boston: Houghton Mifflin Company, 1978), 106.

34. W. A. McConagha, "Politics, Almost as Usual," 5, Declaration of Conscience Speech, McConagha, MCSL.

35. John Cottrell to Elizabeth May Craig, 7 April 1950, McCarthy, Joseph R. Correspondence, Maine Opposition to McCarthy, MCSL.

36. John R. Swanton to MCS, 2 June 1950, Declaration of Conscience Correspondence, MCSL.

37. H. H. Fisher to MCS, 8 June 1950, Declaration of Conscience, Out of State Reactions, MCSL.

38. The Republican dilemma receives attention in "Declaration of Conscience," *Baltimore Sun*, 3 June 1950, Scrapbook, vol. 88, 20, MCSL.

39. Morgan, *Reds*, 274–83; Oshinsky, *A Conspiracy so Immense*, 100. Also, see Haynes and Klehr, *Early Cold War Spies*, 3.

40. W&Y, 1 March 1950, MCSL.

41. "Who Cares?" Scrapbook, vol. 88, 21, MCSL.

42. This was also the view of some conservative newspaper editors. See "Chameleon Republicans," Scrapbook, vol. 88, 59, MCSL.

43. In an interview in the early 1990s, Smith stated: "I have never claimed to be a liberal. That is a label given to me by others, especially by my critics." See Smith-Rhodri Jeffreys-Jones interview, 29 July 1991, MCSL.

44. Smith, *Declaration of Conscience*, 13.

45. Smith, *Declaration of Conscience*, 15–16. The six were: Charles W. Tobey, (NH), George D. Aiken (VT), Wayne L. Morse (OR), Irving M. Ives (NY), Edward J. Thye (MN), and Robert C. Hendrickson (NJ). Ives was the only one who suggested revision—a minor one of changing one word.

46. Declaration of Conscience, Out of State Reactions, 1, 2, 5, 8, MCSL.

47. "Gallant Lady from Down Maine," Scrapbook, vol. 88, 36, MCSL.

48. Scrapbook, vol. 88, 8–10, 14, 23, MCSL.

49. "A Darling Stumbles," Scrapbook, vol. 88, 68, MCSL.

50. "Senator Smith! How Could You?" Scrapbook, vol. 88, 41, MCSL.

51. Sheck, "Margaret Chase Smith's 'Declaration of Conscience,'" 6, MCSL.

52. "The Lady Says it Beautifully, But How Much Good Will it Do?" Scrapbook, vol. 88, 11, MCSL.

53. "Smearing the Innocent and Whitewashing the Guilty," Scrapbook, vol. 88, 21, 25, MCSL. In the eyes of some, the *Boston Herald*'s trivial discussion of appropriate language such as "stateswomanship," "horsewomanship," and "craftswomanship" may have diminished the sincere praise of Smith. See "Stateswomanship," Scrapbook, vol. 88, 20, MCSL.

54. Scrapbook, vol. 89, 100, 169; vol. 90, 201, MCSL.

55. "Stateswoman from Maine," Scrapbook, vol. 88, 22, MCSL.

56. Scrapbook, vol. 88, 12, MCSL.

57. *Portland Sunday Telegram and Sunday Press Herald*, 4 June 1950, Declaration of Conscience, Cartoons, MSCL.

58. *Never Underestimate. . . . The Life and Career of Margaret Chase Smith Through the Eyes of the Political Cartoonist* (Northwood University Margaret Chase Smith Library 1993), 15, 24, 26.

59. *Never Underestimate*, 20, 22.

60. "'Smear' and 'Whitewash,'" Scrapbook, vol. 88, 26, MCSL.

61. Scrapbook, vol. 88, 58, MCSL.

62. "Cart Before the Horse," Scrapbook, vol. 88, 64, MCSL.

63. "Mrs. Smith's Manifesto," Scrapbook, vol. 88, 68, MCSL.

64. Scrapbook, vol. 88, 73, MCSL.

65. MCS to Frederick Nelson, 15 July 1950; Frederick Nelson to MCS, 17 July 1950, Declaration of Conscience Correspondence, MCSL.

66. Scrapbook, vol. 88, 58, 66, MCSL.

67. Scrapbook, vol. 88, 15, MCSL.

68. "Wants More Women Senators," Scrapbook, vol. 88, 20, MCSL.

69. "Plaudits for Senator Smith," Declaration of Conscience, MCSL.

70. "With Kindest Regards," Scrapbook, vol. 88, 65, MCSL.

71. Dean, *Imperial Brotherhood*, 65.

72. "Believes McCarthy Slurred," Scrapbook, vol. 88, 65, MCSL.

73. "Scores Mrs. Smith," Scrapbook, vol. 88, 71, MCSL.

74. Smith, *Declaration of Conscience*, 21.

75. Jackson J. Holtz to MCS, 13 June 1950, Declaration of Conscience, Out of State Reactions, MCSL.

76. Declaration of Conscience, Out of State Reactions. Smith responded to Olewiler stating. "Your sermon on my "Declaration of Conscience" was one of the finest things that has ever happened to me. I am truly grateful" [MCS to Robert Olewiler, 12 July 1950, Declaration of Conscience, Out of State Reactions, MCSL].

77. Walter A. Lynch to MCS, 2 June 1950, Declaration of Conscience, Out of State Reactions, MCSL.

78. Raymond A. Robison to MCS, 2 June 1950, Declaration of Conscience, Out of State Reactions, MCSL.

79. Julius Frandsen to MCS, 5 June 1950, Declaration of Conscience, Out of State Reactions, MCSL.

80. Philip Graham to MCS, 2 June 1950, Declaration of Conscience, Out of State Reactions, MCSL.

81. Virginia Marmaduke to MCS, 2 June 1950, Declaration of Conscience, Press Reports, MCSL.

82. Rose McKee to MCS, 4 June 1950, Declaration of Conscience, Press Reports, MCSL.

83. Llewllyn White to MCS, 2 June 1950, Declaration of Conscience, Out of State Reactions, MCSL.

84. Republican Women of New Hampshire to MCS, 10 June 1950, Declaration of Conscience, MCSL.

85. Sarah Fisher Scott to MCS, 2 June 1950, and Dorothy Heywood to MCS, 4 June 1950, Declaration of Conscience, Maine Reactions, MCSL.

86. Ethel Allen to MCS, 3 June 1950, Declaration of Conscience, Maine Reactions, MCSL.

87. Feddy Marsh to MCS, 16 June 1950, Declaration of Conscience, Maine Reactions, MCSL.

88. For example, one supporter was a Colby College woman and a Sigma Kappa who had worked in politics. She shared that her Oxford-graduate son,

employed by the C.I.A. in Washington, found Smith's speech inspiring. Mrs. William Abbot Smith to MCS, 7 June 1950, Declaration of Conscience, Maine Reactions, MCSL.

89. Louise S. Darcy to MCS, 6 June 1950, Declaration of Conscience, Maine Reactions, MCSL.

90. Ruth M. Vickerg to MCS, 2 June 1950, Declaration of Conscience, Maine Reactions, MCSL.

91. Caldwell Sweet to MCS, 3 June 1950, Declaration of Conscience, Maine Reactions, MCSL.

92. Robert D. Towne to MCS, 2 June 1950, Declaration of Conscience, Out of State Reactions, MCSL.

93. Annalee Stewart to MCS, 16 June 1950, Declaration of Conscience, Women's International League for Peace and Freedom, MCSL.

94. Shirley Johnston to MCS, 2 June 1950, Declaration of Conscience, Maine Reactions, MCSL. Also, an Evanston, Illinois woman shared that someone in her own family suffered because of Communist smear. See Ruth Rideout to MCS, 11 June 1950, Declaration of Conscience, Out of State Reactions, MCSL.

95. Rovere, *Senator Joe McCarthy*, 13.

96. James Lawrence-Fly to MCS, 2 June 1950, Declaration of Conscience, Out of State Reactions. Augustus Bennet to MCS, 5 June 1950, Declaration of Conscience, Out of State Reactions, MCSL.

97. Lewis Pickett to MCS, 2 June 1950, Declaration of Conscience, Out of State Reactions, MCSL.

98. Harry J. Freebourn to MCS, 14 June 1950, and Edward F. Waite to MCS, 2 June 1950, Declaration of Conscience, Out of State Reactions, MCSL.

99. Jesse W. Carter to MCS, 2 June 1950, Declaration of Conscience, Out of State Reactions, MCSL.

100. H. B. Kirshen to MCS, 6 June 1950, Declaration of Conscience, Maine Reactions, MCSL.

101. Arthur Deering to MCS, 3 June 1950, Declaration of Conscience, Maine Reactions, MCSL.

102. Thomas S. Hayes to MCS, 12 June 1950, Declaration of Conscience, Out of State Reactions, MCSL.

103. W. W. Howells to MCS, 3 June 1950, Declaration of Conscience, Out of State Reactions, MCSL.

104. Richard Swift to MCS, 7 June 1950, Declaration of Conscience, Out of State Reactions, MCSL.

105. Richard N. Swift to MCS, 7 June 1950; Ralph Purcell to MCS, 10 June 1950, Declaration of Conscience, Out of State Reactions, MCSL.

106. John G. Donaldson to MCS, 15 June 1950, Declaration of Conscience, Out of State Reactions, MCSL.

107. Paul McGouldrick to MCS, 12 June 1950, Declaration of Conscience, Maine Reactions, MCSL.

108. George B Funderburg to MCS, 7 June 1950, Declaration of Conscience Correspondence, MCSL.

109. W. F. Kennedy to MCS, 7 June 1950, Declaration of Conscience Correspondence, MCSL.

110. Mary Pulsifer to MCS, 2 June 1950, Declaration of Conscience, Out of State Reactions, MCSL.

111. Rebecca Wyncoop to MCS, 2 October 1951, McCarthy Correspondence, Out of State Support for McCarthy, MCSL.

112. John Chapple to MCS, 5 June 1950, Declaration of Conscience, Out of State Reactions, MCSL.

113. Basil Brewer to MCS, 7 June 1950, Declaration of Conscience, Out of State Reactions, MCSL. Surveying the damage she did to the Republican Party, a New Yorker wondered if Smith gave her unpatriotic talk in order to stay on the safe side in case Truman returned to the White House in 1952. See M. A. Ackermann to MCS, 6 June 1950, Declaration of Conscience, Out of State Reactions, MCSL.

114. Alfred Kohlberg to MCS, 26 June 1950, Declaration of Conscience, Out of State Reactions; MCS to Alfred Kohlberg, 28 June 1950, Declaration of Conscience, Correspondence, MCSL.

115. Robert Donner to MCS, 14 July 1950, Declaration of Conscience, Out of State Reactions, MCSL.

116. Clara Speer to MCS, 8 June 1950, Declaration of Conscience, Out of State Reactions, MCSL.

117. Robert Wood to MCS, 21 June 1950, Declaration of Conscience, Out of State Reactions, MCSL. Responding directly to this letter, Smith clarified that "Communism must be rooted out" without flouting the Constitution. See MCS to Robert Wood, 23 June 1950, Declaration of Conscience, Out of State Reactions, MCSL.

118. Helen Randall to MCS, 19 June 1950, Declaration of Conscience, Out of State Reactions, MCSL.

119. John Daly to MCS, 9 June 1950, Declaration of Conscience Correspondence, MCSL.

120. Rovere, *Senator Joe McCarthy*, 21.

121. Donald F. Crosby, *God, Church, and Flag: Senator Joseph R. McCarthy and the Catholic Church, 1950–1957* (Chapel Hill: University of North Carolina Press, 1978), 87. Robert P. Erickson, "The Role of American Churches in the McCarthy Era," *Kirchliche Zeitgeschichte* 3, no. 1 (1990), 47.

122. Warren L. Vinz, "Protestant Fundamentalism and McCarthy," *Continuum* 6, no. 3 (Autumn 1968), 319.

123. Quoted in Warren L. Vinz, *Pulpit Politics: Faces of American Protestant Nationalism in the Twentieth Century* (Albany: State University of New York Press, 1997), 116.

124. S. E. Dubbel to MCS, 27 September 1951, McCarthyism Correspondence, MCSL.

125. Quoted in William Martin, *A Prophet With Honor: The Billy Graham Story* (New York: William Morrow and Company, Inc., 1991), 166–67.

126. Rik Nutt, "For Truth and Liberty: Presbyterians and McCarthyism." *Journal of Presbyterian History* 78, no.1 (Spring 2000), 51–66.

127. Harper Sibley to MCS, 6 June 1950, Declaration of Conscience, Out of State Reactions, MCSL. *Frederick Post* (Maryland), 26 May 1953.

128. G. Duncan Moore to MCS, 2 June 1950, Declaration of Conscience, Maine Reactions, MCSL. Moores concluded his letter, "More power to you."

129. Kingsley W. Hawthorne to MCS, 6 June 1950, Declaration of Conscience, Maine Reactions, MCSL.

130. Ralph Edward Kyper to MCS, 3 June 1950, Declaration of Conscience, Maine Reactions, MCSL.

131. Theodore A. Webb to MCS, 2 June 1950, Declaration of Conscience, Maine Reactions, MCSL.

132. See "Chameleon Republicans," Scrapbook, vol. 88, 59, MCSL. For the "Me Too" cartoon, see *Never Underestimate*, 20. On Republican divisions, see David W. Reinhard, *The Republican Right since 1945* (Lexington: University Press of Kentucky, 1983).

133. Maine led the way with an impressive ratio of about 20 to 1. MCS to Raymond S. Oakes, 15 June 1950, Declaration of Conscience, Maine Reactions, MCSL.

134. "Maine's Woman Senator Wins National Notice," Scrapbook, vol. 88, 11b; Scrapbook, vol. 88, 15, 23, MCSL. For example, see Rinardo Giovanella to MCS, 4 June 1950, Declaration of Conscience, Maine Reactions, MCSL.

135. "Fortunately for U.S., McCarthyism is Getting More in Proper Perspective," Scrapbook, vol. 88, 18, MCSL.

136. Joanne Meyerowitz, "Beyond the Feminine Mystique: A Reassessment of Postwar Mass Culture, 1946–1958," *The Journal of American History* 79, no. 4 (March 1993): 1455–82.

137. W. M. Jeffers to MCS, 5 June 1950, Declaration of Conscience, Out of State Reactions, MCSL.

138. Frank Reilly to MCS, 20 January 1952, Press Relations Correspondence, MCSL.

139. Sherman, *No Place for a Woman*, 111.

140. W&Y, 1 December 1949, MCSL.

141. Conrad Black, *The Invincible Quest: The Life of Richard Milhous Nixon* (Toronto: McClelland & Stewart, 2008), 49.

142. Jack Lait and Lee Mortimer, *U.S.A. Confidential* (New York: Crown Publishers, Inc., 1952), 53, 88. General Perspective—Declaration of Conscience, MCSL.

143. Quoted in Sherman, *No Place for a Woman*, 122.

144. General Perspective—Declaration of Conscience, MCSL.

145. "Sen. Margaret Smith Wins $15,000, a Retraction in 'U.S.A. Confidential' Suit," *New York Herald-Tribune*, 18 October 1956.

146. MCS to E. V. Morgan, 8 October 1951, Communism Correspondence, MCSL. On McCarran, see Oshinsky, *A Conspiracy so Immense*, 207–8.

147. "Readers Vote, 9–1, to Outlaw Communists," W&Y, 28 April 1953, MCSL. Sherman, *No Place for a Woman*, 130–32.

148. "Bill to Outlaw Reds Fails to Win Support," W&Y, 24 August 1953, MCSL.

149. Smith-Rhodri Jeffreys-Jones interview. Republican opposition to McCarthy was rather weak. See Alonzo L. Hamby, *Man of the People: A Life of Harry S. Truman* (New York: Oxford University Press, 1995), 531.

150. "An Old Police State Custom," *I. F. Stone's Weekly*, 1 February 1954, 4, Communism Folder, MCSL. But even liberals such as Hubert Humphrey and Wayne Morse had introduced similar legislation. See Mary S. McAuliffe, "Liberals and the Communist Control Act of 1954," *The Journal of American History* 63, no. 2 (September 1976): 351–67. Others argue that in the late 1940s Truman introduced anti-communist domestic policies that encouraged the rise of McCarthyism. Richard M. Freeland concludes that "The practices of McCarthyism were Truman's practices in cruder hands, just as the language of McCarthyism was Truman's language, in less well-meaning voices." See Richard M. Freeland, *The Truman Doctrine and the Origin of McCarthyism: Foreign Policy, Domestic Politics, and Internal Security, 1946–1948* (New York: New York University Press, 1985), 360.

151. See Sherman, *No Place for a Woman*, 131. Sherman explains that while Smith disapproved the "growing tendency among our people to say. 'I'm more patriotic than you' in order to try to convince their neighbors and their associates of their loyalty to their country," her bills appeared to be guilty of that very tactic. That Cold Warriors defended freedom, but also denied the basic rights of communists is a common criticism among scholars. For example, see, May, *Homeward Bound*, 12.

3

Korean War

The forthright manner Smith demonstrated in the Declaration of Conscience and elsewhere was common in her "Washington and You" newspaper columns to the point that friends advised her to tone down her views and avoid taking a position on sensitive issues. The independent-minded senator disagreed and her public feistiness helped her with Cold War image making. After the North Korean invasion of South Korea, she had good reason to highlight her position on national defense. Attention had shifted away from her Declaration of Conscience and gone were the widespread and glowing congratulations for her criticism of Joseph McCarthy. The only woman in the Senate and outside the circle of conservative Republican Party heavyweights, she expected a rough political ride fueled by resurgent McCarthyism.[1] Still, those who characterized her as a liberal soft on communism were far from the mark.[2] The Korean War was a pressing topic and she voiced Cold Warrior rhetoric at a time when there was an information vacuum due to White House failure to communicate a clear official position on the war.[3]

In an age when polls published in *The Public Opinion Quarterly* indicated that a significant number of Americans lacked a fundamental understanding of important public affairs,[4] Smith forged ahead with strong public statements on national security. She saw herself as "the Average American" and believed her strong views were popular with most Americans and, thus, there was little political danger in expressing herself forcefully.[5] Although wary of polling data as were most mid-century politicians, she shared with readers the results of two polls that demonstrated overwhelming support of 68 percent and 75 percent for permanent peacetime Universal Military Training. These popular views were in line with her thinking.[6]

49

Smith often offered blunt assessments of people and policies. For example, without saying McCarthy's name, she referred to "a Great Lakes–Midwestern Senator" short on courage, thereby questioning his manliness. It was characteristic of her to make public statements such as the Pentagon brass "have no idea what makes a civilian tick. And apparently they don't care."[7] Having experienced a number of confrontations with military leaders who failed to take her seriously, she had limited patience for elite males in the military who were slow to give her the respect she desired.[8] That five of the six Republican senator cosigners of the Declaration of Conscience recanted their support was another example for her of flawed male leadership and character.

If details were incomplete or missing, readers of her column received fascinating insights into Washington politics and personalities from an insider. Rarely verbal herself on the Senate floor, Smith used her column as a weapon to make her views known on the proper direction for the United States, even if it made others uncomfortable. Concerned that Americans often had to rely on politically colored and partisan accounts, she was an advocate for objectivity and allowing ordinary people to hear the foreign policy "facts" so that they could decide for themselves what was appropriate action. She even insisted that the government be more willing to open archives of important information providing there were no sensitive documents; it was wrong for the government to impose "its own Iron Curtain here at home on information that the people were rightfully entitled to have."[9] This position differed from Thomas A. Bailey's *The Man in the Street* (1948) which saw the necessity for deception in order for politicians to direct the "notoriously shortsighted" masses in the proper foreign policy direction.[10] There was a populist tone to her political philosophy that favored a more egalitarian sharing of information. As a result of her working-class background, it was more natural for her to have a closer affinity with Main Street Americans than many of the elites who dominated political life.

In her interaction with ordinary Americans, Smith sought "to talk neither up nor down to anyone, but rather to talk with people." She wrote of her desire to acknowledge and quickly correct any mistakes she made.[11] She even encouraged her readers to examine other columns "to see how much better they are than mine."[12] In the early stage of the Korean War, she shared how some readers were responding to her columns. One critic lamented that most people who read her column did little thinking and naïvely swallowed her statements "lock, stock, and barrel." An Oakland, California, reader declared: "You can do a lot of good if you will stop messing around with a lot of crackpot nostrums." From Lisbon, Iowa, a detractor declared: "It was woman who was first responsible for the loss of peace on this earth—Eve. In your blabbering about freedom you could not go further astray from the eternal truth."

Another critic from Caldwell, New Jersey, wrote that Smith's honesty was outstanding, but her analysis of issues made her look foolish.[13]

It is striking that Smith revealed these harsh assessments in public when she was aware that her lack of education put her at a disadvantage in any analysis of international affairs. While her columns gave evidence of humility, among some journalists and others who disagreed with her she was earning a reputation as being thin-skinned. Her show of confidence masked some of her own insecurities, but she did not doubt herself as a foe of communism. In Bainbridge, Georgia, one man reported that numerous people in the southern states held her in the highest esteem, an impressive compliment given the legacy of harsh feelings that some Southern conservatives had for New Englanders; she was a Yankee, but her vigorous anticommunist views presented throughout the Korean War shared common ground with evangelical Christians in the Bible belt South. In truth, Americans in all regions applauded her political discourse replete with tinges of apocalyptic anticommunism.

There is abundant literature on how Truman and his advisers used overheated rhetoric to scare Americans to accept their Cold War policies, such as the framework of the highly secret 1950 document known as NSC-68 that spurred rapid military rebuilding. A recent study sheds additional light on the relationship between the Truman administration and such scare-mongering tactics arguing that the government was also mindful of not panicking the American people into Cold War hysteria.[14] On the issue of heating up the home front, Smith was different in that she was not selling Truman's specific policies nor did she appear to exercise much caution or restraint with her rhetoric; her anticommunist path was an independent and perhaps more sincere one. The Truman administration could not muzzle her.

Throughout the Korean War there were many people who, agreeing or not, grasped her analysis of foreign policy and, according to Smith, they were very serious thinking people.[15] When she traveled throughout the nation, people expressed their enjoyment of regularly reading her column and it became clear to her that her writing created a feeling among readers that they knew her. She explained, "It was a warm feeling—a feeling of understanding, if not full agreement."[16] Smith embraced a down-to-earth attitude with apparent sincerity, and her "Washington and You" contributed good discussion on the Korean conflict.

The outbreak of the Korean War was a watershed in post–World War II American history. Since achieving its new status as a superpower, the United States faced the task of exercising its global responsibilities without moving in the direction of a garrison state—a bloated, centralized, and regimented state dominated by the military.[17] In the late 1940s, the containment policy of the Truman administration focused on the economic goal of building a stable free-market international order and not on military solutions to block the growth of Soviet communism. The Korean conflict militarized the containment policy and within months America's mobilization and preparedness program went beyond the specific requirements of the Korean War and, in a climate where fears of a garrison state remained, there was the emergence of an institutionalized and permanent national security state.[18] As one scholar explains, "the Korean mobilization was a mobilization within a mobilization" in that the United States armed itself for the Korean conflict "while simultaneously mobilizing for the Cold War in the long-term."[19] From Smith's Washington accounts, Americans read shorthand and simplified versions of important events and developments connected to the evolution of a national security state that saw the permanent alteration of fiscal ideology and policymaking. The goal was to improve the security of the United States against the red menace.

The June 24, 1950, invasion of South Korea by a North Korean army 135,000 strong, supported by planes and Russian-made T-34 tanks, surprised the United States, even though guerrilla war in Korea had been ongoing since 1946. When the Americans and the Soviets withdrew from Korea in 1948–1949, hostility continued between the communist regime led by young Moscow-trained Kim Il Sung in the north and the noncommunist south led by Syngman Rhee, an aged patriot who had been in exile in the United States. The American armed forces had witnessed a major reduction after World War II, Europe was the focus of American policymakers, and North Korea had better and more unified political and military leadership than South Korea. Within days after the invasion across the 38th parallel, South Korea was in serious trouble. Stationed in Japan, General Douglas MacArthur, United States Commander in Chief Far East, received the order to slow the progress of the invading forces while the United States government took the matter to the Security Council of the United Nations. The American political response was prompt; on June 25 their resolution in the U.N. Security Council that North Korea cease hostilities and withdraw from South Korea met approval by all voting members. The Soviet Union missed an opportunity to veto the resolution; it had been boycotting meetings due to the council's refusal to unseat Chiang Kai-shek's Nationalist China and recognize the People's Republic of China. Still, the military situation was dire. Before hasty American aid arrived in Korea in July, the South Korean army suffered heavy losses and appeared on the brink of defeat, with only the southeastern port of Pusan and a small area remaining in the hands of the South Koreans and Americans.

On July 3, 1950, in her first post-invasion installment of "Washington and You," Smith wrote: "No one in this world now can doubt that the invasion orders came from Moscow. It should be crystal clear that Russia has contempt for peace and that it is Russia, not the United States, that is war-minded."[20] Truman believed that the Soviets were behind the aggression, but publicly he said otherwise, thus giving the Soviets a chance to restore the antebellum status quo without losing public face.[21] The position of official government thinking was that the Soviets initiated the Korean clash and, thus, in his memoirs, George F. Kennan wrote of the Soviets unleashing the attack in Korea.[22]

In contrast to Smith's understanding, a number of historians see the Korean War as a struggle between left-wing and right-wing Koreans rather than a contest between the United States and the Soviet Union; they place more blame on the American government for creating a belligerent climate that resulted in the communist response.[23] One notable representative of such thinking argues that the question "who started the Korean War?" should not be asked.[24] Other recent studies that do not attempt to diminish communist aggression argue that while the Soviets were not the main instigators of the conflict they worked in tandem with North Korean and Chinese leaders.[25] Smith's numerous reports on the progress of the war in "Washington and You" continued to hold the Soviets responsible for initiating the conflict, a position that made sense to most Americans. From January to November 1950, the percentage of Americans who believed that the Soviet Union sought world domination rose from 70 to 81 percent.[26]

It was in character for Smith to present a belligerent tone, especially as she faced attacks from McCarthyites who remembered her Declaration of Conscience. No less than any other politicians on the defensive, she had to demonstrate her anticommunist credentials. Yet her militancy toward the Soviet Union was not necessarily a political act of self-preservation; she loathed the totalitarianism of Soviet communism and its threat to national security and to the core values of American life such as liberal-capitalism, freedom of speech, and freedom of religion. In her eyes, communism only promised slavery for the masses caught in its web. There is also the influence of her executive assistant Bill Lewis, a lawyer and military man whose loyal dedication to her also resulted in isolating her from other voices.[27] He remained behind the scenes and it is a difficult task for biographers of Smith to know the full impact of his thinking on her, but his military background and links to the armed forces suggests that his counsel fed her feistiness toward communism.

Scoring a prophecy coup in her column two days before the communist invasion, Smith wrote that "Southern Korea is under the constant threat of Communist attack from the north and is handicapped with critical economic and political difficulties."[28] Opposing the inaction that she perceived to be widely held in Washington immediately after the invasion, she urged that the government act firmly because the attack was nothing less than a direct challenge to national security. Comparisons made to the 1930s Japanese invasion of Manchuria and Benito Mussolini's invasion of Ethiopia underscored the seriousness of "unchecked aggression."[29] In addition to undermining Soviet propaganda that the United States was a warmonger, North Korea's "unprovoked aggression" corrected the misplaced thinking of those who supported American recognition of communist China and its entry into the U.N. As Smith explained, communist action in Korea spoke louder than words; with the Soviets' true aims now apparent (that they were the real aggressors), it was "time for the still-free nations of the world to line up on America's team." Strongly opposing recognition of communist China, she held that red Russia in 1933 was a completely different case: "Red China today is the product more of an outside nation—Red Russia—than of the Chinese people themselves." But *if* the "diplomatic consistency" argument had any merit, then Smith believed it would be "better to withdraw recognition of Red Russia than to grant it to Red China."[30] Recent scholarship reveals that Stalin understood the great possibilities that Asian communism offered; in 1948, he stated that if China fell to Mao's forces "then the victory of socialism in the world will be virtually guaranteed. Nothing will threaten us. Therefore, we cannot withhold any effort or means in the support of the Chinese Communists."[31]

Smith sensed that American foreign policy had been straddling the issue of communist aggression rather than facing it squarely, pointing to the impotent policies concerning Asia. Whereas the Marshall Plan had been successful in Western Europe, the "do nothing, wait and see" policymaking in the Far East was not promoting confidence.[32] Her criticism extended to the Senate which failed to press the White House into action on Far Asian issues in the late 1940s. Using language such as "timid" and "spoon-feeding," she adopted a masculine position to drive her point home. America was "losing" in East Asia because of a "timid, cautious" policy that was a reaction to the money and weapons lost in China. A serious foreign policy error "was putting most, if not all, of our Far East 'eggs' in Chiang's basket, instead of attempting to solidify security in the Far East from an over-all standpoint and inclusion of as many of the Far East and Pacific nations as possible." Missing in the Far East was the "courageous, firm, alert and positive action" that gave victory over communism in Western Europe.[33]

Of immediate importance was American realization that the Korean so-called police action was a genuine shooting war. Truman's failure to ask Congress for a declaration of war was a nonissue for her, but she held the administration responsible for using "frilled" phrases that glossed over the "gruesome reality" of the death and destruction of war. Truman was failing to present "the pessimistic facts of this war" and there was the danger of an overconfident American public expecting "a quick, cheap victory in Korea." When victory came slowly with mounting casualties, "then our national morale will have taken an unhealthy blow." Clarifying that she had no secret information, she saw the real possibility of communist soldiers and materiel being sent into North Korea from Russia, Manchuria, and China, all done while the Americans watched helplessly without taking action such as bombing the supply lines. Smith did not apologize for her criticism; she knew Washington worried and she wanted the American public to be aware of this.[34]

Smith lacked patience for those who believed there were good reasons not to send Americans soldiers to fight thousands of miles across the world. In response to a letter from a constituent asking why American boys were fighting and dying for South Koreans "who hated us," she repeated her standard interpretation that communist aggression threatened American security and placed the peace of the world at risk: "With each bit of territory the Communists gobble up, regardless of how far away from our shores, they come that closer to us." Although Russia had "gobbled up" the Balkans and her "Chinese puppets" had taken control of China without direct American interference, any surrender of South Korea to the communists would represent a policy of appeasement because the United States had assumed responsibility for the South Koreans. "It didn't work with Hitler," Smith wrote, "Why should we expect it to work with Stalin?" The choice was to fight now or fight later when the Soviets had conquered most of the world in the manner of a "cancer." She argued that if the United States backed down, there could be little expectation that Western Europe would be any braver when faced with Soviet aggression.[35] Put simply, it was worse to fight later when the communists increased their military power.

And yet Smith assessed that the United States military needed to increase its supremacy, arguing for better cooperation among American leaders for the effective mobilization of troops.[36] She shared with readers that there was personal bitterness between Defense Secretary Louis Johnson and Secretary of State Dean Acheson, making them incapable of being coldly objective at a crucial time, although she did not reveal that a major difference between the two was that Acheson argued for higher military spending while Johnson, the economizer, desired the opposite.[37] She also wrote of the clash of personalities between Johnson and National Security Resources Board chairman Stuart Symington, who required specific information from the Defense Department in order to have effective mobilization planning. Critical to her thinking was that partial mobilization was inadequate and would not "make Joe Stalin pause and think twice" about continuing "his world wide aggression."[38] In the wake of the communist menace, she painted a clear picture of the America's tragic "weakness" in Korea. The most serious mistake was the rapid demobilization of the armed forces after World War II. More specific, "had we adopted universal training in 1948 we would have a reserve of military manpower today that not only could have been rushed to reinforce our pitifully small force in Korea, but would have made Joe Stalin hesitate more before starting the small fires of war, at vantage points of his choosing, thousands of miles away from American shores." The United States had failed to build the National Guard, failed to have "a 70-Group Air Force," failed to maintain a proper sized Army and Navy, and now it is "time to realize that long, hard years of sacrifice are ahead of us." Smith warned if Americans were unwilling to make the necessary sacrifices "we'll end up making a last ditch stand here in the United States instead of some spot like Korea."[39]

The tone of her reports of the progress of the Korean War became graver as the North Korean army pressed its attack in the month of August with the Americans and South Koreans holding a line with artillery around Pusan. However, she also wrote that perhaps the Korean War was a blessing in disguise. Stalin had made a major tactical error, the United States learned that airpower could not win a modern war, and that American intelligence operations were in dismal shape.[40] In sum, she told readers that the fighting in Korea was a reality check and that the only language the Soviets understood was military might. It was to be a struggle for "preponderant power."[41] There was no other answer for the Soviet leaders who trained their military personnel to be "cold-blooded machines."[42] Targeting the sinister side of communism, such emotional language from a female politician was chilling.

Smith also wrote that elites and others sitting in ivory towers did not always have the right answers for the problems in Korea. Stating in one column the importance of hearing from those in the field who "really know the score," she quoted extensively from a letter sent by a G.I. fighting in Korea. The soldier argued that American support was too little and too late; the United States was in the process of selling the Koreans down the river. While the American government did honor some requests for arms and money, the rationing was so severe that the amount sent was practically ineffective. The soldier compared the action of the government to the stupidity of arguing about the cost of a fire extinguisher when a house is in flames. In her estimation, the soldier she characterized as a deeply religious young American presented worthy ideas on how to combat communism: "What we need now is strong aggressive action to stamp out this insidious force before it enflames the entire world. Possibly then, but not before, will Christianity and democracy do the jobs they were intended to."[43]

By bringing Christianity into the discussion, she provided an interpretation that the tens of millions of churchgoing Americans could appreciate and support. Smith drew on her Methodist values to identify the danger that the communist menace posed to the moral strength of America. Historian Bruce Cumings argues that most Americans were clueless when asked to define communism.[44] In one sense, such a position is misleading. For example, dedicated church-attending Americans, who represented a sizable portion of society, might have fallen short in providing a precise definition of communism, but they understood atheism and its prominent place within communist leadership. In an era when evangelical leaders such as Billy Graham commanded national attention and mass public support, many Americans knew enough to appreciate the threat of communism to freedoms such as free and open worship of Jesus Christ at home or abroad. For many of those who embraced a Christian worldview, the Korean War did not create anticommunist sentiments, but instead drew them out.

The price of victory over communism would be costly, but Smith was confident. She argued that all in all the cost was worth it since victory in Korea would likely encourage free nations in Asia to resist communism, create divisions between communist nations, and "awaken Red China to the crystal clear fact that Red Russia always puts her interests ahead of every other nation, and that Red China cannot hope to do business with Red Russia without being gobbled up." If the Soviets had cared for the Chinese, the invasion would have been of Formosa rather than South Korea.[45] She claimed that everyone knew who was behind the war; North Koreans were fighting South Koreans, but the war was actually "the East against the West." Communism had enslaved hundreds of millions in the East and it sought to do the same in the West. Given this fact, she found it shocking and disheartening that U.N. members were reluctant to send the necessary troops and supplies. By the third week of August, she argued that the U.N. had to step forward, prepare for a northward drive across the 38th parallel, and fight for the occupation of the whole country. Unless there was a united independent nation, there would be no peace.[46] At this stage, Truman maintained that the main objective was to simply force the North Koreans out of South Korea, a position much less militant than Smith's.

A month later, at the time of General Douglas MacArthur's successful landing at Inchon, Smith returned to the theme of what the military should do after pushing the North Korean aggressors north of the 38th parallel. Stating that the key issue was the relationship between the Chinese and the Russians, she informed readers that "Russia has been trying to get Communist China into a war with the United States." The reason was simple: as the Chinese and Americans bled themselves to death, Russia would gain supremacy. She saw the importance of getting "Red China and the other Communist countries to realize that the Kremlin is making suckers out of them today to make slaves out of them tomorrow." But if this failed and the Americans were to go beyond the 38th parallel, they had to be able to wage an all-out war.[47] Judging the proposed Soviet program for peace in Korea, presented in October, as "ridiculous," she argued that the only response to Soviet complaints of

American toughness was to laugh in their face. The Russians had been the international bully, unchallenged for a number of years, but now they were "crying and whining." Americans had initially taken the Russian leaders at their word and the Russians in turn interpreted American compromise as weakness. After a few years of Russian betrayals, the United States was going to be wiser. Smith spoke confidently of American power growing strong enough to stop Russia "from making the earth a slave, godless world ruled by evil men."[48]

Four months after the communist invasion of South Korea, the American people, according to Smith, were now informing their elected representatives that America must get tougher and take the leadership away from the Russians.[49] This strong, militant, and articulate voice of the public, she argued, forced Truman to correctly replace a policy of wait and see with a policy of anticipate and act. She was clear in her support of Truman's authorization for MacArthur to cross the 38th parallel in late September. The recent crossing and northern push by American forces was the proper and courageous step that demonstrated the resolve of the United States, yet while the American forces were successfully gaining control of North Korean territory, she urged caution since history demonstrated the pitfalls of overconfidence that came during times of apparent victory. Military victories in Korea could not hide the reality that the armed forces were operating on a shoestring and, thus, were in "a state of shocking unpreparedness."[50] Taking "the world leadership away from the Communists" with victorious battle in Korea was only the first stage; Americans still faced a relentless Russia in a "world-wide cold war" which might result sooner or later in an attack on the United States.[51]

Three years earlier, Defense Secretary James Forrestal had presented a plan for civil defense, but no action took place and the nation was still lacking a uniform country-wide signaling system. Smith declared that hundreds of mayors experienced disillusionment when they gathered to hear from the National Security Resources Board only to learn that the government had no specific plans for civil defense. As she saw it, the government was warning the people of the potentiality of a Russian air-atomic attack without providing them with a plan in the event of an attack.[52] She urged Americans to stay vigilant and match the sacrifices of the soldiers in Korea and "then surely we will effectively stop the handful of evil men in the Kremlin."[53]

Smith's assessment of the U.N. in the early stage of the war was affirming.[54] Her tone changed, however, with the shifting fortunes of war. In the middle of November, she feared that the inspiring action of pushing the North Koreans to the Manchurian border was for nothing since the U.N. was on the verge of appeasement to China. Smith asked: "Is the U.N. going to lose those hard-fought gains by giving in to the pressure of Red China? Is the U.N. going to become a timid, fearful Caspar Milquetoast?" If the U.N. was going to be like the timid comic strip character, this would be a blow to all freedom-loving people. She wanted an agreement devoid of any tinge of appeasement, which she interpreted as "nothing more than surrender on the installment plan."[55]

After the Chinese troops entered North Korea en masse, she accused the U.N. of listening to ridiculous Chinese charges against American and U.N. forces while Red Chinese troops continued to murder U.N. troops. Using emotional language bound to stir the passions of many Main Street Americans, Smith wrote: "Not only does the U.N. court let the murderer continue ranting, but the U.N. refuses to act to give its own troops that are being murdered a fair chance to defend themselves. The U.N. literally keeps the hands of its soldier tied behind him and yet tells him to stand up and fight the Chinese Communist that is firing a gun at him to kill him."[56] According to Smith, the U.N. was seeking a peaceful settlement with the communists because of the fear of America going to war against China and leaving Western Europe vulnerable to Russian invasion. She opposed this thinking on the basis that the communists always broke their promises and on her belief that "if the whole of the Orient is lost to the forces of communism" then communist forces would certainly attack the rest of the world. Writing that British Prime Minister Clement Attlee and other European leaders were "running away from us as fast as possible," she interpreted the U.N.'s refusal to allow the bombing of Red China bases in Manchuria as Munich all over again, which tragically "made it possible for the Reds to slaughter our handicapped GIs."[57]

Smith kept returning to the appeasement at Munich and other failures to respond meaningfully to aggressive acts by nation-states throughout the 1930s, a line of thinking that made sense to most Americans. Hitler had only been dead for five years. Her warning was that "the admirable trait of being calm can descend into the weakness of lethargy and lack of courage." She wanted peace, but not at the cost of appeasement. Reports predicting any fight with China would become a war of attrition were wrong; she wrote that the United States could defeat China in a few months. The Chinese had 3,000,000 troops, yet they were short on ammunition, had limited steel production, and virtually no navy or air force. Moreover, "Communist Chinese soldiers have not been sufficiently indoctrinated in worship of Communism to be fanatics fighting to the death," and, consequently, propaganda leaflets dropped by American planes would have an effect on the Chinese who "are not a warlike race." At the disposal of the West were 500,000 well-trained soldiers in Formosa and approximately one million anticommunist guerrillas in China. If the U.N. allowed General MacArthur to bomb Manchuria, Red China could be defeated without additional U.N. commitment and any occupation of China. As for the

Soviets, Smith concluded, they would back down.[58] If some considered such analysis of Chinese culture and Soviet leadership foolish and dangerous, its provocative tone made her stand out as a genuine hard-liner.

With American troops experiencing mounting casualties in North Korea, Smith made her voice heard on specific military decisions. She was especially critical of the Air Force and its negligence in the early days when American troops suffered serious losses in the northern part of North Korea. The Air Force had championed the superiority of strategic superbombers, laden with atomic bombs, flying nonstop round trips from a United States airbase, but had neglected the essential development of tactical air support of ground troops.[59] Writing in late December that the United States had "taken a terrible beating in Korea," she discussed changes that were necessary to ensure the security of Americans, namely money spent on sophisticated weaponry, an elaborate radar system, and compulsory universal military service.[60] In the short time, among other Christmas wishes, she desired that General MacArthur receive "all the authority he needs for the protection and defense of the GIs under his command" and that the enslaved half of the world receive "the will and strength to overthrow its evil dictators and to gain freedom."[61] Once again Smith went on record with the suggestion that communist leaders were inherently evil.

The New Year brought intense discussion of America's security and military troubles. In her January 1, 1951, column, she declared that with the exception of Pearl Harbor the United States had suffered no greater military disaster and defeat in its history than what unfolded in Korea in late 1950.[62] Consistent with her Cold Warrior mentality, she supported use of the atomic bomb in Korea. She received opposing letters, but she did not waver in her belief that the dropping of an atomic bomb on Red Chinese military arsenals and production plants in Manchuria might be necessary and the best solution to end the war.[63] After all, given the record of communist atrocities, she reasoned, "maybe the atomic bomb will bring the Red barbarians to their senses as it did the Japanese."[64] That dropping the atomic bomb would be barbaric did not appear to cross her mind. Such provocative rhetoric from a female politician reflects the extent some were willing to go to end a war that frustrated more Americans each day. Even though a January 1951 poll showed that 55 percent still agreed that the United States was correct in sending troops to defend South Korea, the same poll indicated that 66 percent of Americans favored pulling out of Korea.[65]

Smith continued to highlight the shortcomings of the Truman administration. Her forthright views contrasted with the contradictory statements from the White House which she called the "Defense Confusion Capers." Defense Secretary General George Marshall expressed his alarm about the weakness of the defense program on the same day that Charles Wilson, Defense Mobilization chief, painted a rosy picture of American military superiority.[66] She was also critical of Dean Acheson and his lack of awareness that Congress, and particularly the Senate, had a right and responsibility in shaping foreign policy. It was wrong for the White House to be the exclusive architect of American foreign policy: "Our foreign policy is greater than any individual or feuding personalities simply because our country is. For our national security, we can't continue to destroy the unity of our country."[67] Her response to reports of poor morale among American soldiers in Korea included condemnation of defeatism and dishonesty coming from the White House. Using the words "political cowardice and chicanery," she believed that the government avoided admitting defeat while "pussy-footing" and trying to cover up a gradual evacuation, all in the hopes of saving face. As Smith saw it, an evacuation was a poor idea for two major reasons: it would cost lives and damage American prestige by prolonging and emphasizing "our weakness and our defeat by Communist forces."[68]

In the best interest of national security, Smith wrote that Truman needed to remove Acheson as secretary of state. Acheson was not soft on communism and in his book on the Korean War published years later he compared the "fanatical and fighting faith" of the Soviet Union to the dominance of Islam that swept Eurasia centuries earlier.[69] The political attacks on Acheson, justified or not, had reached the point where "many millions of Americans" wanted him fired, relations between Democrats and Republicans were unhealthy, and any sense of unity almost impossible.[70] The person to watch for concerning a revised American foreign policy was not Truman, Acheson, Taft, Governor Thomas Dewey, or former president Herbert Hoover, who promoted an isolationist plan of immediate withdrawal, but rather General Dwight Eisenhower, who might be "in the White House in January 1953."[71] Stating that there was a "near vacuum of leadership" in America, she wrote "we have a floundering hand-to-mouth, day-to-day, off-the-cuff, hit-and-miss—mostly missing—operation that constantly alternates between dire warnings and optimistic reassurances to the American public."[72] In a later column, she repeated her belief that Truman had abdicated his leadership at a critical time, but fortunately, Eisenhower was filling this vacuum with his reports on the situation in Europe.[73]

The rise of Eisenhower appeared to boost the spirits of Smith at a time when she despaired more than ever over the behavior of the U.N. Its loss of courage was a real threat to its "continued existence." Whereas 53 nations had supported the cause of the United States soon after the invasion of South Korea, half a year later "the once-courageous U.N. has turned into a weak, pleading organization that seems intent on having Red China continually slap it." Desiring heroic and bold action, she deplored the U.N.'s "spineless appeasement."[74] Such belittling statements were striking.

She singled out Prime Minister Jawaharlal Nehru, who opposed America's position in Korea and voted on the side of Russia, thus demonstrating that "India is not on our side."[75] It was time to act daringly and she repeated her support for Chinese Nationalist troops based in Formosa to fight in Korea. The argument against the use of such troops in 1950 hinged on the fear of inciting Red China into Korea, but this position had no merit now that the Chinese had already invaded. With U.N. forces rebounding and thus shattering Red China invincibility, she again argued that Chiang's military forces equipped with American weapons and under the capable leadership of General MacArthur could defeat the communists.[76]

In early April, Smith defended MacArthur's ultimatum to the Chinese that contained the implied threat of invasion of China if the communists failed to sign a battlefield truce.[77] Yet, she initially showed restraint on news of Truman's removal of MacArthur from his command, replaced by General Matthew B. Ridgeway. Whatever the resentment for Truman's decision to fire MacArthur, it was crucial for Americans to support Ridgeway, whom Smith characterized as a tactical genius.[78] For Cold Warriors, there was also much to appreciate in Ridgeway's understanding of America's role in the world. On the war, he stated: "Real estate is here incidental. . . . The real issues are whether the power of Western Civilization . . . shall defy and defeat Communism; whether the rule of men who shoot their prisoners, enslave their citizens, and deride the dignity of man, shall displace the rule of those to whom the individual and his individual rights are sacred."[79] Certainly, his understanding of what Americans were fighting for shared common ground with Smith.

However, Smith's column a few days later reflected the lingering fallout over the discharge of a national hero by an unpopular president, an action which compounded rather than clarified American foreign policy in Asia.[80] In her eyes, the British lacked backbone for wanting the removal of MacArthur, and she told her readers that it was high time for the U.N. to live up to its name: "If the member nations are to have as much authority and influence as to cause the dismissal of General MacArthur on the grounds of collective policy on Korea, then those nations exercising that influence and authority must accept the responsibility that necessarily accompanies such authority."[81]

On the eve of Memorial Day, Smith continued her warnings of the dangers of Washington inertia and complacency stating that Russia cared less about victory in Korea and more about the United States becoming weaker. America's failure to arm itself adequately would prompt "the Soviets to attack us herself instead of attacking some small country like Korea through one of her satellites such as North Korea or Red China."[82] Declaring to her readers that wishful hoping for peace was not the answer, she encouraged Americans to support specific action, including giving more money in taxes to finance the rearmament required to make the country strong again.[83] Her warning seemed appropriate when, a few days later, Russia attempted to frustrate progress on a peace settlement: "This time Joe Stalin's evil two cents' worth in trying to muddle up everything is his move to upset the work and progress thus far made on the making of a Japanese peace treaty."[84] As she explained, Stalin sought to jettison all gain made on a treaty and turn the work over to a Big Four Pacific Conference, composed of Russia, the United States, England, and China. With the intent to sabotage real progress, the proposal was preposterous, especially the provision that all decisions would have to be unanimous.[85] The Russians were never serious about peace, but instead utilized any tactic that delayed the rearmament program of the United States and its allies.[86] Given that the communists experienced a staggering defeat, it was folly for the United States to sit back, wait and see, and let Russia dictate the peace terms.[87] Seeing this as a golden opportunity, Smith wanted the United States to show leadership and declare to "the world in no uncertain language, and without the slightest equivocation, on what terms we are willing to end the fighting in Korea."[88]

Almost thirteen months into the war without any peace treaty settlement, Smith shared with readers the results of two of her polls, one by newspaper and the other by radio, showing Americans favored the bombing of enemy installations in Manchuria, the use of Chinese Nationalist troops in Korea, and the blockade of the Chinese coast.[89] Public opinion, even though measured by Smith in an unscientific manner, indicated significant support of her Cold Warrior stand. Believing that her anticommunism was politically sound, she consistently argued that communists were untrustworthy, unmoved by words, and only respectful of "action that hurts them either economically or physically."[90]

In the same month of her polling commentary, Smith devoted three successive articles on "Who Won in Korea?" She identified three major goals in entering the Korean conflict. In the short term, the defense of South Korea was paramount, in the long term, the most important goal was to repulse the communist menace, and the final aim was to see the establishment of a free United Korea. Although successfully reaching the first two, it appeared that the truce talks did not bode well for a United Korea. Smith argued that there was nothing satisfactory about peace if it meant that Korea remained divided.[91] For many Americans there were good reasons to reclaim North Korea. One 1951 report in *The Public Opinion Quarterly* discussed the southward exodus of millions of refugees escaping the tentacles of communism, particularly the system that "marked a member of the family for liquidation or imprisonment by virtue of anti-communist sentiment or action."[92]

Explaining to her readers that "we don't know what all goes on in the evil minds of the men of the Kremlin," Smith did her best to explain the objectives of the communists. Foremost was to seize territory, second was to test the United States, the third "was to tie down as many American forces in Korea as possible once the United States had surprisingly called the Communist bluff," and the final "and perhaps most important objective—the psychological objective." [93] The communists had failed to reach the first three objectives, but they were successful in laying a psychological "booby trap" in Korea. To be more specific, it appeared "that our people and the people of our allies are sinking back into the belief that Russia is acting for peace and that we can let our guard down, slow up and curtail our rearmament program, and conclude that there is no need to fight inflation any more on the false premise that an illusory peace will stop inflation."[94] Even using popular culture to make her point, Smith referred to Irving Berlin's song "Russian Lullaby" and warned Americans to stay strong and not "let a Russian Lullably lull us to sleep."[95] Decades later, one former communist secret agent stated: "The idea of propagating world Communist revolution was an ideological screen to hide our desire for world domination."[96] This was half correct from Smith's perspective; the Soviets wanted world domination *because* their communist ideology required it.

Frustrated by yet more communist delay tactics, Smith, in late August 1951, again promoted the bombing of Manchuria if the communists continued to haggle and seek terms that were unacceptable. The United States had bent over backward for peace, but the time was near for a new forceful approach: "we are taking our gloves off in Korea and untieing our hands and will start slugging with all the power at our disposal." She believed that Americans were willing to bear the consequences, including going to war with Russia.[97] Toward the end of summer 1951, the United States Air Force bombed Rashin, a North Korean town only 17 miles from the Soviet border, and Smith found the lack of Soviet response surprising: "Surely, it is out of character for no protest to come from the Soviets who are used to manufacturing lies and incidents in order to be able to make phony protests." She had two explanations for Soviet behavior: first, they focused on creating confusion at the San Francisco peace treaty conference, including demands related to the Japanese treaty and, second, America's tougher stand had an impact. For Smith, the incident substantiated her position that the United States fight with purpose and not "with one hand tied behind or in fear of what Russia might do."[98]

By the middle of October, she demanded a final decision of whether to fight all-out or abandon Korea (although in reality, this proposition was a false one because she would never agree to leaving South Korea to the communists). Main Street Americans had reached their limit of patience and were open to forceful measures. They abhorred war and wanted the killing on both sides kept to a minimum, but becoming "weary and indignant at battles without victory," they increasingly denounced the "indecisive, one-hand-tied-behind fighting" that caused the climbing toll of casualties near 100,000. Once more Smith bluntly argued that unless the communist leaders took peace more seriously, the United States should consider using all necessary military power including atomic weapons to see the war come to resolution.[99]

With the U.N. forces and communists at a stalemate and few signs of diplomatic progress, Smith had no major military events to assess in 1952. Still, there was no shortage of drama on other issues. Her arguments remained consistent: the bewildered Truman administration continued a policy of confusion demonstrated "by the day-to-day, hit-or-miss—mostly miss—foreign policy" in Asia, the evil communists were bent on world domination, U.N. truce negotiators had to avoid appeasement, and the United States needed long-range thinking and a military buildup that assured both victory in battle and security of the nation.[100] She did include commentary on specific issues such as Truman's ill-thought-out policy that reduced the budget of the Air Force at a time when the Soviets were shooting down more American planes in Korea than vice versa, but most of her treatment of the Korean War concerned diplomatic progress—or lack thereof, including the emotional issue of prisoners of war.[101]

Striking is one historian's sympathetic portrayal of the North Korean Army, notably the communists' "admirable" relations with South Korean peasants during occupation and the communists' restrained policies concerning prisoners of war.[102] The explanation for one case of executed American POWs was that it occurred against the orders of North Korean leaders. Reports by POWs indicated that the executions "occurred when it became onerous or impossible to take American prisoners to the North, and they were done in the traditional battlefield 'humane' manner: one bullet behind the ear."[103] Atrocities in wars take place on all sides, but such apologetic gymnastics would have been heresy to Smith, who saw the communists as ruthless killers. "The reported Korean atrocities inflicted upon our boys by the godless Communists," she wrote, "should make the blood of every American boil in enraged indignation."[104] From journalists such as Marguerite Higgins, who won a Pulitzer for her coverage of the war, Main Street America also received one-sided reports of communists executing helpless wounded. In her book *War in Korea: The Report of a Woman Combat Correspondent* (1951), Higgins recounts the carnage of a hillside "massacre" where a Catholic chaplain courageously chose to stay and pray for American wounded unable to walk as "the Reds shot them anyway" including the chaplain.[105] American commentators on the left who sought to provide balance to such reports did not receive much support from the American public.[106]

Similar to Higgins, Smith could effectively use emotional rhetoric to encourage a passionate response from readers. She discussed Defense Department reports that communists gave American prisoners "intensive treatments of 'brain wash' by intimidation, pressures, arguments, forced indoctrination to break down both mental and physical resistance." Although there were no drugs administered, the communists exposed their victims to relentless bright lights and questioning to the point that the subject believed communist lies. According to Smith's understanding it was essential for the Soviets to have examples of conversions that their propaganda machines could focus on in light of the thousands of communist prisoners of war refusing to return to North Korea.[107]

In March 1952, Smith believed that the communists at Panmunjon outwitted U.N. negotiators when they exchanged lists of names of prisoners-of-war. The communist list was incomplete whereas the U.N. provided detailed lists which the communists used "for prolonging the truce and for great bargaining leverage," specifically the point of forced expatriation. Although the U.N.'s position that no communist prisoner should be forced to go back to North Korea against their will was correct, according to Smith, it meant prolonged imprisonment of American soldiers.[108] In the following month, she returned to the topic writing that communist POWs, embracing democracy, had tattooed anticommunist slogans on their bodies which were nothing less than a death sentence if they returned to North Korea. There was, however, extreme pressure from wives, mothers, and relatives of American prisoners who wanted their loved ones set free even if it meant agreeing to the communist demand for involuntary forced repatriation. Smith understood this position, but she opposed the United States sacrificing its honor for "momentary peace." Explaining that America had promised to protect those who renounced communism, she stated that "to give in on this issue would mean to Asians that it was an admission that our word is worth nothing and that the Communist's word is good." Moreover, it would jeopardize "the confidence of the free half of the world" and the ultimate security of America.[109] Still, millions of Americans asked: "Why do we stay in Korea?" Making matters worse was the undemocratic behavior of South Korean President Rhee, such as his dictatorial acts of imposing martial law, rejecting American authority, and threatening to oust all U.N. agencies from South Korea.[110]

Smith's commentary on Korean issues diminished in the final months leading up to the presidential election, but in late October she began paying greater attention to the war, starting with another critical assessment of the performance of the U.N. Although in its seven years the U.N. had succeeded in comparison to the old League of Nations, a glaring weakness was that the United States was carrying an overwhelmingly high burden while "other nations drag their feet." Smith reminded Americans that, "Other U.N. members have only a pitiful few number of troops in Korea—only token representation." This fact prompted her to ask: If other U.N. nations did not "believe enough in this world organization to provide more troops in the Korean fight against Communist aggression, then can they ever be counted to carry their weight when the big chips are down?"[111] For example, although approximately 25,000 Canadians participated in the war, the Liberal Party in power sought to restrain American aggression. Readers' confidence in the U.N. might have been further hurt by her next column that argued for the ousting of "Reds," not the Soviets but American employees of the U.N. in New York City suspected of communist affiliations.[112]

Communist aggression demanded a forceful response both at home and abroad. When the Soviets shot down an unarmed American B-29 that Smith claimed was not flying over Russian territory, she reiterated the strategic importance of Korea, especially for the security of the Japanese. She warned of Soviet trickery, including a phony proposal declaring the withdrawal of all troops from Korea and Japan: "If, in our understandable eagerness to end the fighting in Korea, we should accept this phony peace proposal, surely it would not be long before we would be faced with a Russian invasion of Japan in a Korea-Kuriles pincer movement."[113] The result would be the loss of Asia. Two weeks later she connected the Air Force's warning to the Soviets that it would return fire if attacked with the "cold-blooded murder" committed by the Soviets who shot down the B-29 plane. Smith found this symbolic of something wrong with American thinking: "These are strange times that we live—times when our country says that it will defend itself against attack in the air by the Russians and such a stand is taken as unusual. What a sad commentary it is that it has become unusual for our country to stand up on its hind feet and say that it will defend itself."[114] She lamented the softness and weakness of American life that she believed was too common. Likewise, Marguerite Higgins worried about American softness and lack of discipline; a North Korean colonel told her, "Your countrymen will be defeated by a longing for a hot shower."[115]

After the presidential election and victory by General Eisenhower uncertainty over Korea persisted.[116] Smith continued her demand that the "Korean Reds" at the truce talks receive an ultimatum and her hard-line position was identical to that of Lewis K. Gough, national commander of the American Legion. Declaring that the United States went into Korea "to destroy force with force," Gough argued that if no peace with honor was possible within a time limit then the United States needed "to serve notice on the enemy that failure to cooperate will bring military disaster" by way of "all effective tactics and weapons." There was risk in provoking the anger of the Soviet Union, but Gough explained that "we must protect the lives and honor and principles of the United States of America."[117] Smith likewise understood that a bolder foreign policy came with more risks, but she preferred it "to standing still or coasting downhill while the Red enemy pushes forward ruthlessly and relentlessly."[118]

All in all, the Soviet Union could not be trusted before or after Stalin's death in March 1953. Because "aggression and subversion and violence" followed conciliatory statements from the Soviets, Georgy Malenkov's soft words for peaceful coexistence and competition were incongruous "with the murderous acts of the Communists."[119] In Smith's estimation, the goal of peace was dismal; there were gloomy reports elsewhere such as the Viet Minh invasion of Laos, one more example of the Reds "carrying on relentlessly their aggression and design to conquer and enslave the world."[120] In mid-June 1953, she responded to inquiries about the finalized Korean truce by stating: "The only honest answer that I can give is that I don't like it but I think that we must realize the possibility that perhaps it is the best solution that we can now get to the Korean stalemated war." Dissatisfied, she nonetheless understood that total victory was not possible under the circumstances,[121] because of America's unwillingness to use "full atomic strength and defeat the enemy quickly."[122] Signed on July 27, the armistice was not, in the words of General Maxwell D. Taylor, Eighth Army commander, "an occasion for unrestrained rejoicing." Approximately 3,000,000 people died during the Korean War, ranking behind only the two world wars for the number of lives lost in a twentieth-century war. And the communists remained a threat. General Mark W. Clark, United Nations commander, gave the grim warning that the United Nations could not relax its vigilance against communism.[123]

Echoing such sentiments since the war began, Smith's newspaper column clarifies that she was a strident Cold Warrior who had no patience with ineffective war policies; she offered a straightforward and consistent Cold War interpretation of Korean War issues, likely a welcome addition for some confused by the Truman administration's handling of an increasingly unpopular war. As she explained: "I've tried to be as simple as possible in my writing because in these times of charges and countercharges there is enough confusion on vital issues without complicating them any more."[124] Like virtually every other politician in Washington, Smith knew and understood little about Korea and its people.[125] But she did not pretend to have sophisticated analytical abilities or a vast source of knowledge.[126] Her use of everyday language and illustrations and her blunt Cold Warrior views gained her supporters across the nation.[127]

By writing about evil communist aggression, Smith was able to arm herself against attacks from McCarthyites. And yet she also wrote on how returning to her home and removing dead plants on her property, getting her hands in the soil to plant flowers, and preparing new grass in the early spring all conveyed a deeper meaning of the American way of life than all the "dramatic orations in Congress." There was the promise of new life and vitality in a communist-free nation. Although Smith was one of the most powerful women in America, her image making in "Washington and You" cast her as a regular Main Street American and fervent Cold Warrior who treasured the core values of the United States.[128] For some Americans, it seemed natural to trust this woman, in her fifties, who lacked the connections and education of most of her male colleagues.

Among those who wrote to Smith were Americans who saw themselves as "just one of the multitude of little guys with their endless questions and problems," desiring to voice their concerns about Korea.[129] Troubled over the state of security of the nation, one letter signed by six people declared: "We are wondering if our boys will be left to pull the chestnuts out of the fire while the other United Nations countries keep their boys safely at home. That question is being asked in every group, and on every street corner in America."[130] A World War II veteran wrote to Smith that he and other Republicans in his community felt that America was asleep and its efforts in Korea where "too little and too late." He opposed recognizing "red China or any other red country," wanted no relations with Russia, and viewed the support of the U.N. as insignificant. His solution was simple: the United States had the atomic bomb and should immediately use it against Russia.[131]

Others questioned the toughness of American leadership. One man writing from Puerto Rico declared: "Words fail me to express my disgust at this outrageous sell out in Korea. Every reasonably informed person should know it will simply defer the inevitable. There will never be anything approaching peace on this earth as long as those revolting barbarous sadistic masters of torture are in the Kremlin." It was long overdue "to get rid of the weaklings in our government" and find men who know "no fear except the fear of Almighty God."[132] A young wife beginning to raise a family worried about world conditions and whether America's defense against communism was strong enough.[133] A school superintendent spoke out against American timidity, demanded a "complete mobilization of the Nation's resources," and asked "What about getting rid of that sissy in the State Department?"[134] One woman of Russian ancestry wrote to Smith: "I vote *no confidence* in Dean Acheson and his foreign policy past or present. . . . And I'm sure the boys in Korea will never understand why the United Nations wasn't pressed into action on giving General MacArthur the necessary orders to allow him to bomb out the sources of the China Reds just as soon as they started in from Manchuria." When it came to the communists, "mommy coddling or appeasing" led to disastrous consequences.[135]

The language in such letters hints that there were a number of Americans upset with America's softness and mindless conformity. Was the United States willing and able to defeat the communist menace? Could there be trust for leaders of questionable strength? In his book *I Saw Your Sons at War: The Korean Diary*, evangelist Billy Graham wrote that the division of Korea at the 38th parallel was a scandalous decision by "men who sold us down the river." The Truman administration was cowardly for preventing MacArthur from seeing victory with an offensive war, including the bombing of China if necessary.[136] It was time for America to exhibit more manliness and a fighting spirit in the face of tough challenges. Mid-century scholars argued that in bureaucratic and business circles the "organization man" and "other directed" white-collar males were deficient of leadership and creative qualities.[137] The dominating forces of consumerism appeared to blunt American initiative and passion. Arthur M. Schlesinger, Jr., lamented in *The Vital Center* (1949) that industrial wealth provided "comfort in undreamed-of abundance" but it also left anxiety and desperation: "We live on from day to day, persisting mechanically in the routine of a morality and social pattern which has been switched off but which continues to run from its earlier momentum. Our lives are empty of belief." On the issue of freedom, America lacked a "fighting faith."[138]

Recent studies refer to the self-absorbed America of the 1950s as a "feminized and infantilized culture." The materialism of post–World War II prosperity and the rise of bureaucratic life caused the softening of American society; Americans took security, liberty, and affluence for granted and there was a decline of the "earlier values of frugality, individualism, self-denial and struggle on behalf of society."[139] Marguerite Higgins argued in a similar vein: "There is a dangerous gap between the mobilized might of the free world and the armaments of the Red world—the Red world which, since 1945, has been talking peace and rushing preparations for war." Korea exposed "our complacency, our smug feeling that all we had to do for our safety was to build bigger atomic bombs. Korea has shown how weak America was."[140] Smith also discussed the general laxness of American society, stating that America suffered two great losses: initiative and public morality. The outcome was that Americans were "too lazy to do [their] own thinking and too cowardly to speak [their] minds." Facing the red menace of communism, Americans had to stop "cry babying" and recapture old glories that were a result of individual initiative.[141] When Smith wrote of the Korean War, her no-nonsense Cold Warrior tone and moral absolutism demanded an emotional response. Given that many men continued to believe it was inappropriate for women to have positions of power over men, her assessments of their "cowardly" actions were conspicuous.[142]

There were the attacks by foes that hated her Declaration of Conscience. It was very difficult, however, for her political foes to doubt her anticommunist leadership and commitment to national security. It was fitting that her first months on the Senate Armed Services Committee consisted of chairing an inquiry on ammunition shortages during the war. Given that the open hearings were among the first ever televised, the American people had the opportunity to see the first woman senator head a major investigation. The subcommittee's criticism of the government's "miscalculation and inability to plan for the defense and security of the United States" was a clear repudiation of fighting a limited war against the communist enemy.[143] Throughout the early fifties, Smith continued to warn Americans that the United States was letting its guard down and drifting from an earlier determination to get strong, all due to an unhealthy attitude of overconfidence and complacency. Although her hard-line posturing contrasted sharply with statements from those favoring "diplomatic pragmatism,"[144] she scored high with hawkish Americans.

Smith's analysis of the war was often simplistic and there were liberals who found her right-wing military views discouraging, but her popularity remained strong. Her Cold Warrior stand on the Korean conflict reflected the emotions and frustrations of those prepared to take serious steps to end and win the war. They understood her support of allowing MacArthur to drop atomic bombs on communist foes, they welcomed communist press reports that denounced her as an aggressive foe of communism, and they praised her for defending the nation.[145] The American people remained strongly anticommunist even as the war grew unpopular. In fact, opposition to the war mostly concerned method and expediency rather than morality and pacifism.[146] Smith's construction of a Cold Warrior image, analysis of the Korean War, and characterization of communist leaders as evil men appeared to resonate with many of those who wanted to see more evidence of a tougher America that could overcome the growing communist menace. She was unapologetic, believing that for the good of all Americans slowing the growth of communism was essential.

NOTES

1. In the climate of war and mounting anticommunism, opponents of McCarthy, such as Senator Millard Tydings (D-MD), met defeat in the November elections.

2. Given the small number of female senators in American history, there is insufficient analysis on how women in the Senate dealt with United States at war. Recent biographies of Smith note her vigilance in warning Americans of the dangers of external communist threats, but the Korean War does not receive much attention: Sherman, *No*

Place for a Woman has one chapter entitled "Amazon Warmonger" (139–64); Schmidt, *Margaret Chase Smith*, 173; Wallace, *Politics of Conscience*, 140.

3. On the ineffective communication of the Truman administration, see Steven Casey, "White House Publicity Operations During the Korean War, June 1950–June 1951," *Presidential Studies Quarterly* 35, no. 4 (December 2005): 691–717.

4. Ralph O. Nafziger, Warren C. Engstrom, and Malcolm S. Maclean, Jr., *The Public Opinion Quarterly* 15, no. 1 (Spring 1951): 105–14. Also, see Thomas G. Paterson, "Presidential Foreign Policy, Public Opinion, and Congress: The Truman Years," *Diplomatic History* 3 issue 1 (January 1979), 6.

5. W&Y, 4 April 1951, MCSL. Her column mail was heavily on the positive side, but she appreciated the constructive criticism of good letters that helped give her "a better balanced picture of what the people are thinking all over the country."

6. W&Y, 19 June 1951, MCSL. On the early reluctance to trust polls, see Susan Herbst, *Numbered Voices: How Opinion Polling has Shaped American Politics* (Chicago: The University of Chicago Press, 1993), 91.

7. W&Y, 4 December 1950, MCSL.

8. For example, see Wallace, *Politics of Conscience*, 133–35, 137.

9. W&Y, 30 June 1953, MCSL.

10. Thomas A. Bailey, *The Man in the Street: The Impact of American Public Opinion on Foreign Policy* (New York: The Macmillan Company, 1948), 13.

11. W&Y, 31 December 1950, MCSL.

12. W&Y, 25 December 1951, MCSL.

13. W&Y, 5 September 1950, MCSL.

14. Steven Casey, "Selling NSC-68: The Truman Administration, Public Opinion, and the Politics of Mobilization, 1950–1951," *Diplomatic History* 29, no. 4 (September 2005): 655–90.

15. W&Y, 5 September 1950, MCSL.

16. W&Y, 17 September 1952, MCSL.

17. Pierpaoli, Jr., *Truman and Korea*, 1–3.

18. Pierpaoli, Jr., *Truman and Korea*, 3–4, 8. Pierpaoli sees the origins of this fear of a regimented state beginning in the New Deal years and continuing during World War II when the armed forces and "huge, overlapping wartime bureaucracies" undermined civilian control (3–4).

19. Pierpaoli, Jr., *Truman and Korea*, 9.

20. W&Y, 3 July 1950, MCSL.

21. LaFeber, *America, Russia, and the Cold War 1945–2002*, 109–10.

22. George F. Kennan, *Memoirs 1925–1950* (Boston: Little, Brown and Company 1967), 395. In 1950, most Americans believed the attack was Soviet sponsored. See Miriam S. Farley, "Crisis in Korea," *Far Eastern Survey* 19, no. 14 (August 16, 1950), 156.

23. LaFeber, *America, Russia, and the Cold War 1945–2002*, 105.

24. Bruce Cumings, *The Origins of the Korean War, Volume II: The Roaring of the Cataract, 1947–1950* (Princeton, N.J.: Princeton University Press 1990), 621.

25. Gaddis, *The Cold War*, 42. Also, see Kathryn Weathersby, "The Soviet Role in the Korean War," in *The Korean War in World History*, ed. William Stueck (Lexington:

The University Press of Kentucky, 2004), 61–92, and William Stueck, *The Korean War: An International History* (Princeton, N.J.: Princeton University Press, 1995).

26. Ralph B. Levering, *The Public and American Foreign Policy, 1918–1978* (New York: William Morrow and Company, 1978), 103.

27. Sherman, *No Place for a Woman*, 6–7.

28. W&Y, 23 June 1950, MCSL.

29. W&Y, 13 July 1950, MCSL.

30. W&Y, 3 July 1950, MCSL.

31. Quoted in Gaddis, *We Now Know*, 66.

32. W&Y, 12 July 1950, MCSL.

33. W&Y, 19 July 1950, MCSL.

34. W&Y, 13 July 1950, MCSL. On Truman bypassing Congress, see Gary R. Hess, *Presidential Decisions for War: Korea, Vietnam, and the Persian Gulf* (Baltimore: Johns Hopkins University Press, 2001), 26.

35. W&Y, 15 July 1950, MCSL.

36. W&Y, 31 July 1950 and 1 August 1950, MCSL.

37. Pierpaoli, *Truman and Korea*, 20–21.

38. W&Y, 1 August 1950, MCSL. On the strained relations between Symington and Johnson, see James C. Olsen, *Stuart Symington: A Life* (Columbia: University of Missouri Press, 2003), 198–203.

39. W&Y, 7 August 1950, MCSL. Elsewhere Smith lamented that because of insecurity caused by war many Americans were living only for today and not for the future. This was not the solution because hiding from tomorrow "is the very thing that those who would conquer our country and enslave us want." To achieve happiness, the United States had to make the necessary sacrifices today and plan for tomorrow. See W&Y, 9 September 1950, MCSL.

40. W&Y, 22 August 1950, MCSL.

41. Leffler, *A Preponderance of Power*, 19.

42. W&Y, 19 March 1953, MCSL.

43. W&Y, 7 September 1950, MCSL.

44. Cumings, *The Origins of the Korean War, Volume II*, 81, 109.

45. W&Y, 8 September 1950, MCSL.

46. W&Y, 21 August 1950, MCSL.

47. W&Y, 22 September 1950, MCSL. Smith discussed the merits of both stopping and advancing. Those who favored stopping pointed out the solely defensive role of the American military force; those who favored advancing believed any standstill meant weakness, and besides, if the Americans were to challenge Russia, it should be in Korea while the United States had superiority.

48. W&Y, 20 October 1950, MCSL.

49. W&Y, 23 October 1950, MCSL.

50. W&Y, 26 October 1950, MCSL.

51. W&Y, 23 October 1950, MCSL.

52. W&Y, 26 October 1950, MCSL.

53. W&Y, 23 October 1950, MCSL.

54. W&Y, 24 October 1950, MCSL.

55. W&Y, 21 November 1950, MCSL.

56. W&Y, 13 December 1950, MCSL. MacArthur had assured Truman in mid-October that "if the Chinese tried to get down to Pyongyang, there would be the greatest slaughter." Quoted in Stanley Sandler, *The Korean War: No Victors, No Vanquished* (Lexington: The University Press of Kentucky, 1999), 112.

57. W&Y, 13 December 1950, MCSL.

58. W&Y, 14 December 1950, MCSL.

59. W&Y, 13 November 1950, MCSL.

60. W&Y, 21 December 1950, MCSL.

61. W&Y, 25 December 1950, MCSL.

62. W&Y, 1 January 1951, MCSL.

63. W&Y, 20 March 1951, MCSL. Chinese leaders publicly dismissed the American nuclear threat. See Michael H. Hunt, "Beijing and the Korean Crisis, June 1950–June 1951," *Political Science Quarterly* 107, no. 3 (1992), 469–70.

64. Quoted in Graham, Jr. *Margaret Chase Smith*, 96.

65. Stanley Sandler, ed., *The Korean War: An Encyclopedia* (New York: Garland Publishing, Inc., 1995), 20.

66. W&Y, 5 April 1951, MCSL.

67. W&Y, 10 October 1950, MCSL.

68. W&Y, 12 January 1951, MCSL. Smith stated that a defeatist attitude that American troops sensed was growing in the United States would only get worse at home and among America's increasingly "timid allies."

69. Dean Acheson, *The Korean War* (New York: W.W. Norton & Company, 1971), 8.

70. W&Y, 18 January 1951, MCSL. Historians point out that there were plenty of people—MacArthur, Truman, Marshall, Acheson, and others—to share the blame for the "fiasco in Korea." For example, see Robert Beisner, *Dean Acheson: A Life in the Cold War* (Oxford: Oxford University Press, 2006), 414–16.

71. W&Y, 15 and 24 January 1951, MCSL.

72. W&Y, 26 January 1951, MCSL.

73. W&Y, 7 February 1951, MCSL. The puritan Smith provided no clue whether she had knowledge of Eisenhower's earlier torrid affair with Kay Summersby, his attractive British chauffeur during World War II. On the Republican strategy to keep the affair from publication, see Conrad Black, *The Invincible Quest: The Life of Richard Milhous Nixon* (Toronto: McClelland & Stewart, 2008), 188.

74. W&Y, 31 January 1951, MCSL.

75. W&Y, 20 February 1951, MCSL.

76. W&Y, 13 February 1951, MCSL.

77. W&Y, 6 April 1951, MCSL.

78. W&Y, 19 April 1951, MCSL.

79. Quoted in Sandler, *The Korean War*, 132. Sandler notes that Ridgeway's "inspiring words" had a positive effect on the Army Chief of Staff, General J. Lawton Collins.

80. W&Y, 24 April 1951, MCSL. On Americans' response to Truman's decision to remove MacArthur, see Stueck, *The Korean War*, 182–84, and Stanley Weintraub,

MacArthur's War: Korea and the Undoing of an American Hero (New York: The Free Press, 2000), 347–48.

81. W&Y, 23 April 1951, MCSL.

82. W&Y, 29 May 1951, MCSL.

83. W&Y, 30 May 1951, MCSL.

84. W&Y, 6 June 1951, MCSL.

85. W&Y, 6 June 1951, MCSL.

86. W&Y, 2 July 1951, MCSL.

87. W&Y, 5 July 1951, MCSL.

88. W&Y, 5 July 1951, MCSL.

89. W&Y, 7 and 16, July 1951, MCSL. The radio poll indicated preference for the bombing of the China coast, 56 percent for and 44 percent against, and the landing of Chinese Nationalist troops in China "without causing all out war," 64 percent for and 36 percent against.

90. W&Y, 14 August 1951, MCSL.

91. W&Y, 25 July 1951, MCSL.

92. John W. Riley, Jr., Wilbur Schramm, and Frederick W. Williams, "Flight from Communism: A Report on Korean Refugees," *The Public Opinion Quarterly* 15, no. 2 (Summer 1951), 274, 277.

93. W&Y, 26 July 1951, MCSL.

94. W&Y, 27 July 1951, MCSL.

95. W&Y, 31 July 1951, MCSL.

96. Quoted in Gaddis, *We Now Know*, 14.

97. W&Y, 28 August 1951, MCSL.

98. W&Y, 4 September 1951, MCSL.

99. W&Y, 16 October 1951, MCSL.

100. W&Y, 2 January 1952, MCSL.

101. W&Y, 18 February 1952, MCSL.

102. Cumings, *The Origins of the Korean War, Volume II*, 682, 697.

103. Cumings, *The Origins of the Korean War, Volume II*, 703.

104. "Americans Should Boil Over Reds' Inhumanity," W&Y, 5 May 1953, MCSL.

105. Marguerite Higgins, *War in Korea: The Report of a Woman Combat Correspondent* (Garden City, N.Y.: Doubleday & Company, Inc., 1951), 91–92.

106. For example, leftist I. F. Stone had a very small following. His "words went largely unread." Norman Kaner, "I. F. Stone and the Korean War" in *Cold War Critics: Alternatives to American Foreign Policy in the Truman Years*, ed. Thomas G. Paterson (Chicago: Quadrangle Books, 1971), 260.

107. W&Y, 23 April 1953, MCSL. Also, see Edwin L. Heller and Hugh Morrow, "I Thought I'd Never Get Home," *Saturday Evening Post* 228, issue 9 (27 August 1955), 34. The story began with the following" "After long months of agonizing pain, mental torture and solitary confinement, the author became ready to 'confess' anything."

108. W&Y, 3 March 1952, MCSL.

109. W&Y, 15 April 1952, MCSL.

110. W&Y, 10 June 1952, MCSL.

111. W&Y, 21 October 1952, MCSL.

112. W&Y, 22 October 1952, MCSL.

113. W&Y, 24 October 1952, MCSL.

114. W&Y, 6 November 1952, MCSL.

115. Higgins, *War in Korea*, 219.

116. According to Smith, women in particular demonstrated their disgust by turn-ing out in record numbers to vote for Eisenhower and his promise to bring American soldiers back home. See, W&Y, 31 December 1952, MCSL.

117. W&Y, 18 November 1952, MCSL.

118. W&Y, 22 December 1952, MCSL.

119. W&Y, 23 March 1953, MCSL.

120. W&Y, 11 May 1953, MCSL. Pointing to the meager assistance in Korea from other member nations of the U.N., Smith acknowledged that while Americans were in no position "to take on another burden like Korea," it appeared that France lacked "a ca-pability to meet the Red invasion" in Southeast Asia. See, W&Y, 7 May 1953, MCSL.

121. W&Y, 17 June 1953, MCSL. Weeks later, Smith wrote: "One of the shames and tragedies of the United Nations is the manner in which most of its members gave little aid in the defense of South Korea and let the United States carry almost all of the burden. These nations will again be on trial. It will be interesting to see if they do as little in rehabilitating South Korea as they did in defending South Korea, or if again they will let us carry all of the burden. It will be especially interesting to see what Great Britain, who appears willing to let Red China shoot her way into member-ship in the United Nations, will do on the rehabilitation of South Korea." See W&Y, 4 August 1953, MCSL.

122. MCS to Lilla Chiavelli, 26 October 1951, Korean War Correspondence, MCSL.

123. "Ceremony is Brief," *New York Times*, 27 July 1953. On the human lives lost, see Allan R. Millett, "Introduction to the Korean War," *The Journal of Military His-tory* 65, no. 4 (October 2001), 924.

124. W&Y, 6 April 1953, MCSL.

125. Her numerous columns on the Korean War rarely gave any attention to the impact that foreign forces fighting against each other had on the Korean peasants. But her lack of understanding did not stop her from demonstrating her sympathy and speaking occasionally of the tragedy that ordinary Koreans faced in their worn-torn country. For example, even though the lives of Air Force flyers would be at risk, she applauded, in late summer 1952, the Air Force's plan of announcing in advance the time and place of bombings targeting military installations, a policy that would save the lives of Korean civilians. See W&Y, 12 August 1952, MCSL.

126. W&Y, 6 April 1953, MCSL.

127. She herself appreciated those who did not communicate to ordinary people with lofty essays of vague generalities and catch phrases. The public was much smarter than politicians realized. See W&Y, 5 February 1951 and 10 October 1950, MCSL.

128. W&Y, 16 May 1951, MCSL.

129. On the paradox of a nation that upheld the ideals of freedom and equality but also witnessed the rise of "great hierarchies of power and wealth," see Steve Fraser and Gary Gerstle, *Ruling America: A History of Wealth and Power in a Democracy* (Cambridge, Mass.: Harvard University Press, 2005), 1.

130. R. P. Robins, et al. to MCS, 18 July 1950, Korean War Correspondence, MCSL.

131. M. A. Brann to MCS, 17 July 1950, Korean War Correspondence, MCSL. Smith replied to Brann, "If you read my column you will see that in the next few days I will raise the question about other nations dragging their feet and not helping out in the situation and criticize England for continuing to sell oil to Red China." See MCS to M. A. Brann, 19 July 1950, Korean War Correspondence, MCSL.

132. L. Aull to MCS, 31 August 1953, Communism Correspondence, MCSL.

133. Virginia Dagget to MCS, 16 July 1950, Korean War Correspondence, MCSL.

134. Howard Hincks to MCS, 18 July 1950, Korean War Correspondence, MCSL.

135. Sophie Lewis to MCS, 6 December 1950, Korean War Correspondence, MCSL.

136. Billy Graham, *I Saw Your Sons at War: The Korean Diary* (Minneapolis: Billy Graham Association, 1953), 63.

137. William W. Whyte, *The Organization Man* (New York: Doubleday, 1956); David Riesman, *The Lonely Crowd* (Garden City, N.Y.: Doubleday & Company, Inc., 1953).

138. Arthur M. Schlesinger, Jr. *The Vital Center: The Politics of Freedom* (Boston: Houghton Mifflin Company, 1962), 243–45.

139. Robert D. Dean, "Masculinity as Ideology: John F. Kennedy and the Domestic Politics of Foreign Policy," *Diplomatic History* 22, no. 1 (Winter 1998), 35–36. Also see K. A. Cuordileone, "'Politics in an Age of Anxiety': Cold War Political Culture and the Crisis of American Masculinity, 1949–1960," *The Journal of American History* 87, no 2 (September 2000): 515–45. Also, post–World War II men "were reluctant to take risks for uncertain rewards or advancement and were more likely to settle for lower-paying but secure jobs." See May, *Homeward Bound*, 85.

140. Higgins, *War in Korea*, 16.

141. Statements and Speeches, Monthly Report, 82nd Congress, 1951, vol. VIII, MCSL.

142. Data collected in the mid-century found that almost half the men viewed it as "'unnatural' for women to be placed in positions of authority over men." See May, *Homeward Bound*, 86.

143. Sherman, *No Place for a Woman*, 128–29.

144. For a helpful discussion of diplomatic alternatives, see Fredrik Logevall, "Bernath Lecture: A Critique of Containment," *Diplomatic History* 28, no. 4 (September, 2004): 473–99. Work needs to be done on the link between western Europeans' low level of religiosity (compared to the United States) and their greater sympathy for diplomacy with the communists.

145. In one letter to a critic, Smith wrote: "I was rated the seventh best (sic) Senator by newspaper reporters that cover Congress in a poll in which Senator Taft was rated Fourth Best Senator." See MCS to Mrs. Shall, 21 January 1952, Korean War Correspondence, MCSL.

146. Sandler, ed., *The Korean War*, 19.

4

Nuclear Credibility

In October 1961, Nikita Khrushchev described Senator Smith as "the devil in a disguise of a woman [who] has decided to beat all records of savagery." Khrushchev's wife also weighed in, stating, "Threats are made to destroy our homes, to kill our husbands, to take the lives of our children . . . just one American name—Margaret Smith."[1] Why such emotional rhetoric? During the Eisenhower administration, Smith regularly condemned Soviet despotism and championed massive retaliation so much so that throughout the sixties few politicians fought harder than she for American nuclear superiority. Her September 1961 Senate speech that opposed "restrictions on the use of tactical nuclear weapons" angered President John F. Kennedy as did her vote against the Nuclear Test Ban Treaty of 1963. Smith's rigid foreign policy did not hurt her at the polls, but her opposition, in the late sixties, to the Safeguard anti-ballistic-missile system suggested that her stand on the communist menace had softened. But this was not the case. She could not escape a hawkish mind-set that only America's offensive arsenal had restrained the Soviets.[2]

In the early 1950s Smith held her ground and often went on the offensive with biting criticism of McCarthyism. The political consequences of such actions included her removal by Senator McCarthy from the Senate Investigations Subcommittee, an act in violation of Senate tradition, replaced by junior Senator Richard Nixon[3] and also her alienation from other Republicans who felt she took a maverick position akin to political suicide. She admitted that the Declaration of Conscience hurt her relationship with "professional politicians," but public support was strong; those who condemned her were people who were already against her.[4] In early 1953, the *New York Times* acknowledged that McCarthy held extraordinary power,[5] yet Smith remained formidable since her hard-line position on the Korean War clarified her anticommunist credentials as did her presented bills in 1953 to outlaw the Communist Party in the United States and her uncompromising support for nuclear superiority over the Soviets.[6] In fact, when it came right down to it, Smith shared many of McCarthy's goals.[7] Of course, she did not have the menacing approach and persona of McCarthy and her stand proved to be more beneficial than detrimental in the Cold War climate of the 1950s.

In October 1954 and February 1955, Smith went on a world tour to evaluate the strength of communism. Not satisfied with past official congressional fact-finding junkets, she desired an unofficial trip that gave her more leeway in gathering information. Two of the most important questions she asked leaders were: what were they doing to combat communism and what could the United States do to assist them in their fight? The tour generated significant publicity, especially since Ed Murrow had a CBS camera crew televise her visits to numerous countries where she talked to many heads of states, high-ranking figures, and various ordinary citizens. The meetings that appeared to have the most impact on her were with Winston Churchill, Francisco Franco, and Chiang Kai-shek, leaders who loathed Marxism-Leninism and who reinforced her own understanding of the dangers of communism.

In Spain, Franco made a good impression on Smith and she judged that he was not "the saber-rattling, fierce militaristic fascist that he has been so erroneously pictured to the American public."[8] She agreed with his belief that stopping the spread of communism began with recognizing it as a destructive agent. As Franco explained to her, communism adopted the mask of a popular movement that promised social and economic benefits for society, but "it is in fact the greatest imperialism known to history, with no moral values to curb it." If not stopped, communism would overcome Europe and Asia.[9] Other leaders and high-ranking figures offered strong statements against communist activity inside and outside their respective nations. Charles de Gaulle told Smith that the Russians' refusal to lift the Iron Curtain would prove that "their talk of peace and coexistence is just dust in our eyes."[10] Clarifying the importance of South Vietnam fighting communism, Minister of Foreign Affairs Tran Van Do maintained that the survival of Vietnam and the entire Free World was at stake. Her conversation with Prime Minister Ngo Dinh Diem and short visit to South Vietnam convinced her that there was less than a 50 percent chance of success against the communists.[11] Gamal Abdel Nasser informed her that communism was a genuine menace to Egypt because the country's low standard of living made it vulnerable.[12] The anticommunist messages that she heard confirmed her stand for greater American support for those nations threatened by communism. For example, in a statement at Manila on whether the

United States would keep its pledge of defending the Philippines from external attacks, she declared: "The United States always keeps her pledge."[13] She repeatedly made it known that America had an obligation to be bold and act against any aggressive communist moves. Given that most Americans saw communists "as the true practitioners of neocolonialism," they dismissed any communist accusations that the United States represented a sinister form of colonialism in the manner it sought other nations to act as surrogates for American control.[14]

In other ways the world trip validated for her the correctness of her understanding of the red menace. Her meeting with Florimond Bonte, the leader of the Communist Party in France, was uncomfortable for he was "a very nervous, emotional and frightened man."[15] She found Czechoslovakia extremely depressive with Prague described as a city "whose soul had been killed, whose heart had been torn out." The Czechoslovakian people "walked as though they have nothing to live for—almost mechanical as the so-called zombies we see in the horror movies." Smith even feared for her safety: the people were slaves "who themselves live in fear that they might fail to be as tough and disagreeable with American visitors as their Russian masters want them to—and in a manner 'trigger happy' looking for ways and excuses to grab American visitors."[16]

While in Berlin, Smith encountered trouble when she and her entourage crossed into the communist sector and window-shopped at a government-operated store with a CBS camera running. After receiving terse warnings from pedestrians that filming was unlawful, they quickly left the area in a fast car while the police tried to stop them. Unknown to them, the police had arrested and held for an hour the other half of their group, including Bill Lewis and U.S. High Commission Public Information Officer Elmer Cox.[17] Following this episode was her visit to Moscow, the first for a United States senator in 18 years. There her interview of Foreign Minister Vyacheslav M. Molotov degenerated into a heated exchange on issues such as freedom of the press and the existence of opposition parties of which the Soviets had neither. Molotov avoided a direct response when she pressed him that the United States permitted the existence of the Communist Party of the United States of America. After a week in the Soviet Union, she flew to Helsinki, where she issued a public statement stating her distrust of communist leaders: the Soviet leaders "talk one way, act another." In her eyes, communism remained an ominous threat.[18] Other American press reports stated that she saw the possibility of relations between the United States and Soviet Union breaking off.[19] Suggesting the sinister character of communist leadership, one report recorded Smith's surprise that Prime Minister Georgy Malenkov "was not liquidated as [Deputy Prime Minister Lavrenty] Beria had been."[20] Victim of a communist power struggle, Beria's execution came less than five months after Stalin's death in 1953.

During her trip to Asia, an incident that attracted much press attention was Smith's meeting with Chiang Kai-shek, who declared on her *See It Now* broadcast that he was ready to free his people "from the Communist yoke through counterattacking the mainland" with American assistance. This came only weeks after Congress overwhelmingly approved the Formosa Resolution of 1955 that committed American protection of Formosa if attacked, thus giving the president "a reserve declaration of war." Chiang explained to Smith that Red China was "a hundred percent Russian-made puppet regime" and the combination of Soviet agents and "brutal suppressive measures of the Chinese Communists" prevented the mainland Chinese people from overthrowing the government. It was essential for Nationalist Chinese troops to counterattack and establish a rallying point for the people. Eisenhower clarified that the United States promised no aid for such a military assault, but the Soviets assumed Smith was behind some of the aggressive rhetoric from Formosa. While inspecting Nationalist Chinese troops she heard from one soldier the tragic story of his whole family being killed by the communists. Her inspection and tour of military installations with Major General William C. Chase provoked the communist press. In the *Red Star*, the Soviet's armed forces newspaper, Smith was one who "waves the atom bomb and calls for war." When Eisenhower invited her to the White House to discuss foreign policy, she repeated her message for America to get tough with communists.[21]

As she explained in a speech to the Overseas Press Club in New York City, communism was modern-day colonialism and Russia sought to make a communist colony out of "every country in the world." Consequently, "*The time has come* when our leadership in world affairs *must* increase in boldness and firmness if *we are* to cope successfully with the threat to the freedom of the world."[22] Reported in the press, her strong and reassuring message to the Asian people she encountered was that the United States "wanted them to be free and remain free from Communist slavery."[23] The conclusions Smith made from her world trip did not offer anything new; there were no flashes of insight to expand her one-dimensional understanding of communism.

Reinforcing Smith's antipathy for the communist menace was the mood of American society toward international communism. In the middle of her trip, she returned to the United States to participate in the Senate's successful vote that "condemned" Joseph McCarthy, but having disgust for McCarthy had no connection to her opposition of communism. The fifties witnessed the disclosure of crucial evidence pointing to communist ruthlessness. For example, an investigation conducted by the United States Congress in 1951–1952 revealed that the Soviets executed over 20,000 Polish prisoners who were mainly businessmen, lawyers, doctors, and other professionals; as potential leaders, they represented a threat to the communists, thus their execution by Stalin's orders.[24] His authorization of the murders was not a difficult decision for someone who had caused the death of millions of his own citizens.[25] Responding to State Department data on Soviet slave labor, Smith explained to her "Washington and You" readers that the "documentary evidence shows that the world has never known slavery" as it exists in the land of Stalin: "the evil men of the Kremlin have made these political prisoners physical slaves and inflicted upon them a living death."[26] Another of a number of examples that Smith reported to her readers was the group murder of Jews by the openly anti-Semitic Stalin regime. In early 1953, she asked: "Can there any longer be any real distinction between the fascism that Hitler espoused and the communism that Stalin attempts to disease the world with?"[27]

The menace of Soviet and Asian communism was on record in numerous newspapers, magazines, and books. The *New York Times* published accounts of Soviet despotism, including the unwarranted imprisonment of John H. Noble, an American held by the Soviets from 1945 to 1955. Noble's imprisonment in the "fiendish" Stolypin prison car (train) and his starvation diet in prison were frightful. He almost lost all hope.[28] On the issue of rape, scholars estimate that Soviet troops in 1945 and 1946 raped as many as two million German women.[29] Noble's *I Found God in Soviet Russia*, published in 1959, presented a passionate and fuller account of Soviet rape, theft, murder, and moral degradation, much of which was due, according to Noble, to the moral erosion that had taken place among the Soviet people: "The terrible truth is that when you remove God from a society, you remove the basis for a moral code; and when men live without a moral code, they live in violence and sin."[30] In Noble's book, there was one story of how a Soviet official ridiculed Christianity and then pointed to a picture of Stalin on the wall and stated, "That is our God, and the only God we have."[31]

Even more influential in the fifties was Whittaker Chambers's best seller *Witness*, a book that revealed the high degree of communist infiltration in government. The circulation of the *Saturday Evening Post* increased hundreds of thousands when they serialized *Witness* prior to publication.[32] Former communist, editor of *Time* magazine, and key witness in the Alger Hiss spy trail, Chambers wrote that communism, holding to a vision of "Man without God," embraced the faith "whispered in the first days of the Creation under the Tree of the Knowledge of Good and Evil: 'Ye shall be as gods.'" Without God, as Chambers understood, communism was "a vicious plot hatched by wicked men" beholden to Marxist-Leninist writing, secret police, labor camps, underground conspiracy, the dictatorship of the proletariat, and coup d'etat. With rhetorical flourish, *Witness* warned of the evil of communism that caused the screams "from husbands torn forever from their wives in midnight arrests . . . from the execution cellars of the secret police, from the torture chambers of the Lubianka, from all the citadels of terror now stretching from Berlin to Canton," and "from minds driven mad by the horrors of mass starvation ordered and enforced as a policy of the Communist State."[33] There were a number of former communists such as Chambers who became fervent anticommunist warriors "when they realized the side they had thought was the bearer of light was really the embodiment of evil."[34] Their voices were louder when Soviet brutality struck, such as the crushing of the Hungarian Revolution in 1956 which resulted in the death of approximately 20,000 Hungarians.

Americans read of repression in Asia of a greater scale. The *New York Times* wrote of "bloody purges" against dissidents by Chinese communists and the *Christian Science Monitor* reported that "many competent observers believe that China as a Communist dictatorship is more dangerous to the Bible and to human freedom than the Soviet Union could ever be."[35] Evangelical literature told of Chinese pastors stoned to death for opposing reform, a woman evangelist pulled apart by horses sent running in opposing directions, the torturing of Christians by forcing water down their throats until their stomachs bulge, the cutting off of women's breasts, and stories of women stripped of their clothing and nailed to a wall left to die.[36] It was difficult to verify the accuracy of the more horrific accounts, but readers believed them to be true. Even Senator Wayne Morse, one of only three senators who opposed the Formosa Revolution of 1955, agreed that Red China ruled "only by terrorism and repression."[37]

In these years when such emotional accounts of communist repression were accessible to most Americans, Smith saw her hard-line views and the angry response of communist leaders as a badge of honor. Some scholars note how rhetoric and military images could conjure up fears and shape perceptions that overestimated threats and actual dangers.[38] Although few Americans were ready to charge Smith guilty of fear-mongering, her aggressive foreign policy views and moral absolutism certainly annoyed Soviet leaders considerably. Even after the Korean War there is no sign that she worried that overheated anticommunist rhetoric might provoke communist leaders to acts of aggression or fuel anticommunism on the home front.[39] She argued that atomic weaponry and all "man-killing" arms were immoral weapons, but this should not hinder the United States from using atomic bombs to stop the communist murderers.[40]

Smith encouraged newspaper mythmaking that portrayed her as a pro-nuclear arms female senator exhibiting more fortitude (misplaced or not) than most of her male colleagues. As early as the mid-1950s, the Soviets referred to her as a warmonger for her consistent stand that only America's superiority in nuclear weapons and the will and purpose to use them, if necessary, would act as an effective deterrent against Soviet expansion. The doctrine of "massive retaliation," formally introduced in 1954 by Secretary of State John Foster Dulles, held that America's capacity to strike aggressors with a massive nuclear arsenal would deter Soviet aggression. It was classic deterrence theory and Smith was a keen student of such thinking. Credibility was crucial, thus the Soviets needed to understand that the United States had the ability and will to unleash devastating nuclear weapons. One scholar of deterrence explains: A country with "massive destructive capabilities" and the will to retaliate was a deadly combination that went beyond bluffing "because an attacker making a mistake on this would be committing suicide."[41] Known for his bluster, Khrushchev improved the Soviet's deterrence credibility by bluffing about its capabilities which in turn spurred Cold Warriors like Smith to fight even harder for a preponderance of nuclear power. Encouraging nuclear buildup in the United States was the widespread fear that the Soviet leaders, who had killed millions of their own people, were capable of sacrificing Soviet citizens in a nuclear showdown. By 1954, both the United States and the Soviet Union had intercontinental bombers and, of course, it did not end there. The nuclear arms race was clearly the most portentous issue in Soviet-American relations and one that Eisenhower found the most troubling.[42]

Actually, Smith argued that Eisenhower spent inadequate money on weapons and too much time on diplomatic initiatives (to the point of almost appeasement). For example, she did not see Josip Tito as a neutralist; he was "tied lock, stock and barrel to the Kremlin" and, thus, Yugoslavia should receive no American money.[43] She took a harder line than Eisenhower, though she believed that his quick responses to the crisis in the Straits of Formosa, caused by Chinese military action in the mid-1950s, and the emergency in Lebanon, where a pro-American government was in peril in 1958, proved that the ever present policy of massive retaliation was successful in producing "the greatest and longest period of peace for the United States since the days of pre–World War II."[44]

Many other hard-line voices argued for nuclear superiority in the late 1950s, notably in the wake of the successful Soviet October 1957 launch of Sputnik, the world's first man-made satellite to orbit the earth. For the majority of Americans, the nation's most urgent problem was the possibility of nuclear war. There was rising fear of a "missile gap" with the Soviets surpassing American nuclear capabilities. Nationally syndicated columnist Joseph Alsop, a fervent anticommunist, cited frightening numbers of alleged Soviet missiles and politicians such as Senator John F. Kennedy used this material to charge that the Eisenhower administration was guilty of allowing a missile gap. In January 1960, Air Force Major General James H. Walsh argued that the Soviets were on track to have 800 intercontinental ballistic missiles by mid-1963, a much larger estimate than other intelligence estimates. These inflated Air Force numbers came to the attention of the nation's leading newspapers, adding fuel to the idea of a missile gap.[45] Of the evangelical Protestant press, *Christianity Today* favored continued nuclear development claiming that "the cessation of nuclear bomb tests is no more the world's real hope for peace in this decade than the organization of the United Nations was in the last."[46] The demands for American science to develop more and better nuclear weapons persisted. In the short term, however, it was paramount for American bombers with nuclear weapons to be airborne day and night. As one Strategic Air Command commander explained in 1960: "We must impress Mr. Khrushchev that we have it and that he cannot strike this country with impunity. I think the minute he thinks he can strike this country with impunity, we will 'get it' in the next 60 seconds."[47]

Assessments that Khrushchev was waiting for the appropriate moment to strike the United States and that the best response was nuclear superiority were common, and, consequently, protests against the nuclear arms race remained mainly within small circles of radicals and pacifists.[48] To placate Americans, the government gave more attention to civil defense than ever before. The nuclear issue was serious enough in the early 1950s to see the creation of the Federal Civil Defense Administration, but it was later in the decade that ordinary Americans learned more about nuclear warning systems, sheltering, and evacuation than ever before, mainly as a result of the increasing threat due to more powerful nuclear bombs and sophisticated bombers and missiles.[49] In particular, civil defense agencies provided strategies to protect Americans against the fallout of nuclear bombs should the military fail to stop them before reaching the United States. Encouraging home bomb shelters, the federal government offered guidelines for families to renovate their basements or patios to improve their chance of survival. In September, 1961, *Life* magazine presented the article "How You Can Survive Fallout" which included an open letter from President Kennedy with the statement "there is much that you can do to protect yourself—and in doing so strengthen your nation." There were 15 photographs, three sketches, and three diagrams detailing the construction of a variety of home bomb shelters. The popular weekly magazine was one of many sources that brought the seriousness of a nuclear-armed communist menace to the attention of households across the nation.[50] The following year, the federal government paid almost 30 percent of the cost of America's first combination underground school and fallout shelter, built in Artesia, New Mexico.[51]

Distrust of communists remained strong into the 1960s, especially during the showdowns between the United States and the Soviet Union in Berlin (1961) and Cuba (1962). For the American people, military spending did not become a controversial issue until after the United States began its ground war in Southeast Asia. In the early 1960s, it was not surprising to have events such as a Dr. Fred Schwarz–led Christian anticommunist crusade at the Hollywood Bowl where film stars such as John Wayne, Jimmy Stewart, and Roy Rogers, genuine heroes for many Americans, were front and center in supporting Schwarz and other "stalwart fighters" of communism.[52]

As for Smith, she continued to be vocal with her hard-line stand against international communism and support for nuclear strength. She gave speeches solely on the "world-wide threat of the Red China–Russia Bloc," the "terrorism" of communism, the desire of communist regimes to destroy the United States, and the need for people to make the necessary individual sacrifices to preserve "our American way of life."[53] She also gave two major speeches in the Senate on September 21, 1961, and exactly one year later, both addressing what she believed was the contrast of President Kennedy's bold words and weak actions. Her first speech expanded a memorandum sent to her from the office of Brigadier General Jerry D. Page. She claimed that ominous signs plagued the United States, particularly communists becoming stronger each day and Khrushchev "vowing to take over the world for communism." In fact, much of her speech focused on answering "What has happened that permits Khrushchev to act as he does?" Drawing on political and military history, she found the answer uncomplicated. There was no support for "a thesis that it is safer to be weak than strong"; the Soviets were bold because America lost nuclear credibility when the Kennedy administration flirted with "the stupidity of limited deterrence," thus communicating to Khrushchev that it lacked the will to use nuclear weapons.[54]

One scholar refers to Kennedy's "mediocre mind," emotional immaturity, and shallow understanding of foreign policy.[55] But here Smith appeared to be questioning his masculinity and her penetrating words seemed to have an effect on policymaking. Democrat Senator Stuart Symington's immediate response to Smith was that the United States would use nuclear weapons if necessary and Kennedy's address to the United Nations General Assembly a few days later stated likewise. Kennedy could not allow a woman to appear bolder than he; clearly, he was upset, characterizing her as "ignorant."[56] Her depiction of him was still on his mind weeks later. In an early October conversation with C. L. Sulzberger, Kennedy admitted it was troubling that Smith categorized him as one who lacked strength.[57] In Moscow, Khrushchev used her speech for propaganda and possible political gain: "Who can remain calm and indifferent to such provocative statements made in the United States

Senate by this woman, blinded by savage hatred toward the community of socialist countries?"[58] Whether or not he could care, his verbal attack gave Smith a sense of pride; she believed Khrushchev was angry because American officials had grown firmer on nuclear weapons since her speech. She also responded with delight to columnist James Reston's assessment: "He [Kennedy] has talked like Churchill and acted like Chamberlain. This is why even so wise and moderate a woman as Sen. Margaret Chase Smith of Maine rose in the Senate last week and, in a remarkable speech, asked whether we had lost our national will to risk everything for our beliefs."[59]

One year later, on September 21, months after the tense showdown between American and Soviet tanks in Berlin and a few weeks before the Cuban Missile Crisis, Smith claimed that the situation was much the same as before; Kennedy's "policy continued to undermine the nuclear credibility of the United States to the detriment of our Nation, and to the advantage and the increasing boldness of Khrushchev."[60] Did Kennedy's rhetoric have any substance? As Smith saw it, his "polished phrases" could not hide from Americans that "we are simply not breathing the air of success." When Secretary of Defense Robert McNamara did present "most encouraging" statements about a "counterforce" that could offset the military capabilities of the communists, she noted the deep silence of the government when McNamara's words received criticism from some academics. Judging the opposition of university and college professors as misguided, she asked, "Do these good and sincere people who are so critical really believe that we would be better off *without* a margin of military advantage across the board?" Deterrence was not "old-fashioned," Smith argued. It was "fiction" that American nuclear buildup indicated "an intention on our part to initiate war against the Soviets by striking first." Those who favored "placating the Soviets at the terrible cost of deliberately downgrading our own military advantage and settling for parity or near parity" did so with shallow reasoning. Smith did recognize the gravity of a nuclear war, but, unlike those who argued there would be no winners, she held that America could win.[61]

However, of considerable concern for more astute thinkers was the mixing of the communist doctrine of inevitability and nuclear weapons. Among communist leaders there was the belief that any future conflict that included nuclear missiles would result in a Marxist-Leninist victory over capitalism regardless of the degree of physical destruction to the world. According to Viacheslav Molotov, communists should not worry or speak about "the destruction of world civilization," but instead focus on "the need to prepare and mobilize all forces for the destruction of the bourgeoisie."[62] In his visit to Moscow in 1957, Mao—manufactured bravado or not—told his communist comrades: "No matter what kind of war breaks out—conventional or thermonuclear—we'll win.

As for China, if the imperialists unleash war on us, we may lose more than three hundred million people. So what? War is war. The years will pass, and we'll get to work producing more babies than ever before."[63] Clarifying what was at stake years later, Adlai Stevenson, the U.S. representative at the United Nations delivered a harsh indictment of the Soviet Union and communism: "Against the idea of diversity, communism asserts the idea of uniformity; against freedom, inevitability; against choice, compulsion; against democracy, dogma; against independence, ideology; against tolerance, conformity." As he saw it, communism's "faith is that the iron laws of history will require every nation traverse the same predestined conclusion."[64]

Fortunately, Khrushchev, in late October 1962, did not shrug off the scientific evidence that painted an ominous scenario of nuclear war between the United States and the Soviet Union. He knew what Fidel Castro did not: the United States had a far greater stock of nuclear weapons than the Soviet Union. Soviet Ambassador Andrei Gromyko could lie to Kennedy's face and deny that the Soviets had offensive weapons in Cuba and Castro could adopt casualness on the prospect of nuclear war, but Khrushchev could not deceive himself as to the reality of Soviet weakness against American nuclear firepower.[65] While Kennedy did not adopt the plans for an immediate air strike on Cuba as promoted by Dean Acheson or a full-scale military invasion recommended by the Joint Chiefs of Staff, he would never allow the Soviets to complete their plans of arming Cuba with missiles.[66] Reflecting on the thirteen tense days and eventual backing down by Khrushchev, Americans could ask, was not the government's tough position to go to the brink during the Cuban Missile Crisis proof that the United States could win? The lesson was clear for Smith: the communists only understood and respected force and it was America's preponderance of nuclear weapons that made the difference.

If there was any question on how far Smith was willing to go in demonstrating her hard-line Cold War views concerning nuclear weapons, the Nuclear Test Ban Treaty ratification vote in the Senate in 1963 settled the matter. As a member of the Armed Services Preparedness Subcommittee, she heard arguments for and against ratification. From the start she was skeptical that ratification was the correct move, especially with a country "which, in recent years, among other things, ruthlessly repressed the Hungarian uprising; erected a shameful wall of tyranny around Berlin; surreptitiously deployed ballistic missiles in Cuba and, after months of stealthy preparations, shattered a moratorium on nuclear testing which had been in effect for 34 months."[67] As for the perceived advantages of the treaty, they were straightforward: moderate the nuclear arms race, thwart additional nations from gaining nuclear arms, encourage better diplomatic relations, and prevent further environmental problems. Taking her interest in national security seriously, she desired to "take a cold, hard, impassionate appraisal of the treaty and all its consequences" before falling in with the wishes of the government. She heard the testimonies of many witnesses who expressed grave reservations on the treaty's negative impact on national security. Edward Teller and John S. Foster, Jr. were two scientists who opposed the treaty, but the Kennedy administration kept anti-treaty testimony from the American public, a position that Smith found disturbing.[68]

National polls indicated a divided America with only a bare majority supportive of the treaty.[69] Seeing that the government's "one-sidedness" gave the treaty momentum, Smith spoke out publicly and made inquiries to key White House people. In her speech of September 9, 1963, she argued that the treaty debate in the Senate failed to adequately assess the potential risks and disadvantages of the treaty. She believed that the United States was behind with scientific data due to the Soviet nuclear testing of 1961 and 1962 which was "massive, sophisticated, and impressive." If the Soviet Union had a nuclear advantage, could the United States be "confident and secure in the knowledge that our ballistic-missile retaliatory second strike force will survive and operate in a nuclear environment?" In total, Smith presented sixteen questions in her speech that demanded close attention for the sake of national security.[70] The response to her stand was respectful, but some press reports made gender comments that detracted from her speech. For example, the *Christian Science Monitor* wrote: Smith "wearing a rose in her blue suit and always an attractive object in the dull chamber, mildly asked" critical questions.[71]

Despite Smith's reservations, ratification of the treaty looked favorable for the Kennedy administration. The Preparedness Subcommittee reported that the Soviet Union had surpassed the United States in the development of large nuclear bombs, but one of the signers was Symington who also planned to vote for ratification. In fact, press reports indicated that in the Senate only eight southern Democrats and four Republicans from Texas and the West voiced outright opposition to the treaty. Within this list, the more powerful senators included: Richard B. Russell (D-GA), Strom Thurmond (D-SC), John Stennis (D-MS), and Barry Goldwater (R-AZ), the latter two on the Preparedness Subcommittee. The Foreign Relations Committee on the other hand recommended ratification with a sixteen-to-one vote. One of the leading proponents for ratification was Senator J. William Fulbright (D-AR), who followed Smith's speech with a 9,000-word address that spoke of the horrors of nuclear war. Expressing his doubts that the Soviet Union "would always seek to conquer the world," Fulbright stated that "the Russian people may turn out to be a powerful ally of the free nations."[72] The thinking of Smith and Fulbright could hardly be more conflicting.

After collaborating with the State Department, Senator John Sparkman (D-AL), second senior Majority member of the Senate Foreign Relations Committee, told Smith that a number of her questions involved highly secret data and thus most answers lacked facts. On September 16, she responded with a second set of questions and two days later Secretary of State Dean Rusk sent her the State Department's answers, again lacking the assurances she sought. At the same time, McNamara followed up a phone call to Smith with a long letter and an attachment that addressed her questions and the position of the White House and apologized for not responding quickly to her letter of September 10.[73] In her September 24 speech to the Senate, just before the vote, she said that her mail from outside Maine showed greater opposition to the treaty than what the Gallup and Harris polls indicated.[74] There was also no certainty that the people of Maine favored the treaty. Representing the position of many, one man wrote, "I am convinced that the test ban treaty serves the Communists and not the United States of America." The *Daily Kennebec Journal* wondered why the "dictator of Russia intensely desires" the treaty.[75] Smith found it troubling that "the national security disadvantages stemming from ratification of the treaty have not been as fully presented out in the open to the public." [76] Still, Kennedy pressured her to support the treaty and the press such as the *Christian Science Monitor* predicted a yes vote.[77] Regardless of the strength of one's convictions, voting openly before the public is not always easy. Assessing that the signing of the treaty represented a greater threat to national security than a rejection of the treaty, she cast a no vote with the nation watching. Only eighteen others voted likewise and, in fact, she was the lone New England senator to oppose the treaty. The final vote had 80 supporting the ratification of the Kennedy-Harriman limited nuclear test ban treaty.

Even though it appeared that many of her constituents favored the treaty, she sided with the opinions of ordinary Americans in other regions of the nation who expressed their opposition to the treaty in correspondence to her.[78] To explain her stand, she told the press that Khrushchev saw the treaty as a way to prevent the United States from conducting open-air tests that would close "the high-yield weapons gap that so heavily favors Russia."[79] Notably frustrating for her was the lack of courage demonstrated by her male colleagues in the Senate: "I have never heard so many speeches that were basically against the treaty end up with the speaker saying that he was going to vote for the treaty even though he felt it presented a grave risk and he was not happy about the way he was going to vote." In the end, Smith believed the treaty signaled weakness rather than strength.[80]

Others agreed with her, including Edward Rozek, an associate professor in the Department of Political Science at the University of Colorado, Boulder, who wrote: "I hope that God will give you enough strength to continue doing what is right."[81] Academics defending Smith on this issue were not common, but there was ample encouragement from a number of newspapers across the nation. *Los Angeles Herald Examiner* columnist George Todt saw Senate ratification of the treaty as "A 'Modern Munich.'" Having strong reservations about the treaty and its safeguards for America, the *St. Louis Globe-Democrat* referred to the nineteen as the "great Senators," and in the eyes of the *Chicago Tribune*, the dissenters possessed "honor and integrity" by taking "their stand against accommodation with the soviet tyranny." In one grim editorial, the *Manchester Union Leader* warned of the day when senators faced "the rifles of a Communist firing squad or the torture chambers of the Communist police." Cited were the words of communist Demitry A. Manuilsky: "The bourgeoisie will have to be put to sleep, so we shall begin by launching the most spectacular peace movement on record . . . [and] capitalist countries, stupid and decadent, will rejoice to cooperate in their own destruction."[82]

Even though Smith's hard-line position situated her in a small group of dissenting senators, she gained a significant amount of national attention and political capital. In the middle of the treaty debate, journalist Vera R. Glaser wrote that there was serious interest "from every state in the union" for Smith to run for president. Some saw her as a good running mate on a ticket headed by Senator Barry Goldwater. One anonymous Democrat acknowledged, "She's got all that a masculine candidate has plus she's the kind of woman women will vote for" and Democratic Senator Maurine Neuberger, the only other female senator, told the press that Smith "would add a lot to the [Goldwater] ticket."[83] In November 1963, when asked how he viewed Smith as a possible opponent in 1964, President Kennedy stated that he would not look forward to campaigning against the "very formidable" Smith, if she was the Republican presidential candidate.[84] One wonders if there was more mischief than sincerity in Kennedy's response given at his last press conference. The *Amarillo Globe-Times* was one of a number of newspapers that argued that America was not ready for a female president or vice president: "the room at the top has a men only sign on it."[85] Still, Smith's possible candidacy did generate serious discussion among Americans which suggests that her Cold War views imparted some masculine credibility to her campaign. In December, moderate Republican Senator George Aiken portrayed Smith to radio listeners across the nation as a strong politician. Honest in her political convictions, she appealed "to people everywhere." [86]

With her reputation as a moderate on domestic issues and a conservative on foreign policy, Smith declared her candidacy in early 1964 and became the first female of a major party to run for the presidency.[87] Yet as impressive as her hawkish views were to conservatives, she lacked the political clout to be a serious challenger to front-runner Goldwater. The high mark of her campaign was 26 percent of the vote at the Illinois primary, where she and Goldwater were the only two on the ballot. The United States was far from ready for a female president and Smith finished a distant fifth in the end, watching Goldwater forces take control of the Republican national leadership. The rise of an "extremist" leader who appeared eager to use nuclear weapons to fight communism confounded many liberals and academics.

While others branded Goldwater a heartless warmonger, Smith offered no criticism of him. Given that her views on nuclear weapons were similar to Goldwater's, it is not surprising that she stated in a radio address that he "is not as irresponsible as his critics say."[88] Chalmers M. Roberts, political writer for the *Washington Post*, hinted that Goldwater's views had significant influence on her in the Preparedness Subcommittee.[89] In 1960, Goldwater's grassroots appeal and rise as a leader of conservative forces gained momentum when his slim book *Conscience of a Conservative*, released in March, became a best seller. Covering foreign affairs in one third of the book, he wrote of policymakers' weak response to the "Soviet Menace." Like Smith, he voiced strong language: America's approach to the Cold War would be better if it disregarded "Mr. Khrushchev's murderous claque as the legitimate rulers of the Russian people or any other people." Again like Smith, Goldwater favored nuclear deterrence and he was willing to take nuclear risks; he wanted to make nuclear war more thinkable because surrender was a worse option.[90]

In the weeks leading up to the 1964 presidential election, the New York advertising firm of Doyle Dane Bernbach produced the famous "Daisy" television commercial. A cute little girl picking daisies in a sunny field plucks the petals as a male narrator counted backward. At zero the screen revealed an atomic explosion and viewers heard President Johnson voice, "These are the stakes. To make a world in which all of God's children can live, or go into the dark. We must either love each other, or we must die." The narrator's final message was for Americans to vote for Johnson. The same advertising firm produced another television commercial that warned Americans not to vote for Goldwater, who voted against the nuclear-ban treaty.[91] Smith, of course, had also voted with him in opposing the treaty, but the Arizona cowboy offered an easier target for liberals. The Maine lady who opposed McCarthyism appeared to have left a lasting impression with many moderates and liberals and they appeared to overlook that she could actually think as Goldwater did on the issue of nuclear arms.

This same year witnessed the release of Stanley Kubrick's satirical film *Dr. Strangelove, Or: How I Learned to Stop Worrying and Love the Bomb* which, in a slapstick comedy manner, portrayed the doctrine of nuclear deterrence as absurd and dangerous thinking. A rogue General Jack D. Ripper, commander of Burpleson Air Force Base, instructs a bomber wing to launch a nuclear attack on Russia. The President of the United States frantically attempts to abort the mission and phones the Soviet premier, who given the circumstances sounds fairly amiable and cooperative. Behind the humor, the movie offered a chilling scenario for Americans who interpreted the nuclear arms race as madness. But for other Americans, Kubrick's interpretation of a likable Soviet leader was not how they interpreted communist leadership, and, thus, the message of the film lost some of its power.

By the mid-1960s, long-range missiles became more important than bombers to both the United States and the Soviet Union and no other national security issue caused greater debate in the Senate in the years Smith was a senator than the anti-ballistic-missile system. A majority of Americans in the 1960s believed that the Soviet Union possessed an ABM system and a 1964 poll revealed that 76 percent agreed with the statement: "Antimissile missiles will make America stronger, and an enemy will be even less likely to attack us than without these missiles."[92] Support for an ABM system had traction because deterrence strategy depended on protecting America's retaliatory capability. If the Soviets had the capability of destroying America's retaliatory forces in a first strike, deterrence was lost.[93] Ideology was important in the Senate voting on the ABM, borne out by the liberal-conservative split of most northern Democrats in opposition to a majority of southern Democrats and a majority of Republicans. Viewing communist expansionism as a grave danger, conservative senators held that it might be necessary to risk war in order to stop communist advancement. Liberal senators, however, feared the possibility of nuclear war more than the threat of communist expansion.[94] In a 1969 Harris poll, 50 percent of Americans agreed and 24 percent disagreed that the "Safeguard ABM anti-missile system is necessary in order for us to keep with the Russians in the nuclear arms race." Two polls in April and July revealed between 78 and 84 percent of respondents agreeing that it was "better to be overprepared militarily than to be caught short without proper defenses," and what appears contradictory, between 47 and 50 percent preferred a focus on peaceful arms control rather than building more ABMs.[95]

As a member of the Senate Armed Services Committee, Smith was a key player in debating and voting on the ABM issue. In his memoirs, Richard Nixon claimed that both sides of the 1969 debate "sought to win her support" to the point that Senator Mike Mansfield stated "he'd never seen so many men publicly woo one woman."[96] In a 1967 Senate speech, she had expressed concern that the proposed Sentinel anti-ballistic-missile system might "become obsolete in the near future." In fact, she wondered if the anti-ballistic-missile defense system in the Soviet Union represented decoys designed to motivate the United States to adopt a very costly and ineffective ABM system. Although her lack of enthusiasm for the ABM placed her in the liberal camp, in the eyes of many her position was more accurately an ultra-conservative one. She wanted something that guaranteed superiority—period. The following year in the Senate Armed Services Committee, she cast her vote against the Sentinel ABM because the Johnson administration's only argument "was that it would strengthen the hand of the President in negotiations with the Russians."[97] Lacking the confidence that many others had for scientists in developing a sophisticated ABM system, she did not want the United States to spend money on something that would be ineffective against the advance of the communist menace.

Even more crucial votes took place in August 1969 on the Safeguard ABM (replacing the Sentinel) designed to destroy enemy missiles targeting American missile sites. Senator George D. Aiken, ranking Republican on the Foreign Relations Committee and a close friend of Smith, assisted the White House in having her consider a compromise amendment. She discussed the draft amendment with Stennis and Russell at the end of a Senate Armed Services Committee session, with the result that all three concluded that the language was too ambiguous. Additional work between the White House and Aiken went nowhere. Notwithstanding her close relationship with Aiken, Smith found the whole episode strange in that the White House's choice of an intermediary was the ranking Republican member of the Foreign Relations Committee, a group opposed to and openly critical of the Armed Services Committee.[98]

The stakes were high for the White House. President Nixon needed the ABM to proceed in order to get the best deal with the Soviets, who he believed outdistanced the United States in 1969 by deploying more intercontinental ballistic missiles, nuclear missile–firing submarines, and ABMs. As Nixon saw it, "the ABM vote represented . . . a philosophical turning point in America's strategic credibility." William Safire, a Nixon speechwriter, claims that the president feared that there could be "a weakening of America's national will" if others perceived him as a "liberal." In the face of his "fairly progressive" domestic legislation and Vietnamization, Nixon desired to disprove any notions of being soft on foreign policy issues: "what Nixon could not abide was an association with post-Vietnam liberalism's soft underbelly, which he considered to be a foolish despair about American values and a debilitating and dangerous boredom with world responsibility."[99] Of course, liberals interpreted the issue very differently. J. William Fulbright, chairman of the Senate Foreign Relations Committee, believed that rather than the issue of anti-ballistic missiles the real point of the ABM debate was the Senate reasserting "some control over the military department."[100]

Smith opposed the "isolationism" of unilateral disarmament and retrench-ment. Consequently, her stand with liberals against the ABM continued to be confusing, inside and outside Washington. In her mind, she could not be any clearer; she was against any allocation of funds for the development and re-search of the Safeguard ABM. When no amendments came forth opposing the spending of one cent for both development and deployment, she introduced what she called her "fish or cut bait" amendment. Observing that both oppo-nents and proponents of the Safeguard ABM were suspicious of her motives, she explained that "in the Machiavellian world of Washington, simplicity and directness is so rare that it is suspect." In a letter sent to each Senator on Au-gust 6, she wrote: "I have no confidence in the Safeguard ABM system and if one has no confidence in it then I cannot see the logic or justification in vot-ing for research and development of it."[101] When the Senate session opened, Senator Albert Gore (D-TN) voiced his opposition to her amendment on the grounds that it might adversely affect other anti-missile developments such as Nike X. Another proposal that received much attention was Senators John Sherman Cooper's (R-KY) and Philip A. Hart's (D-MI) amendment which barred deployment, but allowed research and development of the Safeguard.

In the afternoon, Smith told the Senate that her amendment made more sense than the Cooper-Hart amendment; the proposed Safeguard was too vulnerable and too costly at a time when it was paramount to carefully deter-mine national priorities. If some assumed she favored a liberal direction, her following words corrected this false impression: "I think offensive strength is the better deterrent and as such rates national security priority over the proposed ABM system." If the United States lacked an offensive arsenal, she argued, Russian Kremlin leaders would destroy America without hesitancy. It was tragic that the ABM represented "a self-deluding Maginot Line false sense of security" because any Soviet assault would be a "massive attack with full utilization of all their devastating weapons on cities as well as missile sites." If the United States wanted to pursue defensive projects the answer was the development of a "powerful laser" for protecting missile sites and cities. Her speech generated an intense four-hour session and one veteran who had 40 years of Senate service stated, "In all my years, I have never seen one Senator dominate the Senate Floor as long as she did. And to think that it would be the only woman in the one hundred Senators!"[102]

One issue was that Smith's cool logic of absolutely no money for ABM de-velopment embarrassed some anti-ABM senators who supported the Cooper-Hart amendment. Bill Lewis informed Smith that Gore and others wanted reassurance that her amendment would not apply to any other anti-ballistic systems. In essence, a few changes to her amendment gave "them a chance to save face." She was agreeable to the inclusion of one additional sentence as suggested by Gore, but Goldwater blocked the modification when she asked the Senate for unanimous consent; Stennis did likewise when Fulbright made the same request. With emotions at a peak, the next business was a vote on the original Smith amendment before the presentation of any other amendment. After the Senate rejected her amendment eighty-nine to eleven, anti-ABM senators and Smith crafted another amendment that became "the Senate's all-time cliff-hanger and set a record for the greatest number of votes cast in the history of the Senate."[103] Although pro-ABM senators grumbled that the second Smith compromise was no different from the blocked original, they won the final vote 51 to 50 against. Vice President Spiro Agnew accounted for the additional vote even though it was unnecessary since Senate rules treat a tie vote as a defeat. The critical test remained the vote on the Cooper-Hart amendment. Maintaining her intellectual honesty, Smith refused to support Cooper-Hart and the final vote was 51 to 49 against; her position, according to a recent study on Congress and the Cold War, "sealed the fate of Cooper-Hart."[104] In the end, Cooper and Hart did defend her vote of consistent opposition to any support for the Safeguard ABM, but "much of the liberal press" interpreted her vote as a betrayal.[105]

Smith cared about the response of ordinary Americans, but on this issue she received more opposing than supporting letters. It was her influential position on the Armed Services Committee, her stand on the ABM debate, and the perception that she was an approachable politician with an abundance of integrity in an age when an increasing number distrusted politicians that explains why people across the nation wrote letters to her. Representative of those who found her trustworthy, a Virginia man wrote that Smith's "steadfastness of purpose, devotion to duty and to her Country, and sound judgment help keep alive the faith in our makers of the law that we so badly need" and a Georgian praised her for bravery, depth of character, and integrity.[106] Soon after the key votes on the Safeguard ABM, one of Smith's Maine constituents expressed her affection: "You're quite a gal—and we certainly admire your courage and your spunk and your personal integrity."[107] From Oxford, New York, one man wrote: "I believe it is possibly one of the most sincere stands taken by any member of the Senate."[108]

The ABM issue divided Americans with opponents concerned that the arms race was out of control and proponents worried that the deceptive Soviets were building more missiles and their own ABM system while talking disarmament.[109] Conservatives were more receptive to hard-line attitudes and liberals were more critical of the old policy of handling foreign affairs from a position of superiority. As it was within the Senate, there were Republicans and Democrats at the grassroots on both sides of the issue, but obviously Republican voters showed more inclination to support Nixon on the ABM issue. A Tennessee correspondent expressed it one way: "[I]f the Senate chooses to humiliate our President, and belittle him in the eyes of the world, then it will be the Senate's responsibility for what may happen to our country as a result of weakening the office of the President." Specifically, there was fear that a Nixon defeat to American "defense-abolitionists" would result in foreign leaders questioning him as "the real leader of his country" and expose Americans to the most serious peril in their history—a Soviet attack on the United States.[110]

The Nixon administration also had the support of many of Smith's Maine constituents who likewise believed that the Soviets and Chinese were increasing their nuclear capabilities for world domination. The major arguments were that the Russians only understood force and that the cost of the ABM was a small price to pay for America's "survival." Some comments were apocalyptic: one woman wrote that it was better to save three quarters or half of the United States than none whereas one man claimed Senator Fulbright's views were wrong and he preferred to die trying to defend America than to be "a slave."[111] For some, the North Korean capture of the *Pueblo* (an American intelligence vessel seized in the Sea of Japan) and information necessary to pinpoint the locations of Polaris and Poseidon submarines clarified the importance of installing an ABM system.[112]

Actually, the great success of the Polaris and how detractors had attempted to prohibit its deployment proved to others that the ABM deserved a chance.[113] Another popular point was that the scientific capacity of America was the best in the world and there was no reason to adopt a pessimistic defeatist attitude in the face of Soviet work on an anti-ballistic system.[114] Convinced that the often quoted phrase "military-industrial complex" was done out of context because Eisenhower argued that a strong defense was essential, some of Smith's constituents believed that military people had more integrity than academics, a statement that hinted of the growing gap between conservatives and many professors.[115] One of the few academics who wrote to Smith and declared support for the ABM system was Professor William A. Stanmeyer of Georgetown University Law Center. Fearing the possibility of a "nuclear Pearl Harbor," he gave specific warnings of Soviet arms buildup that had upset the nuclear balance in favor of the enemy. With a reference to George Orwell's *1984*, he wrote that hard-line Stalinists controlled Russia evidenced by the ruthless policies concerning the Berlin Wall, dissenting writers, concentration camps, and "the recent rape of Czechoslovakia."[116]

There were also signs of more conservative-leaning Americans distrusting journalistic reports which allegedly failed to appreciate the sinister ways of communist leaders. An Ohioan supporter of the ABM complained that she found it difficult to get accurate information "from our prejudiced news media."[117] It was confusing to steadfast anticommunists that liberal journalists would fan the flames when they focused on the most radical protesters of nuclear weapons and war and then respond to the threat of communism in a too casual manner. More examples of historical writing and journalistic reports in the 1960s did challenge orthodox interpretations that placed the primary blame for the Cold War on communist leaders.

Consistent with reports of senators receiving mostly anti-ABM mail, Smith received far more anti-ABM letters than pro-ABM letters. Showing little evidence of representing an organized effort of generic or scripted responses, the letters of ordinary Americans across the nation expressed, in good and poor prose, the negative aspects of the ABM system and its linkage to a catastrophic arms race. Correspondence included terms and phrases such as "nuclear Neanderthalism" and "paranoid reaction to communism."[118] A woman from New York City expressed her horror over the expenditures of the "War Department," stating "this Defense title is for the birds."[119] One opponent of the ABM from Washington, D.C. found it disturbing that scientists coldly debated whether "only" 40 or 70 million would perish: "The idea that one finger pressing one button can destroy my family, my life and all that is personally meaningful to me, while at most there will only be a few seconds to realize what is happening, causes me to listen to these experts with complete incredibility to the emotionless way they dispense their knowledge and statistics."[120] Even though the ABM plan was supposedly defensive rather than offensive, it still represented a proliferation of nuclear weapons and a dangerous arms race.

Opponents often specifically stated that the "military-industrial complex" had too much influence, that the expensive project had dubious value, that other pressing needs in America received little attention, and that the Soviets viewing ABM spending as offensive rather than defensive would spend more on weapons. Sample letters making these points are as follows. From Rochester, New York, one man wrote: "Unless something breaks the stranglehold which the military-industrial complex now enjoys, we will have no basis to order our lives in the future except fear."[121] One writer from Caribou, Maine, informed Smith that the three NIKE-AJAX missile sites located within a ten-mile radius of his home had launching pits full of water and weeds, all abandoned by the United States Army. Constructed as the latest in protection, their technological demise foreshadowed obsolete ABMs.[122] Secretary of Defense Melvin Laird's justification of the ABM system on "Face the Nation," prompted an Illinois woman to write that military spending on the ABM was useless, especially in a time when "careful, moderate people" feared the strong possibility of "a truly nasty civil war—a race war."[123] The billions diverted to the ABM program and other military projects resulted in crumbling institutions and a society on the brink of revolution.[124] A Smith constituent stated that the ABM would spur the Soviets: "Russia can only take it as proof that the United States is determined to maintain an even greater superiority of weaponry—which plays right into the hands of the 'hawks' among the Russian leaders who will insist on responding in kind."[125]

Other opponents complained that the message from the government changed wildly. One point was that the government sold the idea of the ABM to protect the United States from a Chinese nuclear threat, but this changed with the realization that the Chinese did not have missiles that could reach America. Next, the government revealed that the ABM was necessary because the Russians "were building a missile defense throughout their own country." When information clarified that the Russian ABM system could not stop the thousands of American missiles, the rationale of having an ABM system in the United States became to "protect our deterrence."[126] The lack of consistent reasoning from the government was frustrating for Americans wanting answers on why politicians were taking huge risks with nuclear weaponry.

A segment of those who pointed out the inconsistencies of government arguments for the ABM nonetheless made it clear that national security remained a major focus. All opponents of the ABM program, a Florida man wanted more bomb shelters, a Maine man believed the best deterrent was the Polaris submarine, and a Kansas man suggested the development of a laser beam to destroy incoming missiles.[127] Thus, some Americans opposed the ABM because they believed that the best defense against communist threats was a good offense.[128] Smith was clearly in line with this type of thinking.

The position of academics was almost always in opposition to the ABM system; peace on the planet depended on a reduction of missiles. Charles Packard, a retired biology professor of Randolph-Macon College, Ashland, Virginia, asked, "Is our world doomed to an insane race for annihilation?"[129] Political scientist Lawrence Peery of San Diego State College wrote that the nation had other, higher priorities.[130] From the California Institute of Technology, William Cook declared that "the entire knowledgeable scientific community *knows* that the ABM system is a complete boondoggle to keep the Military-Industrial complex pot boiling."[131] John Quinn, an instructor at Connecticut College, found it ludicrous that in a time of urban unrest there was support for an ineffective ABM system.[132] Henry Schmidt, an associate professor of German, informed Smith that the government lacked new creative ideas common among young, better educated Americans whose scorn for government emerged with the "panicky" realization that politicians no longer warranted their trust.[133] More than ever before, there were Americans believing it was time for the older generation to step aside and allow young people a chance to improve society, notably in light of the lunacy of nuclear missile stockpiles.

Many writers thanked Smith for her opposition to the ABM without acknowledging or understanding that her position remained that of a Cold Warrior. A lady from Tacoma, Washington wrote she would have voted for Smith as president because she had bucked the military establishment and another from Brandeis University appreciated Smith's stand "in helping to make a few people aware of this game of insanity called defense."[134] Expressing gratitude for her vote against the ABM system, a Michigan man wrote "it will earn the ever increasing thanks of your countrymen long after you have ceased to serve them," a prediction that was at odds with the liberal criticism of her vote against the Cooper-Hart amendment and her hard-line stand on other defense issues.[135]

Others were aware that her position on the ABM was unique for her. Writing of Smith's Cold Warrior leanings and specifically her vote against the nuclear test ban treaty, a Virginian shared her pleasant surprise that Smith opposed the ABM in an Armed Services Committee vote.[136] From Maine, one woman acknowledged Smith's view on national security issues and that her opposition to the ABM did not represent a liberal perspective, but she was happy nonetheless that Smith was against the ABM. Even though one man knew her views on the "morality" of the Pentagon differed 180 degrees to his beliefs, he respected the consistency of her vote against the Cooper-Hart amendment.[137]

But more common was criticism of Smith for not doing enough to kill the ABM system. Among others, women from Tennessee, Virginia, and Texas wrote that they found it impossible to understand how she took a clear stand for no research, development, and deployment of the ABM, but voted against the Cooper-Hart amendment.[138] Disappointed and puzzled Americans found her vote against the Cooper-Hart amendment inconsistent and judged the failure of the Senate to pass the amendment as "a tragic mistake."[139] Sending a clear message, an Ohioan wrote: "As a woman, interested in politics, I am ashamed of your defection to the ABM proponents, at the last moment."[140]

The manner in which Smith responded to her critics did not place her in a good light. To those who were critical of the industrial-military-complex and showed their displeasure for her vote against the Cooper-Hart amendment, she reacted with anger. To one constituent, Smith wrote: "I find that many who claim they can't understand simply don't want to understand but rather are looking for an opportunity to accuse me of ulterior motives or stupidity."[141] Here the thin-skinned Smith failed to see that the optics were not in her favor. If one was unaware of her reasoning and her foundational hard-line views, her vote against the Cooper-Hart would have appeared to be either an act of stupidity or duplicity. She also appeared to lack patience for those who struggled to understand Cold War assumptions of American nuclear superiority—those who could not continue to see the issue in such a simple and stark manner as staunch Cold Warriors did when they high-lighted the evil nature of communism.

Debates on nuclear credibility placed Smith at center stage and by the late 1960s she came under more sustained attacks for her hawkish stand. There was an increasing number of Americans questioning a Cold Warrior position on the nuclear arms race and much of the correspondence sent to her opposed nuclear weapons. To the dismay of those who found Smith's hawkish views dangerous, she was an unrepentant and leading hawk in the Senate. If more women than ever before "claimed that saving American children from nuclear extinction was the essence of 'Americanism,'" the unmarried and indepen-dent Smith viewed it another way. Others using the ideology of domesticity as a weapon against Cold War assumptions had less influence on her because she never fully embraced the notion of domestic containment which upheld traditional gender roles and the belief that security was found in the home.[142] For those more in the conservative camp, her consistency stood out against the male leaders who came across as fickle when tough decisions were before them on how to respond to communist enemies. Letters do not reveal the whole story since polling indicated that there were many Americans favor-ing nuclear superiority.[143] A number of her strongest supporters who were in agreement with her Cold Warrior stand on the communist menace believed she was greatly in error on the ABM issue, [144] but she would be forgiven for this transgression.

Assured that she had the support of a significant number of people, Smith had no regrets for her hard-line stand for nuclear superiority, including her opposition to the test ban treaty of 1963. In 1971, journalist Don Larrabee explained that the treaty unfortunately worked in favor of the communists by preventing the United States from fully testing and developing a success-ful ABM system, an interpretation that gave Smith's position legitimacy.[145] Seeing communism as an evil and destructive force, she could be as tough as a Cold Warrior like Barry Goldwater. In the confusion of the ABM de-bate, many failed to see that her position was not dovish but very hawkish; her point was for the United States to spend money on *effective* weapons. There were signs in the media that she was becoming out of touch with the growing number of Americans who questioned the fundamentals behind nuclear credibility, but she could count on conservatives and the fact that the anti-nuclear movement lacked the necessary traction to gain strong and widespread support among Americans. A far-reaching and much more emotional issue was American involvement in Southeast Asia and Smith's stand would result in more difficult times for her in her final two years in the Senate.

NOTES

1. Smith, *Declaration of Conscience*, 257. One other translation refers to her as "Satan in the guise of a woman." See Sherman, *No Place for a Woman*, 174.

2. Smith, *Declaration of Conscience*, 413.

3. "Key Senate Place Lost by Mrs. Smith," *New York Times*, 27 January 1951.

4. Declaration of Conscience Speech, Senator Smith's Reaction, MCSL.

5. "McCarthy Senate Power Now Deeply Entrenched," *New York Times*, 18 January 1953.

6. Sherman, *No Place for a Woman*, 130–32.

7. This is a major theme of Gallant's, "Margaret Chase Smith, McCarthyism and the Drive for Political Purification," vi.

8. World Trip Report, Part IV, World Trip 1954–1955 Folder, MCSL.

9. Franco-Smith Interview; *See It Now* Scripts, World Trip 1954–1955 Folder, MCSL.

10. De Gaulle-Smith Interview, World Trip 1954–1955 Folder, MCSL.

11. Memorandum of Conversation, Ministry of Foreign Affairs, World Trip 1954–1955 Folder; World Trip Report, Part V, World Trip 1954–1955 Folder, MCSL.

12. Nasser-Smith Interview, World Trip 1954–1955 Folder, MCSL.

13. "Senator Smith Confirms Dulles PI Defense Pledge," *Evening News*, 23 February 1955, Scrapbook, vol. 169, 101, MCSL.

14. Neil Sheehan, *A Bright Shining Lie: John Paul Vann and America in Vietnam* (New York: Random House, 1988), 131.

15. World Trip Report, Part II, World Trip 1954–1955 Folder, MCSL.

16. World Trip Report, Part III, World Trip 1954–1955 Folder, MCSL.

17. "Berlin Reds Try to Hold Sen. Smith," *Washington Daily News*, 20 October 1954, Scrapbook, vol. 149, 25, MCSL.

18. Sherman, *No Place for a Woman*, 139–42.

19. "Sen. Smith Declares U.S.-Soviet Relations Near Breaking Point," *Portland Herald Press*, 29 October 1954, Scrapbook, vol. 149, 41, MCSL.

20. "Formosa Must be Protected, Sen. Smith Tells the NEWS," *Temple University NEWS*, 18 February 1955, Scrapbook, vol. 155, 146, MCSL.

21. Senator Margaret Chase Smith–Madam and Generalissimo Chiang Kai-Shek Interview, World Tour Folder, MCSL; Sherman, *No Place for a Woman*, 144–45.

22. Margaret Chase Smith, "Impatience and Generosity," Scrapbook, vol. 158, 131, MCSL.

23. "Senator Margaret Chase Smith Reports on Recent Overseas Trip," *The Richmond Bee*, 20 May 1955, Press Reports, World Trip 1954–1955 Folder, MCSL.

24. Haynes and Klehr, *In Denial*, 19–20.

25. Gaddis, *We Now Know*, 19.

26. "Slave-Labor Charges Against USSR Backed," W&Y, 15 July 1952, MCSL. For Dwight Eisenhower's discussion of communist despotic rule, see "U.S. Won't Rest Till Reds' Victims are Free, Ike Says," *New York Times*, 26 August 1952.

27. "Stalin Regime Now Openly Anti-Semitic," W&Y, 21 January 1953, MCSL.

28. "Jailed American Caged in Rail Car," *New York Times*, 4 April 1955, 6. On rampant crimes, see "Russia Re-Viewed: Crime Wave Goes Unchecked," *New York*

Times, 1 October 1954. In an earlier period, "Lenin had closed the churches of Russia and executed thousands of priests and active believers." See Peter Grose, *Operation Rollback: America's Secret War Behind the Iron Curtain* (Boston: Houghton Mifflin Company, 2000), 54. According to one source, "tens of thousands of believers died in prison or in exile between 1929 and 1961." See David E. Settje, "'Sinister' Communists and Vietnam Quarrels: The *Christian Century* and *Christianity Today* Respond to the Cold and Vietnam Wars," *Fides et Historia* 32, no. 1 (Winter/Spring 2000), 88. Also, see Eric Crouse, "New Evangelicalism, *Christianity Today*, and U.S. Foreign Policy, 1956–1965," *Canadian Evangelical Review* 30–31 (Fall 2005–Spring 2006), 47.

29. Gaddis, *We Now Know*, 45.

30. John Noble, *I Found God in Soviet Russia* (Grand Rapids, Mich.: Zondervan Publishing House, 1971), 30.

31. Noble, *I Found God in Soviet Russia*, 96.

32. Nash, *The Conservative Intellectual Movement in America*, 103.

33. Whittaker Chambers, *Witness* (New York: Random House, 1952), 7–9, 14.

34. Perlstein, *Before the Storm*, 104.

35. "Protestant Missionary Exodus from Red China Reported Near," *New York Times*, 6 January 1951. "Christianity Faces Up to Grim Challenge of Communist Rule in China," *Christian Science Monitor*, 13 February 1954.

36. Hollington K. Tong, "Christianity in China," *Christianity Today (CT)*, 21 January 1957, 13. "Red Atrocities," *CT*, 22 June 1959, 29.

37. "Against the President's Action: A Way to War," *Newsweek*, 7 February 1955, Scrapbook, vol. 154, 116, MCSL.

38. See Melvyn P. Leffler, "National Security," in *Explaining the History of American Foreign Relations*, 2nd ed., ed. Michael J. Hogan and Thomas G. Paterson (Cambridge: Cambridge University Press, 2004), 125.

39. These were concerns during the Korean War. See Casey, "Selling NSC-68," 668.

40. "GI's Should Decide Use of A-Bomb on Reds," W&Y, 27 August 1953, MCSL.

41. Patrick M. Morgan, *Deterrence Now* (Cambridge: Cambridge University Press, 2003), 24.

42. Robert A. Divine, *Eisenhower and the Cold War* (Oxford: Oxford University Press, 1981), 110.

43. Sherman, *No Place for a Woman*, 148.

44. Smith, *Declaration of Conscience*, 259. For a critique of the doctrine of massive retaliation, see Egar Bottome, *The Balance of Terror: Nuclear Weapons and the Illusion of Security, 1945–1985*, revised and updated ed. (Boston: Beacon Press, 1986), 18–25. For more discussion of nuclear deterrence, see John Foster Gaddis, *The Long Peace: Inquiries Into the History of the Cold War* (Oxford: Oxford University Press, 1987).

45. May, *Homeward Bound*, 26. Christopher A. Preble, "'Who Ever Believed in the 'Missile Gap'?': John F. Kennedy and the Politics of National Security," *Presidential Studies Quarterly* 33, no. 4 (December 2003), 803, 805, 809–10. Also, see

Sheldon Ungar, "Moral Panics, the Military-Industrial Complex, and the Arms Race," *The Sociological Quarterly* 31, no. 2 (Summer 1990), 175.

46. "Christ and the Atom Bomb," *CT*, 2 September 1957.

47. Quoted in Morgan, *Deterrence Now*, 9.

48. Maurice Isserman and Michael Kazin, *America Divided: The Civil War of the 1960s* (New York: Oxford University Press, 2000), 64.

49. For the popularization and privatization of military preparedness in the fifties, see Luara McEnaney, *Civil Defense Begins at Home: Militarization Meets Everyday Life in the Fifties* (Princeton, N.J.: Princeton University Press, 2000). Also, see May, *Homeward Bound*, 1.

50. Susan Stoudinger Northcutt, "Woman and the Bomb: Domestication of the Atomic Bomb in the United States," *International Social Science Review* 74, issue 3/4 (1999), 132, 134.

51. Kristina Zarlengo, "Civilian Threat, the Suburban Citadel, and Atomic Age American Women," *Journal of Women in Culture and Society* 24, no. 4 (1999), 937.

52. Perlstein, *Before the Storm*, 148–49. On John Wayne's right-wing politics, see Garry Wills, *John Wayne's America: The Politics of Celebrity* (New York: Simon & Schuster, 1997), 201–2.

53. Senator Margaret Chase Smith Public Speech, 25 July1960, MCSL.

54. Smith, *Declaration of Conscience*, 261–72.

55. Michael Hunt, *Lyndon Johnson's War: America's Cold War Crusade in Vietnam, 1945–1968* (New York: Hill and Wang, 1996), 50–51.

56. Smith, *Declaration of Conscience*, 273.

57. Michael R. Beschloss, *The Crisis Years: Kennedy and Khrushchev 1960–1963* (New York: Edward Burlingame Books, 1991), 320.

58. Quoted in Gallant, "Margaret Chase Smith, McCarthyism and the Drive for Political Purification," 218.

59. Smith, *Declaration of Conscience*, 273–74.

60. Smith, *Declaration of Conscience*, 274.

61. Smith, *Declaration of Conscience*, 275–84.

62. Quoted in Gaddis, *We Now Know*, 228–29.

63. Quoted in Gaddis, *We Now Know*, 249.

64. Quoted in Congressional Record—Senate, 2 August 1963, 13222, MCSL.

65. Gaddis, *We Now Know*, 266–68, 277–78.

66. The subsequent naval blockade of Cuba was also very risky; however, it received 84 percent support from Americans (who knew about the blockade), according to an October 23 Gallup poll. See Ungar, "Moral Panics, the Military-Industrial Complex, and the Arms Race," 177.

67. Senator Margaret Chase Smith, broadcast for WGAN, 25 August 1963, MCSL.

68. Smith, *Declaration of Conscience*, 313–14.

69. Randall Benett Woods, *Fulbright: A Biography* (Cambridge: Cambridge University Press, 1995), 319–20. By mid-September, the number jumped to 81 percent of Americans favoring the treaty.

70. *Congressional Record*, 9 September 1963, 15,657, MCSL.

71. *Christian Science Monitor*, 11 September 1963.

72. *Chicago Tribune*, 10 September 1963.

73. Robert McNamara to MCS, 19 September 1963, Armed Service Committee Correspondence, MCSL.

74. Smith, *Declaration of Conscience*, 323.

75. "Voice of the People," Scrapbook, vol. 260, 167. "Smith Wants Answers," *Daily Kennebec Journal*, Scrapbook, September 12, 1960, vol. 260, 156.

76. Smith, *Declaration of Conscience*, 318–321.

77. "Test Ban Treaty Debate," Scrapbook, vol. 260, 152, MCSL.

78. Senator Margaret Chase Smith, broadcast for WABI, 21 October 1963, MCSL. She told her audience that the mail outside Maine was "94 percent against the treaty."

79. "Why Woman Voted 'No' on Treaty," *Houston Chronicle*, 24 September 1963.

80. Senator Margaret Chase Smith, broadcast for WABI, 21 October 1963, MCSL.

81. Edward Rozek to MCS, 2 October 1963, Armed Services Committee Correspondence, MCSL.

82. "A 'Modern Munich,'" *Los Angeles Herald Examiner*, 29 September 1963; "The Test-Ban Vote," *St. Louis Globe-Democrat*, 25 September 1963; "The Honor Roll," *Chicago Tribune*, 2 October 1963; "Can't Sleep With Rattlesnakes and Live," *Manchester (N.H.) Union Leader*, 25 September 1963. The 19 opposed were: Byrd (VA), Byrd (WV), Eastland (MI), Lauche (OH), Long (LA), McCulden (AR), Robertson (VA), Russel (GA), Stennis (MI), Talmadge (GA), Thurmond (SC), Bennett (UT), Curtis (NE), Goldwater (AZ), Jordan (ID), Mechum (NM), Simpson (WY), Smith (ME), and Tower (TX).

83. Vera R. Glaser, "Senator Smith Possible '64 Sleeper," Scrapbook, vol. 260, 164; "Sen. Neuberger Backs Maine's Smith as Veep," *Oregonian*, Scrapbook, vol. 260, 20, MCSL.

84. Smith, *Declaration of Conscience*, 361.

85. *Amarillo Globe-Times*, 12 November 1963, 16.

86. "Opinion in the Capital," Aiken-Smith Correspondence, MCSL.

87. Her final decision was kept a secret. See "Margaret Chase Smith Seeks Presidency," *New York Times*, 28 January 1964.

88. Senator Margaret Chase Smith, Radio Press International Panel Program, 10 February 1964, MCSL.

89. Chalmers M. Roberts, "Lady from Maine," *Washington Post*, Scrapbook, vol. 260, 172, MCSL.

90. Robert Alan Goldberg, *Barry Goldwater* (New Haven, Conn.: Yale University Press, 1995), 139–40; Perlstein, *Before the Storm*, 62–63, 67.

91. Barry M. Goldwater, *With No Apologies: The Personal and Political Memoirs of United States Senator Barry M. Goldwater* (New York: Berkley Books, 1980), 201–2.

92. Thomas Graham and Bernard Kramer, "The Polls: ABM and Star Wars: Attitudes Toward Nuclear Defense, 1945–1985," *The Public Opinion Quarterly* 50, no. 1 (Spring 1986), 126–27. The breakdown of the 76 percent was 61 percent (agree) and 15 percent (strongly agree).

93. Robert A. Levine, "Deterrence and the ABM," *World Policy Journal* 18, no. 3 (Fall 2001), 23.

94. Robert A. Bernstein and William W. Anthony, "The ABM Issue in the Senate, 1968–1970: The Importance of Ideology," *The American Political Science Review* 68, no. 3 (September 1974), 1198.

95. Graham and Kramer, "The Polls," 128.

96. Richard Nixon, *RN: The Memoirs of Richard Nixon* (New York: Grosset & Dunlap, 1978), 417.

97. MCS to Ronald Wells, 11 July 1968, Armed Services Committee Correspondence, MCSL.

98. Smith, *Declaration of Conscience*, 394–96.

99. William Safire, *Before the Fall: An Inside View of the Pre-Watergate White House* (New York: Da Capo Press, 1975), 135–36.

100. Claude Witze, "The ABM Showdown: Rationality Wins by a Single Vote," *Air Force/Space Digest* (September, 1969), 46.

101. Smith, *Declaration of Conscience*, 396–98.

102. Smith, *Declaration of Conscience*, 398–401, 404.

103. Smith, *Declaration of Conscience*, 405–8.

104. Robert David Johnson, *Congress and the Cold War* (Cambridge: Cambridge University Press, 2006), 157.

105. Smith, *Declaration of Conscience*, 409–12. For a fair account, see Nathan Miller, "The Making of a Majority: The Senate and the ABM," *The Washington Monthly* 1, no. 9 (October 1969): 60–72.

106. Henry Wise to MCS, 9 September 1969; Leonard Hizer to MCS, 11 July 1969, Armed Services Committee Correspondence, MCSL.

107. Carolyn Blouin to MCS, 14 August 1969, Armed Services Committee Correspondence, MCSL.

108. Gary Nicholson to MCS, 13 August 1969, Armed Services Committee Correspondence, MCSL.

109. In the press, there had been discussion of the GALOSH ABM setup around Moscow. See Steven C. Haas, "Reassessing Lessons from the ABM Treaty," *International Affairs* 64, no. 2 (Spring 1988), 234.

110. Neely Coble to MCS, 28 April 1969, Armed Services Committee Correspondence, MCSL.

111. Mabel Brooks to MCS, 7 May 1969; Ruth Smith to MCS, 27 May 1969; Marguerite Pendergast to MCS, 20 June 1969; Phil Saucia to MCS, 19 July 1969; Herbert Provencher to MCS, 8 June 1969; Nelson Pryor to MCS, 25 March 1969, Armed Services Committee Correspondence, MCSL.

112. A. R. Silvester to MCS, n.d. Armed Services Committee Correspondence, MCSL.

113. Lawrence Doughty, Jr. to MCS, 26 March 1969, Armed Services Committee Correspondence, MCSL.

114. John Gunther to MCS, 14 May 1969, Armed Services Committee Correspondence, MCSL.

115. Gerald Griffin to MCS, 17 July 1969, Armed Services Committee Correspondence, MCSL.

116. William Stanmeyer to MCS, 3 and 6 June 1969, Armed Services Committee Correspondence, MCSL.

117. Grace Griffith to MCS, 11 August 1969, Armed Services Committee Correspondence, MCSL.

118. Roger Garrison to MCS, 11 March 1969; R. N. Gallup to MCS, 11 March 1969, Armed Services Committee Correspondence, MCSL.

119. Cecile Carver to MCS, 14 May 1969, Armed Services Committee Correspondence, MCSL.

120. Eric Hooglund to MCS, 1 May 1969, Armed Services Committee Correspondence, MCSL.

121. Richard Briggs to MCS, 3 May 1969, Armed Services Committee Correspondence, MCSL.

122. James Miller to MCS, 10 June 1969, Armed Services Committee Correspondence, MCSL.

123. Margaret Tyler to MCS, 27 July 1969, Armed Services Committee Correspondence, MCSL. Smith was for civil rights. See Sherman, *No Place for a Woman*, 210.

124. Helen Lear to MCS, 1 July 1969, Armed Services Committee Correspondence, MCSL.

125. Gene Bonyun to MCS, 16 March 1969, Armed Services Committee Correspondence, MCSL.

126. Doreen Thompson to MCS, 9 June 1969, Armed Services Committee Correspondence, MCSL.

127. John Perkins to MCS, 31 March 1969; Donald Rogers to MCS, 22 March 1969; W. Richard Souza to MCS, 19 March 1969, Armed Services Committee Correspondence, MCSL.

128. For another example, see E. Curtis to MCS, 7 August 1969, Armed Services Committee Correspondence, MCSL.

129. Charles Packard to MCS, 20 March 1969, Armed Services Committee Correspondence, MCSL.

130. Lawrence Peery to MCS, 11 August 1969, Armed Services Committee Correspondence, MCSL.

131. William Cook to MCS, 22 March 1969, Armed Services Committee Correspondence, MCSL.

132. John Quinn, 28 March 1969, Armed Services Committee Correspondence, MCSL.

133. Henry Schmidt to MCS, 20 April 1969, Armed Services Committee Correspondence, MCSL.

134. Phyllis Dana to MCS, 9 June 1969; Claire Tinker to MCS, 15 October 1969, Armed Services Committee Correspondence, MCSL.

135. James Alexander to MCS, 12 August 1969, Armed Services Committee Correspondence, MCSL.

136. Chouteau Chapin to MCS, 9 May 1969; Harriet Shepardson to MCS, 3 July 1969, Armed Services Committee Correspondence, MCSL.

137. Arthur Conner to MCS, 10 August 1969, Armed Services Committee Correspondence, MCSL.

138. Dorothy Pike to MCS, 26 February 1970; E. McNall to MCS, 12 August 1969; Eleanor Heilbron to MCS, 13 August 1969, Armed Services Committee Corre-

spondence, MCSL. Dorothy Pike of Tennessee appreciated Smith's integrity, but she found it difficult to accept the losing vote for the compromise amendment.

139. Charles Allen to MCS, 8 August 1969; Charles Packard, 25 August 1969, Armed Services Committee Correspondence, MCSL.

140. Dorothy Franke to MCS, n.d., Armed Services Committee Correspondence, MCSL.

141. MCS to Perley Clarke, 29 September 1969, Armed Services Committee Correspondence, MCSL.

142. For further discussion, see May, *Homeward Bound*, 209.

143. One study claims that "many (if not most) Americans" saw nuclear superiority as "the clearest manifestation of their country's status as the world's preeminent power." See Ronald Powaski, *Return to Armageddon: The United States and the Nuclear Arms Race, 1981–1999* (New York: Oxford University Press, 2000), 5–6.

144. For example, Hugh Frey to MCS, 6 June 1969, Armed Services Committee Correspondence, MCSL.

145. Don Larrabee, "Sen. Smith's Vote at Camera Time," Armed Services Committee Correspondence, MCSL.

5

Vietnam War

Responding to a letter written by a Utah junior high school teacher in December 1969, Senator Smith stated: "I feel that the United States is justified in being in Viet Nam, and in my opinion, we are in Viet Nam to stop the communists from conquering the world." In the aftermath of America's attack on Cambodia the following year, she made clear her support for Richard Nixon in numerous letters. She opposed any attempts of the Senate "to straightjacket" Nixon's decisions on Vietnam and even in her final full year in the Senate, she still claimed that he was doing "an excellent job" with a position on the Vietnam War superior to that of Democratic presidential candidates.[1] Public statements and her correspondence sent to ordinary Americans demonstrate her persistent Cold Warrior views when others, including some hawks, were rethinking their positions on American foreign policy.

After the assassination of President John F. Kennedy by an American communist who had lived in Russia, a point that Smith highlighted in a speech to the Women's National Press Club, the succession of Lyndon Johnson did not alter America's position to support the Republic of Vietnam (South Vietnam) in its struggle against the communist Democratic Republic of Vietnam (North Vietnam).[2] Within President Johnson's first year, the North Vietnamese Army and the guerrilla arm of the communist National Liberation Front (Viet Cong) increased their military operations and most weeks there were 400 to 500 incidents a week of terrorism, sabotage, and propaganda.[3] In early August 1964, following the command of Le Duan (a North Vietnamese leader who favored military confrontation with the United States), North Vietnamese PT boats (Soviet built) attacked the USS *Maddox*, an American destroyer in the Gulf of Tonkin that North Vietnamese radar had been tracking for days. After another episode two days later involving the *Maddox* and the USS *C. Turner Joy* (another destroyer), Johnson responded by securing congressional approval of the Southeast Asia Resolution better known as the Gulf of Tonkin Resolution, in essence a blank check for the administration "to take all necessary measures to repel any armed attack against the forces of the United States and prevent further aggression."[4] Senate support for the resolution was overwhelming with only two dissenting votes by Democratic Senators Wayne Morse (OR) and Ernest Gruening (AK). Did Senate acceptance reflect American public opinion that embraced a "Cold War Consensus," particularly the conviction that the defense of South Vietnam was essential to U.S. security?[5]

Smith went on record in the fifties that America's "principal world struggle with Communism is in Asia—particularly Southeast Asia" and she considered the Viet Minh "to be hated Communists" attempting to impose a "Communist colonialism far worse than the European colonialism they hate."[6] Although she expressed doubts of the United States getting involved in a ground war in Vietnam, having the communists conquer all of Vietnam was a worse scenario.[7] For the pre-1965 period when Vietnam was off the radar for most Americans (almost two-thirds knew little), it is difficult to measure the level of commitment that ordinary Americans had for the defense of South Vietnam, but by 1965 Smith and most politicians did fall in line and support the American mission in Southeast Asia, including Harry S. Truman, who gave his full support for the government's policy to stop the communists in South Vietnam and thus prevent communist growth in other countries. In June, 47 percent of Americans surveyed favored sending more U.S. troops to Southeast Asia, 19 percent favored no change, and 11 percent favored withdrawal of troops. One reason for public support of increased intervention was reports of atrocities by communists against American personnel.[8]

Some scholars claim that the notion of America as a City upon a Hill compelled the United States to intervene in Vietnam to provide a moral example to the world.[9] There is clear evidence of many evangelicals and conservative Catholics consistently showing a willingness to support all American military activities which confronted the communist menace anywhere in the world. For theological conservatives, there was an enduring perception that communism was an evil force and that communist leaders would be unwilling to negotiate any agreement that compromised their Marxist worldview. Consequently, conservative Christians were skeptical that diplomacy could succeed without any show of force. Concerning Southeast Asia, they believed, as later scholarship demonstrated, that both the Soviets and the Chinese supported the North Vietnamese cause.[10]

Regarding the role of Congress in its call for greater military commitment, Smith did not regret voting for the Gulf of Tonkin Resolution, explaining to one soldier, "I was under no misunderstanding when I voted for the Gulf of Tonkin Resolution."[11] To an Ohioan man almost eight years later, she explained her interpretation of the "completely legal" resolution: "it was only an expression of the sense of the Senate and was not at all necessary for President Johnson had full power to do what he did without this Senate resolution." In her opinion, all Johnson wanted was for Congress to share the responsibility of greater American involvement in Southeast Asia.[12] Other senators did not view it in such a benign manner; instead, they believed Johnson had manipulated them. Singled out by Johnson to sway others to support the resolution, Senator J. William Fulbright was one who "performed beautifully" in reassuring like-minded liberals that the resolution was a moderate measure designed to prevent a wider war.[13] Fulbright's later claim that the Gulf of Tonkin Resolution was an exercise of deception demonstrates the growing polarization in political circles that unfolded on the issue of America's involvement in Southeast Asia.[14]

By 1965 America's military involvement in Vietnam escalated quickly, most clearly the bombing campaign against North Vietnam called Operation Rolling Thunder. Following the February raid on the communist army north of the Demilitarized Zone was the arrival of the Marines in March, thus ending America's "advisory role." When American troops began ground operations, attitudes favoring commitment increased with most Main Street Americans supporting the war. The ground war saw troop levels rise from 59,000 at mid-year to over 184,000 in December, and at the end of 1966 there were 385,000 American troops in Southeast Asia.[15]

In 1966, Smith was 68 years old and ready to take her record before voters in a period when fortunes changed for Republicans in Maine. In her home state, the people elected a Democratic legislature in 1964, the first one since early in the century. Once considered "the citadel of Republicanism," Maine also gave Lyndon Johnson almost 70 percent of the vote, among the highest in the nation. On the 1966 campaign trail, Smith interpreted foreign policy, and even domestic relations, through the prism of Munich; she championed firmness and resolve and she won reelection with 59 percent of the vote. Her Democratic opponent waged a "virtually hopeless fight."[16] She was the "grand old lady" with consistent and solid support in Maine. With the exception of a small number, her constituents lacked knowledge of her less than attractive trait of overreacting to any perceived slights. If some critics were correct in claiming she lacked vision and was in politics for self-serving reasons, the majority of the people of Maine apparently thought otherwise.

As the only female in the Senate, Smith's vantage point on the Vietnam War was remarkable. As noted in the mainstream press, she was the ranking Republican on the powerful Armed Services Committee and a senior member of the Appropriations Defense Subcommittee and the Central Intelligence Subcommittee. She remained fairly quiet in the Senate, but there were those who viewed her as "a woman worth hearing and reading" and one deserving of trust.[17] On the Vietnam War, she continued to stubbornly follow her conscience on what she believed was correct in a politically charged environment. Given both her history of taking bold stands—right or wrong—and her political stability of not facing another election for six years, Smith's statements on the war are valuable for shedding light on the persistency of basic Cold War assumptions which critics argued had little room for more nuanced understandings of global politics. She did not fear the consequences of speaking on contentious war issues. Her masculine, hard-line position garnered the approval of conservative Americans disgusted with "no-win" war policies and irritated with those who opposed American military action against communists in Southeast Asia.

For Smith and politicians seeking reassurance for their anticommunist stand, there were government documents available that highlighted the "ruthless intimidation and threat of violence" practiced by communists in Southeast Asia. For example, one 1967 Department of State report sought to discredit the position that there was popular support in South Vietnam for the Vietcong. Citing historical material, statistics, and an unofficial public opinion survey, the State's Bureau of Public Affairs claimed that the Vietcong had to rely on "terror" to maintain their "precarious" control of the South Vietnamese in various regions of the country. Almost 60 percent of South Vietnamese survey respondents identified the reality of Vietcong terrorism and sabotage and 83 percent claimed that after the war a government led by the nationalists would be better for them.[18] If the accuracy of such reports was questionable, the emotions they engendered were undeniable. For Smith, there was sacredness to independent thought. In her "This I Believe" statement, she wrote: "I believe that no one has a right to own our souls except God."[19] Any softening of attitudes toward communism, in the belief that a liberalization of communist doctrine had occurred, made little difference to those Americans who saw all forms of communism as atheistic and repressive systems that robbed people of freedom. As one evangelical put it, regardless of the doubts over American involvement in Southeast Asia and contrary to ecumenical semantics, "Americans are unconvinced that totalitarian Communism is a benevolent historical force."[20]

When Smith began her term in January 1967, her private letters to ordinary people on United States involvement in Southeast Asia clearly opposed any "appeasing surrender" that gave South Vietnam to the "Viet Cong."[21] If the American people showed determination, she declared, it would not be a hopeless war.[22] Repeated in many letters were her words to one Connecticut man:

"We are in Viet Nam to stop the Communists from conquering the world." Given her typical response that "we must stay in Viet Nam," one had to look elsewhere to find any sophisticated articulation of communist strategies and realistic responses available to the American government.[23]

Smith's Senate speeches offered more detail and analysis than her correspondence to the American people. For example, her statement on the Senate Floor on February 23 outlined "seven tragedies" in the Johnson-McNamara handling of the war: a lack of pilots and resources of the Tactical Air Command; bomb shortages; deterioration of combat readiness; Reserve and the National Guard becoming havens for too many draft dodgers; promotions of officer-rank Reservists to General without much chance of them seeing active duty; promotions of those who make no effort to meet training requirements; and the lack of academic freedom in military colleges. Almost half of her speech focused on the last "tragedy" concerning academic freedom that involved Major General Jerry D. Page, Commandant of the Air War College, who allegedly lost his college position for his forthright lecture on bomb shortages in Vietnam. The Page episode likely interested Smith because of her experience of lecturing at the Air War College, her appreciation for independent thinking, and the message itself that the Johnson administration's bomb shortages represented a less than a total effort to defeat the communists. In her final assessment, she viewed the tragedies as "examples of why the credibility gap of the Johnson Administration is widening instead of narrowing."[24] The credibility issue had serious implications for American morale when, according to Smith, the only correct option for the government was to continue fighting for victory.

In a much cited and talked about article entitled "Why I Worry about the War in Vietnam," published in April 1967, Smith accepted the "stark fact" that America was in Southeast Asia and that it could not "pull-out and leave South Vietnam and its people to the mercy of the Viet Cong and North Vietnam." Put simply, American and South Vietnamese surrender was "unthinkable."[25] Having had a warm relationship with Johnson since 1945 when they served together on the House Naval Affairs Committee, she favored his Texas hill-country pragmatism over the urbanity and intellectualism of Washington's best and brightest.[26] In her Vietnam War article, she focused her criticism on Secretary of Defense Robert McNamara for the administration's "contradictory policies." She questioned America's national resolve when McNamara stated on the one hand bombing in the north showed North Vietnamese leaders "the price they pay for their continued efforts to subvert the south," but on the other hand admitted that bombing had no major impact on slowing infiltration. In her eyes, it was predictable that Americans experienced confusion when Senator Robert Kennedy quoted the Secretary of Defense as an authoritative source for a bombing pause, while President Johnson quoted the Secretary of Defense as "an authoritative source against another bombing pause." Believing that the United States was winning in Vietnam, Smith argued for more patience and determination in *forcing* Ho Chi Minh to the peace table. Specifically, the American military had to go beyond limited and restrained operations and strike the supply lines in North Vietnam.[27]

The stakes were higher than the freedom of South Vietnam alone; the war measured the resolve of America to confront Soviet and Chinese strategy "to destroy freedom of the peoples of Asia." Also worrisome to Smith was the polarization unfolding in the United States, particularly how "extreme leftists" were "accusing anyone who supports a firm and determined stand in Vietnam with being warmongers delighting in the napalm killing and injury of natives of Vietnam." Seeing similarities with the McCarthyism of the 1950s, she worried that the emotion and the hatred of the "extreme left" paralyzed many senators in getting involved in the debate: "No Senator," she wrote, "wants to be called a 'warmonger,' even by a draft card burner." Smith's greatest fear was that lack of political leadership and hesitancy to inform Americans of the full and unpleasant details of the war reflected "a potential indecisiveness, and perhaps a lack of national resolve on the war in Vietnam, on the part of the American people themselves."[28] The issue of national resolve was an important one for her, but by labeling certain opponents "extreme leftists" she in effect unfairly cast doubt on the character and loyalty of all opponents of the war, most of whom were moderate, supportive of the American political system, and against violent protest actions.

Responding to Smith's worry article, some defended their antiwar position in passionate letters. One common argument against American involvement in Vietnam reasoned that if the main opponent was the Vietcong, then the United States was wrongfully interfering in a civil war. Another point was that American retreat might be "unthinkable" as Smith claimed, but was it right that 200 American boys died each week because politicians lacked "the guts" to admit an error? Declaring that the war distressed him and that he knew no one who approved America's foreign policy, one man wrote: "I care no more about my present or my future, sick with a conscience that cries out day and night to know what I could and should have done to prevent the awful sin of the United States."[29] The choice of the word "sin" hints that traditional theological constructs were a component of some antiwar arguments, something more explicit than general references to the lack of morality in American actions.

Those more in line with Smith believed that a restrained military approach was not going to end the war. A veteran at Fort Carson, Colorado, claiming to be a witness to communist terror in Vietnam, encouraged Smith to persuade

Americans to support the "fight to bring freedom to the South Vietnamese people."[30] With the communists committing ruthless acts of violence on peasants, some Americans wondered why the United States was fighting a limited war that restricted bombing of North Vietnam to only selected targets. A correspondent asked Smith: "When the enemy throws a grenade at a bus or taxi carrying innocent children and women, has it too been selected not to inflict civilian casualties?"[31] A common outlook was that no one except advisers should have been sent at all, but, now that the politicians had committed to a ground war, American troops could not retire until they completed the mission.[32] This position had enough traction in the Johnson administration that the number of American troops reached the stunning figure of 436,000 by May 1967, as General William Westmoreland, the United States Commander, prepared the way to victory.

Even if details were often missing, Smith's letters to ordinary Americans continued to be blunter than her public articles on the issue of American victory in Southeast Asia. In private letters she argued that American allies were not helping the United States because they were selfish and unappreciative of past American assistance.[33] In a letter to the Ohio State University Young Republican Club, she was critical of "policy formulators" for failing to provide a clear and consistent program for General Westmoreland to follow.[34] While she was a tough critic of some of the government's strategy and tactics, she agreed with Johnson on basic objectives and she wrote of her appreciation for those who defended Johnson's determination to defeat the communists in Vietnam.[35] She was hopeful that Johnson would get on track and take consistent and forceful action. Close to Johnson were Secretary of State Dean Rusk and consultant General Maxwell Taylor who both portrayed the war, in the words of one scholar, "as just another noble U.S. Cold War effort to contain evil communism."[36]

On the issue of the draft, Smith's correspondence explained that volunteer enlistments were too few to end the draft and that Americans should support the troops "instead of pampering the draft card burners and the flag burners."[37] She told a Michigan woman that America's national security depended on the draft.[38] To those worried that deferment for college students was unfair, she gave assurance that "deferment does not mean that they will not ultimately be caught by the draft."[39] She heard from many who were angry about draft dodgers. For example, an Albuquerque, New Mexico, woman voiced her resentment for the level of anti-Americanism openly flaunted and her disgust for the "cowardly men" who went to Canada to avoid serving their country: "The acts of these men constitute an insult to all our men who have accepted their responsibilities and are serving in Viet Nam, and an affront to their families at home."[40] Smith took a tough stand on draft dodgers who left the country and it was shocking to her when a senator referred to draft dodgers in Canada and Sweden as "patriots."[41]

Troublesome were letters received by Smith that indicated a lack of patriotism or worse. One letter she received told the story of a Marine who, while searching for his four dead buddies, found a cache of blood plasma and other medical supplies stamped Berkeley, California, that students attending the University of California at Berkeley allegedly sent to the Vietcong. The Marine wanted his parents to explain to him why there were Americans helping to kill Americans.[42] Whether or not the story was accurate, there was the perception among some that the antiwar actions of a number of college students bordered on treason. As a woman who experienced two world wars, Smith found it upsetting that there were young Americans promoting an antiwar message of radicalism and violence. It is important to point out that by the late 1960s she was more prone to be very judgmental and, thus, she was often guilty of an oversimplification of the categories of war protesters. Of course, she had plenty of company on this point since President Johnson himself believed there was a strong link between international communism and the antiwar movement.

In contrast to those who wanted the American military out of Southeast Asia, Smith argued it was essential that any peace had to be on honorable terms: "I refuse to do what Ho Chi Minh wants—to call for us to give up and pull out." The solution for ending the war was "an all-out effort" rather than the "half-hearted holding action" that was "chewing up our boys in fatalities and injuries." But she again repeated her fear that too many Americans lacked principle and courage in the "age of miniskirts and beatniks" to support an all-out military effort against communism.[43]

Scholars note that the "beatniks" were the small but growing number of mostly young Americans who rejected a "rigid, authoritarian order." For those who embraced adventure through sex, drugs, and rock 'n' roll, there was more emphasis on individual fulfillment than on older ideals of service to country and commitment to traditional religious values. Smith found this troubling and she was not alone. Contrary to some stereotypical views of the rebellious sixties, attitudes toward sex, for example, remained surprisingly traditional at the end of the 1960s with almost 70 percent of Americans disapproving of premarital sex.[44] The Southern Baptist Convention had evangelists speaking the language of the counterculture, but solely for the purpose of bringing young people into the church fold. For the Southern Baptist Convention, the country's largest Protestant body, there was a clear link between communism and counterculture behavior. As Mark Oppenheimer writes, "Communism was, after all, the philosophy of atheism and, in its earliest, Leninist incarnation, free love."[45] As was the case for evangelicals throughout the nation, the

Southern Baptists clearly rejected the counterculture and supported the war effort against the Vietnamese communists.

Smith praised a Baptist minister for his courage in supporting the war effort, especially because he had two teenage sons who faced the possibility of serving and because of the disturbing trend that most liberal clergy who made their voice heard were against government policy on Vietnam. Her view of the antiwar clergy was not favorable: "[W]hile I am sure that the protesting ministers do not represent the majority of their profession in this country, by their vigorous and heavy articulation they certainly do give the image that the overwhelming majority of ministers in this country condemn our Government on the Viet Nam issue."[46] Her assessment was correct: the liberals were vocal, but they did not represent a majority. In the years Christian leaders became more vociferous against the war, the liberal churches within Protestantism and Roman Catholicism experienced declining church membership (unlike conservative churches which continued to show vitality).[47] Conservative Catholic and Protestant clergy viewed the antiwar views of liberal clergy as "a cause of rapture to the men in the Kremlin and to all who wish the cause of freedom ill." Escalating the war or continued bombing had the support of 73 percent of conservative clergy.[48] Giving high praise to American troops fighting in Vietnam, Cardinal Francis Spellman spoke of the "soldiers of Jesus Christ" who demonstrated "the best traits of human courage and endurance in the annals of history."[49]

What happened on college campuses remained a more pressing issue for many Americans than the war views of liberal clergy. Given that many of the foot soldiers for the antiwar movement came from the colleges, politicians found plenty to say about the conduct and character of college students. Smith agreed with Governor Ronald Reagan that college demonstrators undermined "our boys who are fighting in Viet Nam."[50] One Californian woman wrote of the influence that the well-organized and well-financed antiwar movement had on many college students and the importance of counteracting this force. Conservatives voiced their concerns that too many colleges were victim of an unchecked secular liberalism that spawned student radicalism. As early as 1964, there were signs of the formation of revolutionary groups at elite universities such as the Maoist-backed May 2nd movement at Yale University, but often missed is that they represented the fringe.[51] The *Wall Street Journal* declared that the most prestigious universities in the United States poured out "authoritative statements that American society and its institutions are utterly undeserving of respect."[52] One example is C. Douglas McGee, a philosophy professor at Bowdoin College, who stated his disapproval of "obsolescent anti-communist rhetoric" that insulted the intelligence of people with "good minds," by this implying that only rational people were correct in not seeing atheistic communism as a significant threat.[53] In opposition to America's "fascism" and "belligerent (sic) war machine," a senior at Bowdoin College stated his amazement that Smith believed "the antiquated 1950 view that Communism, 'that cancerous growth which is diseasing the world,' must be defeated."[54] At the end of the sixties, only one out of every five college students polled claimed to have attended at least one antiwar demonstration and by the end of the war only ten percent of colleges and universities had experienced violent disturbances.[55] But it was the small number of radicals among college protesters who captured the thinking and stirred the prejudices of Smith to view college antiwar protest as mainly disloyal.

As political and cultural debates heated up, Smith showed signs of less tolerance for critics of her stand. In letters with a biting edge to them, she complained to ordinary Americans of how some newspaper editors attempted to "tar" her with "snide and distorted news stories" and how certain Democratic politicians questioned her patriotism.[56] Biographers write of Smith's cool relations with various members of the press and her growing sensitivity to being challenged by others with opposing opinions, so much so there was the suggestion that she had a "persecution complex."[57] Sherman notes Smith's acute attention to image making and how she was wary of the power of the press to hinder her political success.[58]

Hawks like Smith did face severe criticism in the *New York Times*. In a story entitled "The Hawks Fly Off-Course," the *Times* targeted the Preparedness Subcommittee, singling out Senators John Stennis, Henry Jackson, and Smith, for their "demagogic and misleading report" that argued the necessity of unrestricted bombing of North Vietnam in order to quickly and successfully end the war. The senators were wrong to hold to a "delusive hope" of a quick war: "Those who favor unilateral withdrawal or immediate negotiations can reasonably talk of an early end to the war, but those who support the war cannot responsibly tell the American people anything except to dig in for a long, hard struggle." Basing its opposition to the senators' report on World War II bombing results, the *Times* article argued that not even Hanoi leveled and Haiphong's harbor sealed would stop supplies from reaching South Vietnam. A "disservice" to the country, the Armed Services report was a "cruel trick" played upon parents of men killed in the war and a dangerous strategy that risked intervention by the Chinese. In a twist to a popular adage, the *Times* concluded that war is too important to be left to both generals and senators.[59]

To be sure, the Armed Services Subcommittee did provide a nurturing environment for Smith's Cold Warrior views; she was the lone female among powerful hawks with consistent hard-line views toward the communist enemy.[60] Addressing the "rising hawkishness" of the subcommittee, Robert McNamara states that facing the senators' questions over a seven-day period in August 1967 was one of the most stressful episodes of his life.[61] Understandably discouraged, McNamara and others critical of the Armed Services Subcommittee faced polling data suggesting that Smith and her committee colleagues had the support of many Americans; in December 1967, a Harris poll found Americans supporting escalation rather than de-escalation of the war by a margin of 63 to 37 percent. While the lack of progress in Vietnam discouraged most Americans, only 10 percent were calling for an immediate withdrawal.[62]

The challenge for antiwar activists was to convince more Americans that the war was un-winnable; the problem was that there were countless Americans who demanded total victory, and this was achievable, according to a California woman, if the government turned the war over to the military.[63] One Kentucky woman spoke for others when she wrote that the United States "must have total victory" against the North Vietnamese invaders so that the South Vietnamese could "unite and form a government of their choosing."[64] Any harkening back to the American Revolution had resonance with those who equated the South Vietnamese struggle to America's fight for democracy against the British. Yes, the war was becoming increasingly unpopular, but one letter-writer, stating one could not judge a war's "righteousness" by the degree of its popularity, wrote that the Revolutionary War (high rate of desertions), the War of 1812 (New Englanders considered secession), and the Civil War (Copperheads spearheaded antiwar activities) were all unpopular wars. More applicable, the Korean War was also a detested war, yet American troops kept the communists out of South Korea and now South Koreans were free and proud of their government, hard fighting army, and booming economy.[65] An observation especially important for American evangelicals, who remained steadfast anticommunists, were signs that South Korea was also on its way to becoming an evangelical stronghold of the world.[66] Could not South Vietnam also witness Christian revival once the dark, atheistic forces of communism met defeat as they did in South Korea less than twenty years earlier?

At any rate, convinced that diplomacy was not working and not accepting the arguments of those who opposed the war on the moral grounds that many innocent civilians died as a result of collateral damage, Smith showed no signs of wavering from her hard-line position. She wanted to see more bombing. Ho Chi Minh, she wrote, regarded the bombing pauses by the American government and antiwar demonstrations as signs of "weakness and lack of resolve."[67] A communist who was in the Soviet Union in the 1930s and who had survived the Stalin purges apparently only by virtue of support from the right people,[68] Ho was a survivor with an indefatigable resolve to see victory with a revolutionary system that bred antagonism and violence. Historian

Mark Moyar argues that Ho, strongly influenced by Lenin's writings, which argued for "the subordination of the interests of the proletarian struggle in one nation to the interests of that struggle on an international scale," put communism ahead of nationalism.[69]

Smith believed she correctly understood the menace of those doggedly driven by communism and, as was the case for the other Cold Warriors in the Armed Services Committee, the domino theory continued to be central in her thinking. If the United States did not take a stand in Vietnam, she argued, it would have to do so in Thailand, or some other place, but by then it would be in a less formidable position. Communist sources also reveal that many communists believed that victory in South Vietnam would bolster communism throughout the world.[70] She rejected leftist claims that the war represented an uprising of the lower class and that America's fight against the Vietcong meant support for a South Vietnamese aristocracy.[71] When the number of American troops in South Vietnam reached one half million in January 1968, she approved. Two weeks before the Tet Offensive, she wrote that "Munich clearly proved that appeasement only whets the appetite of aggressive dictators."[72] Withdrawal was not an option.

The launching of a series of coordinated assaults by the North Vietnam Army and the Vietcong on many provincial capitals and major cities in South Vietnam began on January 30. The fierce attacks of the Tet Offensive were a psychological blow to the United States, even though militarily the offensive was a tactical disaster for the communists. American and South Vietnamese troops eventually crushed the communist offensive, but the magnitude of the communist operation shocked many Americans who had believed the government's message that the United States was winning the war. The dominant perception in the mainstream press was that the Tet Offensive was a massive military defeat for the United States. Disagreeing, others lamented that the United States missed a golden opportunity to finish off the communists in the South. U.S. military historian Brigadier General S. L. A. Marshall argued that "a potential major victory" for the United States was lost due to "mistaken estimates, loss of nerve, and a tidal wave of defeatism."[73]

Evangelical Christian reports on the Tet Offensive gave emotional stories of the deaths of American missionaries, ironically at the same time that liberal Christians released a report declaring that in Vietnam the United States "must be guilty of having broken almost every established agreement for standards of human decency in times of war." Readers of *Christianity Today* read how, in Ban Me Thuot, the Rev. Robert Ziemer and the Rev. C. Edward Thompson, of the Christian and Missionary Alliance, appealed to the Vietcong to allow them to transport badly injured Carolyn Griswold to a hospital. "They were shot dead on the spot," and consequently Miss Griswold died. At the same time, Ruth Wilting, a nurse from Cleveland, died when the communists strafed a garbage pit where she and others sought sanctuary after bombs destroyed the missionary compound. Ruth Thompson, wife of Edward, also lost her life, but fortunately the couple's five children survived because they were in Malaysia. Other reports told of atrocities such as the communists entering an orphanage in Mi Tho and gunning down the children and super-intendent. The response of Dr. Harold John Ockenga, evangelical minister of Park Street Church in Boston, was for the United States to "go for victory" by blockading Haiphong harbor, destroying strongholds in Laos and Cambodia, and "chancing a bigger war and an encounter with Russia and China."[74] For many evangelicals, the failure of the South Vietnamese to support the invad-ing communists was proof that America's fight to save South Vietnam was a worthy cause.

Smith confronted the issue of the Tet Offensive in her March 1968 article titled the "Vietnam Crucible," published in a number of newspapers. She wrote that she fully understood why Americans experienced confusion over the war because she herself—even with access to much more information on the war—found it difficult to reconcile the disparity between government and press reports. In her view, news reporters were guilty of contributing to the confusion of war developments. With bluntness she stated: "I cannot con-clude that war correspondents report with complete objectivity and without bias." She preferred that Americans withhold accepting both the news reports that interpreted the Tet Offensive as evidence of the United States having "no hope of victory" in Vietnam and the military perspective that viewed the com-munist operation as "a tactic of desperation" against American forces close to victory. In her mind, all that was certain was that the communists had failed to take the cities; weeks or months would have to pass before there was any accurate assessment of the impact of the Tet Offensive. Smith concluded her article by predicting no major change of American policy after the November election. Instead, it was "more probable that there will be a change of policy before the election."[75]

Days later, Johnson went on television to present the shocking news of his decision not to run for reelection. For the first time, over 50 percent of Americans polled said that the war was a mistake. In the following weeks, the American people had to cope with the assassinations of civil rights leader Martin Luther King. Jr. and presidential hopeful Senator Robert Kennedy. Funding for social programs declined 35 percent as a result of the rising costs of the war.[76] In the months leading up to the Chicago Democratic convention, to choose a presidential candidate for the November election, the Democrats were in disarray with one camp prepared "to stick it out in Vietnam" versus a camp of insurgent liberals who had the support of antiwar Americans hopeful that constitutional remedies were possible. The Chicago convention in August witnessed a brutal crackdown on antiwar protesters by police, but polls indicated that the majority of Americans favored the actions of the cops and Mayor Richard Daley. Simply put, most Americans desired law and order.[77] With the emergence of Alabama governor George Wallace as a third-party candidate, the Republican Party's Richard Nixon scored a close victory over Democrat Hubert Humphrey, 43.7 percent to 42.4 percent of the total vote.

The pressure was on Nixon, who was not a doctrinaire conservative. Desiring an honorable peace without increasing American troop buildup, he outlined the plan of "Vietnamization" whereby South Vietnamese troops would replace American troops. There were approximately 540,000 American troops in South Vietnam and soldiers returning to the United States would take place in stages. While the South Vietnamese armed forces began the process of gaining strength, Nixon ordered more bombing in North Vietnam, Laos, and Cambodia.

With the pace of change too slow in the eyes of antiwar activists, they organized major protests across the nation, a decentralized approach that involved over 200 urban centers. Before the planned mass demonstrations of October 15, 1969, took place, led by the Moratorium peace coalition, Nixon voiced his criticism: "Whatever the issue, to allow government policy to be made in the streets would destroy the democratic procedure. It would give the decision not to the majority, and not to those with the strongest arguments, but to those with the loudest voices."[78] But try as he did, Nixon could not slow the momentum of antiwar activists who sought to end the wrongs of the hawks; approximately two million Americans participated in the October 15 Moratorium to end the war in Vietnam, including 100,000 in Boston, a city located not far from southern Maine. It was clear that the antiwar protests reached beyond college students, capturing the attention and support of many moderates. A worried Nixon responded with an important television address; his "great silent majority" speech of November 3, which asked patriotic Americans to be patient with the government's policy of peace with honor, went "over the heads of the press to the people."[79] Although generally well received by many ordinary Americans, the speech also galvanized the support of others for another major antiwar protest planned for mid-November. The March Against Death saw approximately 40,000 demonstrators, each holding a placard with the name of an American soldier killed in Southeast Asia, march past the White House, call out the names of the dead soldiers, and deposit the placards in coffins at the Capitol. Also striking was the gathering of 250,000 that convened at the Washington Monument to hear both politicians and celebrities proclaim peace. The influence of such demonstrations, however, suffered due to the media attention focused on radicals carrying Vietcong flags and pictures of communist icons and militants clashing with law enforcement. Law-abiding demonstrators found it frustrating that radical protesters were more detrimental than beneficial to the antiwar cause. In late 1969, polling indicated that only 21 percent of Americans favored immediate withdrawal.[80]

As for Smith, her earlier distrust for Nixon, because of his link to Joseph McCarthy, did not cause her to lessen her public support for his Vietnam War policy which promised not to abandon the South Vietnamese. She had several personal talks with Nixon maintaining it was vital that the United States did not surrender to aggressive communist forces.[81] There were a growing number of ordinary Americans, not connected to leftist antiwar groups, who bemoaned the inflexibility of hard-line politicians such as Smith, but she also had strong support. In December 1969, one conservative letter-writer pleaded to her: "Won't you please heed the military counsel and do all in your power to unleash the full offensive power of the great nation to bring these cruel North Vietnamese butchers to their knees and thus insure the freedom of self determination of all peace loving people."[82] As had been the case in the Johnson years, "half-hearted" approaches to fighting a war frustrated Smith and her response to Americans was consistent. To a Massachusetts man she wrote: "Either do it right and clean up the mess—or don't do it at all and don't get involved in something you have no intention at the outset of trying to win."[83]

The early months of 1970 witnessed a slight cooling-off period, but this changed after April 30 when Nixon delivered his speech, live on television and radio, informing the public that an American and South Vietnamese incursion into Cambodia was in progress.[84] The antiwar backlash to this announcement was a major test for Smith. Many Americans found it shocking that Nixon was widening the war with the escalation of military engagements in neutral Cambodia. Capturing the anger of many, one letter-writer asked: "How long must we endure this Alice in Wonderland logic of expanding to contract; destroying to build; wounding to heal and spending to save?"[85] Characterizing Nixon's decision as typical of the "Cold Warrior mentality," a Chicago resident wrote the following warning to the president: "May I advise you, Mr. Nixon, that just as Lyndon Johnson's obsession with victory in Vietnam returned him to geriatric fantasies on the Pedernales, so can your obsession with exacting obedience from your equals in Asia and at home return you, along with Ronald Reagan, S.I. Hayakawa and Disneyland, to your proper niche among California's more aberrant excesses."[86] Especially stunning were the responses on college campuses. The number of universities that took action against Nixon's policy especially mushroomed after National Guardsmen killed four students at Kent State University in Ohio on May 4.

Responding to antiwar protest, the burning of the Reserve Officers Training Corps building, and other acts of property damage, the Ohio governor had called out the National Guard to restore order and peace. The tragic deaths resulted in an unparalleled eruption, in American history, of hundreds of campus demonstrations from coast to coast.[87] Appalling but less talked about was the death of two African Americans (one high school and one college student) by Mississippi police who shot many rounds at a demonstration at Jackson State College, ten days after the Kent incident.

Smith herself faced a crowd of an estimated two thousand at Colby College in Maine five days after the Kent killings. Even as early as November 1967, half of the Colby College faculty and administrative staff were against the war, much to the disgust of one Commander of Veterans of Foreign Wars.[88] Because of the Cambodian "incursion" and Kent State episode, Colby students overwhelmingly approved a campus strike that led to marches, rallies, sit-ins, and workshops. The Students for a Democratic Society (SDS) showed *Salt of the Earth* (1954), a controversial film on class conflict produced by blacklisted Hollywood radicals. Colby President Robert Strider stated that the Nixon administration was insensitive to "the deadening impact the war" had on young Americans.[89] He could have said the same of Smith.

In this politicized atmosphere, striking college students representing a number of Maine colleges told the press that they had notified Smith by telegram to return home and address her constituents. She claimed not to have received the telegraphed demand directed from the president of the Colby College student body (a Massachusetts resident, she later pointed out), but she responded and arrived at the Colby campus more out of a sense of duty than for any desire to better understand the concerns of those with opposing views. Experiencing intense pain in her right hip on the steps of the Colby library, she faced taunts and obscenities for 90 minutes as she defended Nixon's Cambodian decision. Even though other accounts suggest that most of the crowd was respectful, she wrote that it was "perhaps the most unpleasant experience of my entire public service career."[90] One especially difficult moment was when some students asked, "How could anyone trust a president who lied about the presence of U.S. troops in Laos?"[91] Certainly, there is danger in trying to deceive a democracy; the communist leaders had the upper hand in managing the media or controlling policy decisions.[92] Only a few weeks earlier, Smith had inquired about American military involvement in Laos and the response from the Department of Defense was that there were "no U.S. ground troops in Laos."[93] When she gave this message to the students, a young retired army lieutenant came forward testifying that he had fought and received combat injuries in Laos. "They calculated to embarrass me," she wrote later. Contrasting her confrontation with students was the next day's "warm praise" that Senator Edmund Muskie received at Colby for attacking Nixon's foreign policy,[94] a response that suggests the influence of antiwar activists in organizing letter-writing campaigns to protest Nixon.

Nixon wrote in his memoirs that this period was "among the darkest" of his presidency and in a letter to Smith he expressed his gratefulness for her support for his policy.[95] Of the Americans who voiced their admiration for Smith's defense for the government's course of action in Cambodia a typical response was that Nixon's course was the only logical one.[96] Some letters suggest that support for Nixon was strong. Viewing himself as "one of the great president's silent majority," one constituent assured Smith that there were many supporting the fight against "the enemies of freedom in Vietnam and Cambodia."[97] In his letter from Camp Lejeune, North Carolina, one Vietnam veteran wrote: "I think that we are right in being there, not because I am a career Marine but because I have served in Viet Nam and have seen the Communist oppression first hand."[98] Despite the death and destruction portrayed in horrifying detail by the press, many Americans maintained, albeit mostly silently, that it was a worthy goal to stop a brutal communist system that denied human rights and freedom.

If not totally supportive of Smith's message, many others found her performance at Colby impressive. Responding to her defense of the Cambodian incursion, the New Jersey parents of a daughter who attended Colby College and opposed the strike wrote that their daughter judged Smith to be "the only sane sensible person whom she heard on campus all that week!"[99] An assistant finance officer of the Maine government shared: "It takes a lot of courage to stand up before an audience such as you did and state your convictions as you always have."[100] Angry on how television slanted the news on America's involvement in Southeast Asia, one Maine politician commended Smith for her "straight-forward, courageous speech."[101]

In the wake of such support for her stand, Smith even claimed that the confrontation with college antiwar protesters was a good experience. As she stated in one letter, "I would have rather gone there and frankly and directly disagreed with them and faced their verbal abuse than to have defaulted. I try to practice what I preach—even when I say it is time to stand up."[102] In one letter to a family that had offered encouragement, Smith wrote "that it was worth it to stand up to the invectives, insults, and even obscenity. . . . You make me feel as though I stood taller than my junior colleague. God bless you for your kindness!"[103] Her assessment of the verbal abuse she received suggests a large rabble of belligerent students rather than a small minority which was probably more accurate. Her trepidation that radical extremism was growing explains in large part her own reactionary responses, but a problem for her was the appearance that she was losing touch with many moderate young Americans who opposed the war but who were not asking for radical political change. The Report of the President's Commission on Campus Unrest, chaired by Republican William Scranton and delivered later that year, found that most protesting students were peaceful.[104]

In her correspondence, Smith argued that Muskie's attack on Nixon made no sense given the senator's support for Johnson who had accelerated troop involvement. She had more respect for someone like Senator George McGovern who consistently opposed the war during the Johnson and Nixon administrations, unlike "those who supported the Johnson Vietnam plank at the 1968 Democratic National Convention and then so suddenly reversed their positions immediately after Nixon became President."[105] Her assessment of Muskie's change of heart appears disingenuous, particularly when it was clear she disliked him, but her admiration for those who took a stand and did not waver was sincere. Also, she believed that partisanship should not supersede the importance of supporting the president when it came to the serious business of war and national security. She continued to argue that the Cambodian incursion was the type of military action needed to end America's involvement in Southeast Asia.[106] Yes, she loathed communism and expressed her resistance to any American "appeasement" to North Vietnam, but she also wanted to see the "boys" home.

Smith did not view herself as a warmonger, especially when she saw evidence of hypocrisy concerning the use of military force. For example, in a letter to a Vermont woman, she noted: "It is very ironic that so many who so militantly demand an immediate unilateral withdrawal from Vietnam, in the same breath demand our unlimited involvement in the Middle East."[107] However, such a comparison is tenuous since it was not realistic in 1970 that the American government would send large numbers of troops to the Middle East. With Nixon as president, Smith was clearly much more defensive of her position than was the case during the Johnson years.

One vocal critic was John Cole of the *Maine Times*, who suggested that Smith was unaware of what was happening in the war and had a flawed understanding of college protest. Her response was that Cole had personally attacked her "ever since he came to Maine from the south."[108] The reference to the "south" was one way of undermining the influence of an outsider who opposed her conservative values and understanding of the Vietnam War. She had also found it annoying that Katherine Graham, publisher of the *Washington Post*, demonstrated "an extremely critical attitude toward the sole woman Senator."[109]

Within a month of the Colby episode, Smith went on the NBC-TV *Today* show arguing that left-wing "extremism produced not only violent reactions but a tendency, among the great moderate majority of Americans to draw back in disgust into their mental shells and not speak up," a statement similar to

Nixon's great silent majority.[110] While there was truth to this observation, she failed to clarify that in addition to the extremists and the "great moderate majority of Americans" there were moderate antiwar demonstrators who had no taste for radical political solutions. Whether in the media or in her correspondence, she echoed Nixon's concerns about those "with the loudest voices" whose demonstrations in the streets were a threat to the democratic process.[111]

Smith's television appearance prompted a repeating of standard arguments against communism by ordinary Americans coast to coast. A Decatur, Georgia, woman informed Smith that loath to be silent, she was ready and willing to defend the government.[112] The television show also provoked a Portland, Oregon, woman to voice her opinion that communists operated freely in the United States, including on campuses where they were "stirring up our young people." Moreover, it frightened her that there might be communist professors "teaching our children." Desiring an end to the war, she found it "incongruous to fight them in foreign lands and give them free license right here at home."[113]

Of course, no legitimate research university should have censured the free exchange of ideas, including Marxist doctrine taught in various disciplines such as English, history, political studies, and sociology, to name only a few. In the years of domestic discord and college teach-ins, radical historians challenged those White House interpretations that narrowly focused on communist aggression in global terms with little or no appreciation for a Vietnamese self-determination guided by indigenous communist leadership. In Gabriel Kolko's *The Roots of American Foreign Policy* (1969), American intervention in Vietnam represented "an effort to preserve a mode of traditional colonialism via a minute, historically opportunistic *comprador* class in Saigon."[114] One of the more noted books in this period that offered a romantic version of the Vietcong was Frances Fitzgerald's *Fire in the Lake: The Vietnamese and the Americans in Vietnam* (1972).[115] In such studies, it was the United States that must accept "the responsibility for the torture of an entire nation" since it sustained corrupt South Vietnamese governments. They argued that it was the Americans rather the Vietnamese communist leadership who were guilty of spurning negotiation and escalating the war.[116] It is imperative, however, to clarify that only the most unbendable left academics argued that the foreign policies of communist nations were morally better than that of the United States. In 1972, historian William Appleman Williams, certainly no conservative, acknowledged that communist "revolutions extracted a terrible price in terror and hardship."[117]

For all the fear there was for the influence of leftist professors, radicals numbered only 5.1 percent compared to 27.7 percent conservatives (41.5 considered themselves liberal), according to a study of 60,000 faculty during the war. In the late 1960s, more acceptable critiques of American intervention in Southeast Asia came from realist scholars. For example, arguing that the containment of communism in Vietnam did not further American interests, Hans J. Morgenthau wrote, in late 1968, that it made no sense for the United States to continue fighting a war in Vietnam which was "politically aimless, militarily unpromising, and morally dubious."[118]

Important to note is that only a small number of college students viewed the cause of the communists as an honorable one that warranted their support. There were young protesters who chanted slogans like "Ho, Ho, Ho Chi Minh/The NLF is gonna win," but such "extravagant rhetoric of revolutionary cultism" was unwelcome among most protesters, a fact often lost to the many Americans who loathed campus demonstrations.[119] There was a clear distinction between those who opposed the war, including a number of those who voiced leftist rhetoric without carrying out radical action, and the tiny number of antiwar protesters who made an intellectual and passionate decision to embrace revolutionary Marxism or another form of radical politics. Some impressionable young minds caught up in the excitement of challenging a flawed capitalistic system with provocative ideas new to them were sure to fall under the spell of Marxist and other left-wing professors, but the next step of embracing full-blown radicalism is one that very few students took. In fact, one did not necessarily need to be a radical to believe that Ho Chi Minh was a nationalist—that is, a legitimate and rightful leader supported by the will of the people to unite Vietnam.

Undoubtedly, it was difficult for many Americans to understand how students could pay any homage, serious or not, to communist ideas. Without knowing a student's motives or true beliefs, ordinary Americans found it upsetting that any student would wear a Mao-adorned T-shirt or chant provocative antiwar slogans. Just as there were naïve students who flirted with radicalism without becoming true followers of the cause (compared to the tiny minority who did), there were Main Street Americans who jumped to the wrong conclusion and believed that radicalism and ideas indifferent to law and order were dominating the colleges. Unwilling to abandon the Cold War mind-set of an earlier age and publicly stating that communists played an important role in organizing college protests, Smith was one who erred with simplistic assessments of those against the war.[120]

The orthodoxy among policymakers for almost two decades was that the Soviets and Chinese were using Ho and his "Viet Minh rebellion" to achieve communist domination of all of Southeast Asia. The Chinese and Soviets had supplied North Vietnam with troops, engineers, economic aid, and military supplies including advanced aircraft (MiG-17 and MiG-21 fighters) and surface-to-air missiles.[121] Whether they were certain Ho was a pawn or not, conservatives in particular saw him as ruthless; there was something behind the words of Ngo Dinh Diem that Ho was "as pure as Lucifer."[122] He was a ruthless and, according to one historian, a "devout, if idiosyncratic, Marxist who relished his nation's role as the vanguard of revolution in the developing world." Belying the benevolent uncle image were his words, "All those who do not follow the line which I have laid will be broken."[123] During his early rise to power, he had many of his rivals murdered.[124]

When the communists executed a cruel landlord some Vietnamese peasants may have viewed this as a type of rough justice, but killing a respected teacher and committing other violent acts on innocent peasants represented wanton terror. Using terrorism effectively, the Vietcong eliminated many Vietnamese "traitors" by slowly disemboweling or beheading them in front of their families and other villagers. Mark Moyar argues that Marxist-Leninist ideology did not cause peasants to join the Vietcong. One communist official explained: "If the Party were to say: in the future you will be a laborer, your land will be collectivized, you will no longer own any farm animals or buildings, but will become a tenant farmer for the Party or the socialist state—if the Party were to say that, the peasants would not heed them . . . according to the teaching of Lenin, the peasant is the greatest bourgeois of all: he thinks only of himself. Say one word about collectivism, and he already is against you."[125] Often forcing the Vietnamese peasants to fight, the communists embraced coldhearted methods to ensure they reached their goals. Behind the communist struggle there was more cruelty and despotism than romance. One remarkable case is the warning that a Hanoi official gave his nephew: "Why are you joining? Don't you know that the war in the South is a colossal sacrifice of troops? They're sending soldiers to the South to be killed at a merciless rate. . . . If you go now there's only one fate—unbearable hardship and possibly death—a meaningless death."[126]

As the war dragged on and the number of deaths escalated, more college students wrote to Smith and questioned the correctness of fighting the North Vietnamese and Vietcong. Did the Vietnam War make any sense? Exactly why were young Americans fighting and dying there? Was it wise to support the corrupt South Vietnamese regime? Were not some of the war activities of the United States criminal?

Other Americans likewise voiced their disgust for an "immoral" and "evil" war against Vietnamese communists which resulted in the murder of innocent people. Numerous critics deplored the use of American napalm bombs that caused a horrible, burning death to men, women, and children. An Indiana man saw "madness" in America's wiping out Vietnamese villages, destroying the countryside, and "measuring its military progress by the historically unprecedented standard of dead bodies counted rather than territory taken."[127]

Proud of her participation in peace marches, one woman wrote that it was imperative to protest the United States for fighting "an imaginary enemy," killing "countless innocent civilians," and supporting "an evil and corrupt South Vietnamese government."[128] In the opinion of one New Yorker, retired from the Foreign Service, the American support of warlord dictatorships in South Vietnam, Cambodia, and Laos was "morally reprehensible."[129] An Iowa mother of a son who served in Southeast Asia wrote of gangs of "South Vietnamese" who attacked American servicemen when they went into some of the hamlets. She wanted to know who the real enemy in Vietnam was. And more direct: "How can you senators sleep at night, knowing that our young men are dying over there for vague, ill-defined reasons?"[130]

As a defender of freedom of expression, Smith more or less tolerated people's choice to oppose the war, even if she did not like it. She, however, could not accept any hint of domestic "anarchism" that triggered acts of trespass, arson, violence, killing, and other crimes. Twenty years to the day after her famous declaration, Smith's Declaration of Conscience of June 1, 1970, addressed the ills of American society beset with dangerous polarizing forces. Petitioning for moderation, she warned that extremism was forcing the American people to choose between anarchy and repression, and of this narrow choice cornered Americans, with misgivings, would decide on the latter. It was a call for Americans not to fall "mute by the emotional violence of the extreme left" because the end result would be "a reaction of repression." As she declared to a Utica, New York, woman, if forced to make a decision, she would choose repression over anarchy. Hubert Humphrey was one who approved of Smith's declaration: "Once again, you have said in your own quiet, concise, and persuasive manner what many of us have been thinking and all too few have been able to clearly articulate."[131] The truth is many Americans sincerely believed that leftist radicals were willing to carry out revolutionary actions such as kidnapping top governmental officials. Revealing is the fact that Smith's declaration generated mostly favorable responses from the press.[132]

The correspondence of Americans ran approximately eight to one approving her speech,[133] with many echoing her criticism of left extremism. One of her female constituents, who was a member of Americans for Patriotism, wrote that antiwar protesters had "the earmarks of the old time Communism."[134] Agreeing with Smith and disgusted with the weak political response to "anarchy," a San Jose, California, family suggested that politicians were "waiting for the Communists to take over from the inside."[135] Professing to have studied communism for over 50 years, an Indiana judge wrote: Communists "will build their stands on our weaknesses and as long as we have men like Jerry Rubin and Abbe Hoffman, who are anarchistic people, who state it is their intention to destroy this nation, they mean what they say."[136] Tired of being one of the silent majority, a Florida woman asked what she could do to help Smith and others fight the extremists who sought to overthrow the government.[137] There were also equally alarming letters critical of her understanding of the right. In a particularly passionate and harsh letter criticizing "such a stupid speech," one California woman declared her love for the United States and her commitment to fight communism "without pay, with no hope or desire for honor or glory, with the full knowledge my life is in constant jeopardy."[138] A Dallas veteran of World War II, who took offense to Smith's depiction of "so called right wing (sic) extremists," suggested that pro-communist coddlers in the government and the media used the term to discredit "patriotic Christian Americans" who opposed them. In his view, there were "millions upon millions" of right-wingers in the nation, and he found it galling that the three networks made little attempt to balance the news with notable conservative voices.[139]

Smith's declaration might have balanced criticism of the extreme left and right, but it fell short in offering a nuanced perspective of the forces of anarchism and repression. While Americans did witness tense moments in May 1970, much would have to happen to realistically see the emergence of a comprehensive police state. She was wrong to suggest that America was on the verge of anarchy with society controlled by the extreme left. Regardless what she and some of her supporters thought, Abbe Hoffman and other radicals and communists were nowhere close to taking over the government. Within her declaration lay the foundation that college antiwar protesters were driven by dangerous ideology.

From Washington, D.C., one critic of Smith wrote that her comments on the "radical left" were false, that college students only wanted a decent life, and that Smith and Nixon desired to "dragoon them" into the "WAR Department" to become "skilled assassins" in Southeast Asia. This forced the "kids" to rebel.[140] Judging her declaration as biased against opponents of the war, a Maryland man asked: "Who are the greater criminals, Presidents who violate the Constitution to send the young to a war, or a few of the young who break windows?"[141] While these are also overheated comments, many more moderate Americans had more faith in the common sense of the overwhelming majority of college students.

Holding strong for Nixon, Smith believed that his strategy showed greater promise than what Johnson and his decision-making "whiz kids" had achieved. In an earlier day, when the scapegoat was commonly and unfairly "the much maligned military officers of our nation," she blamed the Pentagon civilian chiefs of the Johnson administration for the "disastrous decisions" on the war and criticized their "open contempt" of the military.[142] With the

Nixon administration in place that showed more respect for military leaders, Americans needed to be patient and allow the White House and the Pentagon to do their work effectively. Smith consistently opposed amendments by Frank Church/John Cooper and George McGovern/Mark Hatfield that sought to limit or terminate funding for military operations in Southeast Asia.[143] As she stressed to one Tennessee man, there was no way she could support any proposals to "straight-jacket" Nixon's Vietnam strategy.[144] In his study of foreign policy warrior intellectuals, Robert Dean writes that the "identity narrative of the imperial brotherhood demanded relentless defense of boundaries and an utter rejection of appeasement."[145] It appears that Smith was even more relentless than key members of the imperial brotherhood who rethought their anticommunist convictions.

For conservatives, in addition to the problem of dovish politicians, there was the liberal media. Scholars concede that the majority of journalists were antiwar liberals. However, this did not guarantee fair treatment of the antiwar movement. In demonstration after demonstration, the press focused on the radical fringe, and thus contributed to the perception that violence was the norm for protest events.[146] Where the media was truly damaging for conservatives and those supportive of the war effort was its considerable attention to the terrible incidents of civilian murder and loss of life and widespread destruction due to major bombing operations. One *New York Times Magazine* story revealed how Lieutenant Colonel Anthony Herbert was the victim of military demotion because he had reported atrocities committed by American and South Vietnamese against defenseless women and children.[147] The *New Yorker* gave a harsh assessment of the government's mass deportation of South Vietnamese from the northern to southern provinces; this "final solution" project represented an "openly totalitarian act" with the machine-gunning from helicopters of those who did not participate. According to the article, most of the South Vietnamese in the northern provinces supported the communists and regarded the United States Marines "as the real invaders."[148] With the exception of one sentence mentioning that the Vietcong captured two American pilots, hung them by their thumbs, and skinned them alive, an article in the *Maine Times* was replete with horrific examples of American brutality on the Vietnamese people. In the words of four returning veterans, there were American soldiers who slaughtered wildlife, violently injured children and women, and tossed grenades into civilian huts, all "for the fun of it." Appalling also was the murder of all prisoners and the cutting off of the ears of dead bodies.[149]

Televisions reports such as the Huntley-Brinkley show of November 1969 that presented film evidence of South Vietnam soldiers beating and kicking a bound prisoner had a profound impact on television viewers, including one Florida man who assumed that such violations of the Geneva Convention were typical in Vietnam, a point he made in a letter to Smith.[150] The most stunning television clip was the cold-blooded murder of a Vietcong by General Nguyen Ngoc Loan, chief of South Vietnam's national police, on the streets of Saigon during the Tet Offensive. The communist invaders had killed several of his men, but the chief's action was horrific and indefensible.[151] Presenting very powerful images, many sensational and sickening reports captured the horrors of war with the Americans and South Vietnamese often alone playing the lead role of malevolence.

Conservative voices in the media sought to present another perspective that saw evil more broadly. As early as September 1963, Joseph Alsop was critical of the Saigon press corps, "the crusaders" who appeared to hail communist leaders as saviors. One of those crusaders representing the *New York Times* was David Halberstam, who reacted angrily to pro-Diem reports of journalists such as Marguerite Higgins. When his editors suggested he tone down his dispatches in light of conflicting reports by Higgins, he replied: "If you mention that woman's name to me one more time I will resign repeat resign and I mean it repeat mean it."[152] While not agreeing with Higgins's position, Neil Sheehan, Vietnam War correspondent for the *New York Times*, acknowledged that Higgins "had the professional stature that Halberstam lacked in 1963."[153] However, years later Higgins was mostly forgotten, including by most historians. Receiving much more attention are Halberstam and Sheehan, who were instrumental, according to Mark Moyar, in undermining Diem's regime in the eyes of influential Americans and South Vietnamese.[154]

Presenting a different picture than that of much of the *New York Times* reports, Higgins's book *Our Vietnam Nightmare* (1965) argued that Buddhist counterinsurgency against the government of South Vietnam was political rather than religious, that Ho Chi Minh was a callous killer, and that the United States was in Vietnam to counter the communist armies sent south by Ho "to terrorize, bomb, burn, trick, and bleed the Vietnamese nation into submission."[155] Providing numerous examples of communist atrocities against Vietnamese peasants, she explained that it was difficult for Americans to understand the "terror of the kind perpetuated by the Viet Cong."[156] For Americans who agreed with her, she was someone who knew Vietnam better than any other American reporter and who upheld the domino theory.[157]

In a later period, journalist Paul Greenberg found it exasperating that critics of the United States government were quick to use the Pentagon Papers "as indisputable proof of Washington's wickedness" while dismissing the revelation of secret documents revealing that the North Vietnamese in late 1963 had plans to use regular forces in South Vietnam.[158] Before an investigation of the My Lai atrocity took place, when American soldiers under the command of Lieutenant William Calley brutally executed some 350 unarmed Vietnamese civilians, the *National Review* wrote: An ex-GI "described it as a 'dark' event—as it may well have been; but, most assuredly, there is something dark and sick about much of the reaction from the liberal Left." In its analysis of the media's "irresponsible comment," the *National Review* questioned whether the American people were guilty of the slaughter and whether the incident called in question American involvement in Vietnam as argued by others: "Do the innumerable atrocities committed by both sides in World War II add up to the proposition that resistance to the Nazis ought to have been abandoned?"[159] The conservative journal had also defended unrestricted bombing of the communists arguing that "Hanoi itself orders the bombing—by continuing to fight in South Vietnam."[160]

Admiral U. S. Grant Sharp, USN (Ret.) used the *Reader's Digest* (May 1969) to present his arguments that the United States could have won in Vietnam "long ago" had there been proper use of airpower: "To concentrate on infiltration and to refrain from hitting primary targets—as we were required to do—emasculated our war effort." Sharp argued that it was possible to both bomb effectively and avoid killing large numbers of civilians, a stark contrast to the communist enemy who "repeatedly lobbed rockets blindly" into populated cities, killing over 27,000 South Vietnamese civilians in the 1957 to 1968 period. The U.S. armed forces appeared to be at the mercy of communist sympathizers who effectively pushed "the propaganda buttons."[161] Ideology was often a fairly accurate predictor of how communism played out in the media.

There is no denying that American troops randomly committed war crimes,[162] yet one historian suggests that "cold-blooded murder was probably relatively rare."[163] Whatever the true number, such murders were terrible, as were the atrocities committed by the communists. Those who judged the South Vietnamese government and the American war effort as immoral might say little of the cases of communist terror and brutality of their own people.[164] And for all the talk of the harsh methods of President Ngo Dinh Diem, a Roman Catholic inspired to fight the spread of communism, there were still Americans years after his assassination in November 1963 who viewed his administration in a positive light.[165] It should not be surprising that a significant number of Americans expected a follower of Christ to ultimately follow Christian principles.

On the horrific communist treatment of American prisoners of war, one career Marine officer sent several letters to Smith. Finding the "silence over the POW issue" disgraceful, he wanted her to condemn, in a Senate resolution, "the atrocities and inhuman treatment being perpetrated by the North Vietnamese."[166] A Californian, whose brother was a prisoner of war since

1965 when he was shot down in his F-4, pleaded for Smith to help pressure North Vietnam to treat their POWs humanely.[167] One New Jersey woman suggested that too many Americans were unaware of the ill treatment of American POWs; she wanted the politicians to act and "excite our people and show the North Viet Namese we mean business."[168] Smith received one poem entitled "How Shall She Tell Him" written by a Texas woman concerned over the emotional distraught of a mother and her four-year-old boy whose birth came after the father's capture by the North Vietnamese; the message that followed the poem indicated helplessness: "But does she really *know* he'll be home? What *can* be done for the prisoners of war and men who are missing in action? The men are treated cruelly! *What can be done?*"[169]

The communists remained unresponsive to efforts by the United States to see the practice of acceptable standards for the treatment of prisoners of war. In violation of the terms of the Geneva Convention, North Vietnam and the National Liberation Front failed to provide a list of prisoners, release sick and wounded prisoners, allow appropriate international inspection, or permit regular mail between prisoners and their families. In the eyes of the communists, captured Americans were criminals rather than legitimate prisoners of war.[170] The contrast to how the Americans and the South Vietnamese and their communist enemies operated their prisoner-of-war camps was stark. In a case of American and South Vietnamese failure to adhere strictly to Geneva standards, policy dictated that there was a thorough investigation in which guilty servicemen received judicial sentences.[171] North Vietnam and its agents rejected offers by the United States and South Vietnamese governments for an exchange of prisoners that would favor thousands more communist prisoners released than American and South Vietnamese prisoners. In his letter to Smith, Deputy Assistant Secretary of State Armistead I. Selden, Jr. stated that "the enemy seems to be utterly disinterested in the fate of its own men."[172]

How was the United States to negotiate with an enemy that drafted women and 13-year-old boys into the communist war cause? How did one bargain with communist leaders who appeared to be willing to commit as many of their people to death as necessary for victory? One study estimates that the communist crimes against Vietnamese civilians accounted for approximately one million deaths.[173] When it came to military battles, Ho Chi Minh stated: "You can kill ten of my men for every one I kill of yours. But even at those odds, you will lose and I will win."[174] A Chinese official had stated that "war in Southeast Asia would not be such a bad thing."[175]

For Smith and other Americans, the war against communism was unique. The enemies of World War II—the (West) Germans, Italians, and Japanese— were no longer America's enemies, but this was because German Nazism,

Italian Fascism, and Japanese militarism fell in defeat. Americans who feared the threat of communism understood, even if only on a superficial level, that it was a worldview constructed with more lasting and ambitious goals of conquest, clearly spelled out in Marxist literature if one researched. Not so much concerned over the issue of the United States saving face in the eyes of the world, what mattered to Smith and other Americans was a commitment to confront an evil ideological system. In his book *The Just War* (1968), Paul Ramsey argued that Christian love of the neighbor demanded American action against communist aggression.[176] If America let the South Vietnamese fight the communist menace by themselves, the resulting bloodshed, chaos, and communist repression would be unjust. Smith believed that pulling out of Southeast Asia immediately was wrong; it would stop the fighting, but not the fight. Victory over the communists was only possible with a full military effort. Smith's support for Nixon did not waver in 1972 when he escalated bombing in North Vietnam in order, as explained by the Department of State, "to provide the necessary protection for our remaining forces in South Vietnam until we have achieved the President's goal of ending the American involvement in Vietnam."[177] Whatever the reason, military resolve was crucial because signs of weakness only invited Hanoi to stay the course. On Memorial Day, she charged that a "shocking number of political leaders" acted in a manner that encouraged the Vietnamese communists to prolong the conflict as long as possible. What the communists could not win militarily, they could win politically "back in the United States."[178] Another problem she saw was that flawed political decisions prevented the military from securing a victorious conclusion, a position consistent with Mark Moyar and the revisionist school of Vietnam War historiography.[179]

Smith's masculine hard-line position did not waver in the face of the antiwar movement which consisted of many pacifists, liberals, social democrats, and others who opposed revolutionary actions. Actually, countless Americans erred in believing that many antiwar protesters, those who dismissed the domino theory as nonsense, were budding Marxists. The antiwar movement was hurt by the perception that elite antiwar activists sneered at the working class and "ridiculed the symbols and values of patriotic Americans."[180] It did not matter that the majority of antiwar protesters, who were neither violent nor destructive, saw themselves as loyal and patriotic citizens. There was a conservative backlash and many average Americans who viewed the war as a mistake or as an exercise in futility also held leading activists in contempt: "No matter what they did, activists never escaped the grip of that irony."[181] For example, fundamentalist Carl McIntire referred to the antiwar group Clergy and Laymen Concerned About Vietnam as "the advance guard of Ho Chi Minh." The CALCAV's failure to raise the necessary funds for its antiwar activities is an indication of the difficulties such groups faced in garnering broader support.[182]

When dozens of antiwar activists, notably people such as actress Jane Fonda and SDS cofounder Tom Hayden, visited North Vietnam over the course of the war, the government and most Americans viewed such visits as acts of betrayal or worse. Quoted as saying "Now we're all Vietcong," Hayden, and the others who met with North Vietnamese and Vietcong leaders, was proof in the eyes of many Americans of a warm relationship between communists and antiwar activists. At some demonstrations, activists unwisely read public greetings sent by North Vietnamese leaders, thus substantiating the worst fears of the Americans who believed that antiwar activists favored a communist system of government. A revolutionary SDS leader, Bill Ayers believed it possible for the government to fall. The "Third World romanticism" of radicals clearly hurt the antiwar movement, a fact that Hayden admitted years later. The photograph of activist Jane Fonda in North Vietnam behind an antiaircraft gun used to shoot down American airplanes infuriated many. Politicians did their part by linking urban racial riots and other violent protests with antiwar activities. Government agents who infiltrated the antiwar movement also promoted violence within. It is no wonder that the antiwar "movement engaged the active support of only a minority of Americans, with perhaps as few as six million participating in its major events and twenty-five million on the sidelines sympathizing with them." During Smith's final six years in the Senate, there was never a majority of Americans favoring immediate withdrawal from Vietnam. In May 1972, Nixon took a gamble shortly before his trip to Moscow and announced the mining of Hanoi's and Haiphong's harbors. The antiwar movement escalated its protests, but 59 percent of Americans polled supported the mining.[183]

In 1972, one historian critical of American foreign policy recognized the complexity of the Vietnam issue as it pertained to the voting public. In the late 1960s, "contrary to the images on the television screens, voting analyses showed that young people under thirty were more 'hawkish' than the over-fifty generation." It was noncollege, conservative Americans rather than radical students that determined Nixon's victory in 1968.[184] A recent study suggests that many historians of the antiwar movement fail to realize that "the protesters would have remained a tiny insignificant minority if American soldiers had been winning in Vietnam."[185]

After the Cambodian episode in 1970 the strategy of the antiwar movement was to favor congressional politics rather than urban protest.[186] Smith's 1972 memoirs appeared in print as she prepared her bid for another term in the Senate. Bill Lewis edited and wrote most of the book, which clearly presented the Cold Warrior views she held over the years. It was the belief of many on the left that those who failed to get beyond mindless anticommunism were dupes of outdated thinking. Still, Smith soldiered on and defeated the Harvard-educated, multimillionaire executive Robert A. G. Monks in her first primary contest since 1954. Facing her Democratic challenger William Hathaway in the general election was another matter. A four-term Congressman and opponent of the war, Hathaway defeated Smith by a tally of 224,270 to 197,040.[187]

Smith's curt and defensive reaction to antiwar protest suggests that she incorrectly believed that radical beliefs were common in the broader antiwar movement. There is evidence of a clear failure to offer a judicious response to those opposing the war or at least giving the average college student more credit for responding to the war in a reasonable, law-abiding manner. Writing from New York, one student claimed that a "far greater" threat than communism was the polarizing attacks against antiwar protesters by Nixon, Vice President Spiro Agnew, Attorney General John Mitchell, and Governor Ronald Reagan. Some believed that Smith belonged in this group, since her rhetoric of toughness also polarized and overcharged the war issue.[188] In addition, having characterized communist leaders as evil throughout her years in the Senate, her stand appeared outdated to some in light of Nixon's 1972 visits and talks with communist leaders in China, where he sought normal relations, and the U.S.S.R., where he signed agreements which banned deployment of antiballistic missile systems. There was irony that Smith, who detested Nixon's alliance with McCarthyites in the 1950s, appeared more conservative than Nixon after his triumphant visits with communist leaders. The fact that she was no ideologue outside the issue of national security only confused the matter.

And yet her Cold Warrior stand was not the deciding factor in her electoral loss, since many of her constituents appeared to find the stereotypes of the Cold War acceptable for understanding American involvement in Southeast Asia. Political scientist Christian Potholm claims that her defeat was mainly due to her refusal to embrace modern campaign techniques, particularly powerful thirty-second television commercials and the expertise of media consultants.[189] Biographers Janann Sherman, Patricia Schmidt, and Patricia Ward Wallace list additional factors for her defeat: Smith's health issues including failing eyesight, listless campaign activity, the heart attack and illness of her trusted assistant Bill Lewis, the opposition of Maine feminists, and the desire among many Mainers for change, believing Smith had lost contact with her constituents. In the end, it was her advanced age, overconfidence, and lackluster campaign rather than her Cold Warrior record and reactionary manner that cost her dearly.[190]

If it is accurate that pre-1965 Congress and the mainstream media did not overwhelmingly favor a firm commitment to defending South Vietnam only to come on board after being caught up in the momentum of war with the introduction of American ground troops in 1965, by 1968 and beyond the mood had shifted, with many politicians and the mainstream media questioning the correctness of defending South Vietnam. For the first time more than 50 percent of Americans polled answered "yes" to the question "Do you believe United States involvement in the Vietnam War to have been a mistake?"[191] And an increasing number of Americans viewed communism in a more benign manner.[192] Still, anticommunism persisted and Cold Warriors such as Smith remained viable winning candidates despite the difficulties that antiwar activists caused them. Almost 75 years old, she had only lost by a 53 to 47 percent margin.[193] In the end, even with her shortcomings she could have won had she fought hard to win.

NOTES

1. MCS to Kenneth Van Otten, 3 December 1969; MCS to Mrs. John T. Rowland, 13 May 1970; MCS to Rosellyn Waterhouse, 18 May 1970; MCS to Steven Wilson, 21 February 1971; MCS to Ted Moon, Jr. 13 October 1971; MCS to A. T. Sawyer, 29 February 1972,Vietnam War Correspondence, MCSL.

2. Smith Statement, 27 January 1964, Press Relations, MCSL. She told the press club that "it was not a Southern anti-negro extremist that shot President Kennedy but instead a Marxist, a mentally deranged Communist." Some studies hold that Kennedy had no intention of withdrawing from Vietnam. For example, see Moyar, *Triumph Forsaken*, 277.

3. David Kaiser, *American Tragedy: Kennedy, Johnson, and the Origins of the Vietnam War* (Cambridge, Mass.: Harvard University Press, 2000), 294–95.

4. For a revisionist perspective on the Gulf of Tonkin episode, see Moyar, *Triumph Forsaken*, 310–11. Eric Crouse, ed., *Dear Senator Smith: Small-Town Maine Writes to Senator Margaret Chase Smith about the Vietnam War, 1967–1971* (Lanham, Md.: Lexington Books, 2008), 18.

5. Fredrik Logevall challenges this "inevitability thesis" and argues that Congress and the mainstream media, up to early 1965, did not overwhelmingly favor a firm commitment to defending South Vietnam. See Logevall, *Choosing War*, xvii–xviii.

6. World Trip Report, 18 April 1955, World Trip 1954–1955 Folder, MCSL. "West Can't Afford to Lose Indo-China," W&Y, 14 August 1953. In this column, Smith added economic and strategic reasons for preventing the communists from taking Vietnam.

7. In a 1967 article published in various newspapers, she stated that Eisenhower had been against a ground war in Asia, having witnessed "the tragic failure and mistakes of France and her resulting ignominious defeat in Vietnam." See Margaret Chase Smith, "Why I Worry about the War in Vietnam," Vietnam War Press Reports, MCSL.

8. Michael Hunt, *Lyndon Johnson's War: America's Cold War Crusade in Vietnam, 1945–1968* (New York: Hill and Wang, 1996), 100. Moyar, *Triumph Forsaken*, 390, 414.

9. For example, see Loren Baritz, *Backfire: A History of How American Culture Led Us into Vietnam and Made Us Fight the Way We Did* (New York: Ballantine Books, 1985), 10–11.

10. Moyar, *Triumph Forsaken*, xiv. Kaiser, *American Tragedy*, 339. By mid-1965, Chinese units totaling approximately 250,000 men began to arrive in North Vietnam. See Hunt, *Lyndon Johnson's War*, 87–88.

11. MCS to Paul Norton, 22 December 1969, Vietnam War Correspondence, MCSL.

12. MCS to Steven Wilson, 21 February 1972, Vietnam War Correspondence, MCSL. Historians such as Mark Moyar support this interpretation. See Moyar, *Triumph Forsaken*, 313.

13. Logevall, *Choosing War*, 203.

14. Randall Bennett Woods, *Fulbright: A Biography* (Cambridge: Cambridge University Press, 1995), 472–79.

15. Crouse, ed., *Dear Senator Smith*, 18–19.

16. Sherman, *No Place for a Woman*, 204.

17. Michael S. Harris to MCS, 25 March 1968, Foreign Relations Correspondence, MCSL. One college group, for example, who wanted to hear her view was the Ohio State University Young Republican Club. See Gary Allen to MCS, 13 January 1967, Vietnam War Correspondence, MCSL. One New York City man wrote: [I]t is clear that you command the respect of the Senate and of the country in an unusual degree." See Matthew Zuckerbraun to MCS, 16 May 1970, Vietnam War Correspondence, MCSL. For a sampling of correspondence from small-town America, see Crouse, ed., *Dear Senator Smith*. For additional views of Main Street America, see Michael S. Foley, ed., *Dear Dr. Spock: Letters about the Vietnam War to America's Favorite Baby Doctor* (New York: New York University Press, 2005).

18. "Popular Support for the Viet Cong," Department of State, MCSL.

19. Smith, *Declaration of Conscience*, 447.

20. "Why Thanksgiving?" *CT*, 24 November 1967, 23.

21. MCS to Arthur Conner, 5 January 1967, Foreign Relations Correspondence, MCSL.

22. MCS to Howard Norton, 5 January 1967, Vietnam War Correspondence, MCSL.

23. MCS to John Lynch, 27 January 1967. Also, MCS to G. Nelson, 25 January 1967, Foreign Relations Correspondence, MCSL. MCS to Joy Cox, 6 January 1967, Vietnam War Correspondence, MCSL.

24. Senate Speech, 23 February 1967, MCSL.

25. Smith, "Why I Worry about the War in Vietnam."

26. Schmidt, *Margaret Chase Smith*, 304. The term "best and brightest" is from David Halberstam, *The Best and Brightest* (New York: Fawcett Crest, 1972).

27. Smith, "Why I Worry about the War in Vietnam."

28. Smith, "Why I Worry about the War in Vietnam."

29. Crouse, ed., *Dear Senator Smith*, 50, 52, 55.

30. Roosevelt Montgomery to MCS, 3 May 1967, Vietnam War Correspondence, MCSL.

31. Francis Westrack to MCS, 24 April 1967, Vietnam War Correspondence, MCSL.

32. Crouse, ed., *Dear Senator Smith*, 53.

33. MCS to Florence Blodgett, 22 May 1967, Foreign Relations Correspondence, MCSL.

34. MCS to Gary Allen, 13 January 1967, Vietnam War Correspondence, MCSL.

35. MCS to Alton Robinson, 16 June 1967, Foreign Relations Correspondence, MCSL.

36. Joseph A. Fry, *Debating Vietnam: Fulbright, Stennis, and Their Senate Hearings* (Lanham, Md.: Rowman & Littlefield Publishers, Inc., 2006), 73.

37. MCS to Florence Blodgett, 22 May 1967; MCS to Francis Westrack, 27 April 1967, Foreign Relations Correspondence, MCSL.

38. MCS to Linda Shumaker, 16 February 1967, Vietnam War Correspondence, MCSL.

39. MCS to Clifton Greenleaf, 22 May 1967, Foreign Relations Correspondence, MCSL.

40. Charlotte Haynes to MCS, 4 May 1967, Vietnam War Correspondence, MCSL.

41. On the topic of the world heavyweight boxing champion who refused to fight in the Vietnam War, she wrote: "I will say this much for Cassius Clay. He stayed in this country and took his case to court instead of going to Canada to evade the draft or deserting to Sweden." See MCS to Stilman Brewer, 20 November 1970, Vietnam War Correspondence, MCSL.

42. Owen Kincaid to MCS, 2 July 1967, Vietnam War Correspondence, MCSL.

43. MCS to Donna Aldrich, 16 May 1967; MCS to Priscilla James, 11 August 1967, Vietnam War Correspondence, MCSL.

44. Isserman and Kazin, *America Divided*, 149–51. May, *Homeward Bound*, 210.

45. Mark Oppenheimer, *Knocking on Heaven's Door: American Religion in the Age of Counterculture* (New Haven, Conn.: Yale University Press, 2003), 173, 195. For further discussion of evangelicalism and the counterculture, see Larry Eskridge, "Billy Graham, the Jesus Generation, and the Idea of an Evangelical Youth Culture," *Church History* 67, no. 1 (March 1998): 83–106.

46. MCS to Philip Mather, 3 February 1967, Foreign Relations Correspondence, MCSL.

47. Glenn T. Miller, *Piety and Profession: American Protestant Theological Education, 1870–1970* (Grand Rapids, Mich.: William B. Eerdmans Publishing Company, 2007), 728, 748.

48. E. Brooks Holifield, *God's Ambassadors: A History of the Christian Clergy in America* (Grand Rapids, Mich.: William B. Eerdmans Publishing Company, 2007), 261–62, 267. For his category "fundamentalists," Holyfield notes that there was 91 percent support for an escalation of war and continued bombing.

49. Holifield, *God's Ambassadors*, 305.

50. Melvin Small, *Antiwarriors: The Vietnam War and the Battle for America's Hearts and Minds* (Wilmington, Del.: Scholarly Resources, Inc. 2002), 85. MCS to Owen Kincaid, 5 January 1967, Foreign Relations Correspondence, MCSL.

51. Mrs. Douglas Coppin to MCS, 28 March 1967, Vietnam War Correspondence, MCSL. Also, Nash, *The Conservative Intellectual Movement in America*, 302–3. On early radical college groups, see Small, *Antiwarriors*, 13.

52. Cited in *Manion Forum*, 17 May 1970, Vietnam War Press Reports, MCSL.

53. C. Douglas McGee to MCS, 6 April 1967, Vietnam War Correspondence, MCSL.

54. Whitman Smith to MCS, 27 October 1967, Vietnam War Correspondence, MCSL.

55. Small, *Antiwarriors*, 7, 86.

56. MCS to Alvin Settle, 27 April 1967, Foreign Relations Correspondence, MCSL.

57. Wallace, *Politics of Conscience*, 171–72, 176. Also, see Schmidt, *Margaret Chase Smith*, 283.

58. Sherman, *No Place for a Woman*, 168.

59. "The Hawk Fly Off-Course," *New York Times*, 3 September 1967, Vietnam War Press Reports, MCSL.

60. Fry, *Debating Vietnam*, 85–86, 94.

61. McNamara, *In Retrospect*, 284. The members included: John Stennis (D-MS), Stuart Symington (D-MO), Henry Jackson (D-WA), Howard Cannon (D-NV), Robert Byrd (D-WV), Strom Thurmond (R-SC), and Jack Miller (R-IA).

62. Fry, *Debating Vietnam*, 141. Small, *Antiwarriors*, 55.

63. Yvonne Barber to MCS, 26 April 1967, Vietnam War Correspondence, MCSL.

64. Marjorie Fink to MCS, 5 December 1967, Vietnam War Correspondence, MCSL.

65. L. S. Elliot to MCS, 14 September 1967, Vietnam War Correspondence, MCSL.

66. Philip Jenkins writes that "one of the great Christian success stories in Asia is South Korea." In South Korea, Christians represent a solid majority of those professing a religion. The Full Gospel Central Church in Seoul has the distinction of having the world's largest single congregation in the world, according the *Guinness Book of World Records*. See Philip Jenkins, *The Next Christendom: The Coming of Global Christianity* (Oxford: Oxford University Press, 2002), 71.

67. MCS to Earl Freeman, 23 October 1967, Foreign Relations Correspondence, MCSL. After Ho's death, Hanoi remained encouraged by the dissent against the war in the United States. See Jeffrey Kimball, *Nixon's Vietnam War* (Lawrence: University Press of Kansas, 1998), 221.

68. William J. Duiker, "Ho Chi Minh and the Strategy of People's War," in *The First Vietnam War: Colonial Conflict and Cold War Crisis*, ed. Mark Atwood Lawrence and Fredrik Logevall (Cambridge, Mass.: Harvard University Press, 2007), 156.

69. Pierre Brocheux, *Ho Chi Minh: A Biography*, trans., Claire Duiker (Cambridge: Cambridge University Press, 2007), 187. Moyar, *Triumph Forsaken*, 9.

70. MCS to Whitman Smith, 27 October 1967, Vietnam War Correspondence, MCSL. Moyar, *Triumph Forsaken*, 377.

71. MCS to Linda Wheeler, 6 November 1967, Foreign Relations Correspondence, MCSL.

72. MCS to Mary Parker, 18 January 1968, Foreign Relations Correspondence, MCSL.

73. Quoted in Spencer C. Tucker, ed., *The Encyclopedia of the Vietnam War: A Political, Social and Military History* (Oxford: Oxford University Press, 2000), 397. CBS news anchor Walter Cronkite disagreed and he viewed the military's version as "more of the old siren song." See Walter Cronkite, *A Reporter's Life* (New York: Ballantine Books, 1996), 256–58.

74. "Viet Nam: The Vulnerable Ones," *CT*, 1 March 1968, 16–17. "Six Missionaries Martyred in Viet Nam," *CT*, 1 March 1968, 37. "Report from Viet Nam," *CT*, 15 March 1968, 35.

75. Margaret Chase Smith, "Vietnam Crucible," Vietnam War, MCSL.

76. Small, *Antiwarriors*, 58, 90.

77. Isserman and Kazin, *Divided America*, 231, 234.

78. Quoted in *RN: The Memoirs of Richard Nixon* (New York: Grosset & Dunlap, 1978), 402.

79. Quoted in Melvin Small, *Johnson, Nixon, and the Doves* (New Brunswick, N.J.: Rutgers University Press, 1989), 188. Comparing social status, "More modestly situated citizens remained more hawkish (and supportive)." See William L. Lunch and Peter W. Sperlich, "American Public Opinion and the War in Vietnam," *The Western Political Quarterly* 32, no. 1 (March 1979), 40.

80. Small, *Antiwarriors*, 114–16.

81. MCS to Richard E. Fortier, Jr. 26 September 1969, Views and Issues Correspondence, MCSL.

82. Crouse, ed., *Dear Senator Smith*, 122.

83. MCS to Philip Diming, 19 January 1970, Miscellaneous out of State, MCSL.

84. Crouse, ed. *Dear Senator Smith*, 119.

85. George DesRoberts to MCS, 1 May 1970, Vietnam War Correspondence, MCSL.

86. Anthony Moulton to Richard Nixon, 1 May 1970, Vietnam War Correspondence, MCSL.

87. Small, *Antiwarriors*, 122–23. As one University of Wisconsin student wrote: "It took the killings at Kent State on Monday to really get things going. The word arrived here about noontime, and at seven that evening there was a student rally to decide on a strike." See Crouse, ed., *Dear Senator Smith*, 183

88. R. J. Meehan to MCS, 24 November 1967, Vietnam War Correspondence, MCSL.

89. Crouse, ed., *Dear Senator Smith*, 173.

90. Smith, *Declaration of Conscience*, 428–29.

91. Quoted from Sherman, *No Place for a Woman*, 212.

92. Gaddis, *We Now Know*, 269.

93. Dennis Doolin to MCS, 3 March 1970, Vietnam War Correspondence, MCSL.

94. Smith, *Declaration of Conscience*, 428–29.

95. Nixon, *RN*, 457. Richard Nixon to MCS, 19 May 1970, Vietnam War Correspondence, MCSL.

96. This is a point clearly expressed by one Alabama resident. See Gary Huffman to MCS, 30 April 1970, Vietnam War Correspondence, MCSL.

97. Donald Anderson to MCS, 8 May 1970, Vietnam War Correspondence, MCSL.

98. C. P. Barker to MCS, 13 May 1970, Vietnam War Correspondence, MCSL.

99. John and Vivian Hannon, 18 May 1970, Vietnam War Correspondence, MCSL.

100. Samuel Hinds to MCS, 26 May 1970, Vietnam War Correspondence, MCSL.

101. Lowell Henley to MCS, 11 May 1970, Vietnam War Correspondence, MCSL.

102. MCS to John Baxter, 5 June 1970, Cambodia Correspondence, MCSL.

103. MCS to Munroe Rinfret, 29 May 1970, Cambodia Correspondence, MCSL.

104. The Report of the President's Commission on Campus Unrest, Superintendent of Documents, U.S. Government Printing Office, Washington, D.C. 20402, 1970.

105. MCS to Arnold Tobin, 27 May 1970, Cambodia Correspondence; MCS to Philip De Velder, 17 May 1971, Vietnam War Correspondence, MCSL.

106. MCS to Mr. and Mrs. Eberhard Schmidt, 12 May 1970, Cambodia Correspondence, MCSL. For a revisionist account that argues that Nixon was correct in describing the Cambodian incursion as "the most successful military operation of the Vietnam War," see John M. Shaw, *The Cambodian Campaign: The 1970 Offensive and America's Vietnam War* (Lawrence: University Press of Kansas, 2005), 153.

107. MCS to Rosellyn Waterhouse, 18 May 1970, Cambodia Correspondence, MCSL. Some conservative Christians wondered the same. See "Cambodia and Israel," *CT*, 22 May 1970, 21.

108. Wallace, *Politics of Conscience*, 180. MCS to Robert Easton, 22 May 1970, Cambodia Correspondence, MCSL.

109. MCS to Mrs. George Frame, 12 January 1967, Press Relations Correspondence, MCSL. On Graham and the war, see Katherine Graham, *Personal History* (New York: Vintage Books, 1998), 399–401. In 1951, Philip Graham wrote to Smith stating that "both Mrs. Graham and I are wild-eyed fans of yours," a statement that speaks of the impact of her "Declaration of Conscience." See Philip Graham to MCS, 3 July 1951, Press Reports Correspondence, MCSL. In Katherine Graham's memoirs there is no mention of Smith.

110. Smith, *Declaration of Conscience*, 431.

111. For Nixon's statements, see Nixon, *RN*, 403.

112. Kathleen Hinkley to MCS, 2 June 1970, Declaration of Conscience Correspondence, MCSL.

113. Donna Peterson to MCS, 1 June 1970, Declaration of Conscience Correspondence, MCSL.

114. Gabriel Kolko, *The Roots of American Foreign Policy* (Boston: Beacon Press, 1969), 89–90. Also, see Gabriel Kolko, *Anatomy of a War: Vietnam, the United States, and the Modern Historical Experience* (New York: Pantheon Books, 1985).

115. Frances Fitzgerald, *Fire in the Lake: The Vietnamese and the Americans in Vietnam* (Boston: Little, Brown, 1972).

116. Kolko, *The Roots of American Foreign Policy*, 131–32.

117. Leo P. Ribuffo, "Moral Judgments and the Cold War: Reflections on Reinhold Niebuhr, William Appleman Williams, and John Lewis Gaddis," in *Cold War Triumphalism: The Misuse of History After the Fall of Communism*, ed. Ellen Schrecker (New York: The New Press, 2004), 305n60.

118. Small, *Antiwarriors*, 88. Hans J. Morgenthau, *A New Foreign Policy for the United States* (New York: Frederick A. Praeger, Publishers, 1969), 27, 138. Morgenthau explained: "Communism in South Vietnam is irrelevant to the containment of Soviet or Chinese Communism since Vietnamese Communism is not controlled by either of them. Our fight against the South Vietnamese Communists is relevant only to our relations with South Vietnam, which, even if it were governed by Communists, is unlikely to affect the balance of power in Asia" (132). According to one historian, in these years, there was little scholarly attention paid to critics of the Cold War. See Thomas G. Paterson, "Introduction: American Critics of the Cold War and Their Alternative" in Thomas G. Paterson, ed., *Cold War Critics: Alternatives to American Foreign Policy in the Truman Years* (Chicago: Quadrangle Books, 1971), 4.

119. Isserman and Kazin, *Divided America*, 183.

120. On the Senate floor, for example, Smith stated that communists played "an important role in organizing and directing these youngsters." Quoted in Wallace, *Politics of Conscience*, 179.

121. Hunt, *Lyndon Johnson's War*, 11, 87–88.

122. Quoted in Brocheux, *Ho Chi Minh*, 178. Diem was fearless face-to-face with Ho, telling his capturer: "You are a criminal who has burned and destroyed the country, and you have held me prisoner. . . . You speak a language without conscience." Quoted in Jacobs, *America's Miracle Man in Vietnam*, 30.

123. Gerard J. DeGroot, *A Noble Cause? America and the Vietnam War* (New York: Longman, 2000), 102–3. Also, see Moyar, *Triumph Forsaken*, xiv, 9–10.

124. Moyar, *Triumph Forsaken*, 17–19. Richard Nixon wrote of intellectuals "looking at idealized portraits of Ho Chi Minh gazing beneficently upon the children gathered around him and seeing a mythical national father figure rather than the brutal dictator he really was." See Richard Nixon, *No More Vietnams* (New York: Arbor House, 1985), 22.

125. Moyar, *Triumph Forsaken*, 91, 93.

126. Quoted in DeGroot, *A Noble Cause?* 124.

127. "Vietnam Policy," Vietnam War Press Reports, MCSL.

128. Crouse, ed., *Dear Senator Smith*, 106–7.

129. Ralph White to MCS, 1 May 1970, Vietnam War Correspondence, MCSL.

130. Wilma Nichols to MCS, 8 March 1969, Vietnam War Correspondence, MCSL.

131. Smith, *Declaration of Conscience*, 430–35, 437. Also, see "Mrs. Smith Warns of Repression," *New York Times*, 2 June 1970. MCS to Helen Huzarewicz, 22 July 1970, Declaration of Conscience Correspondence, MCSL.

132. Small, *Antiwarriors*, 128–29. Sherman, *No Place for a Woman*, 213.

133. MCS to Robert Curran, 3 July 1970, Declaration of Conscience Correspondence, MCSL.

134. Laura Laviaster, 6 June 1970, Declaration of Conscience Correspondence, MCSL.

135. The Theobald family to MCS, 3 June 1970, Declaration of Conscience Correspondence, MCSL.

136. Richard Kaplan to MCS, 18 November 1970, Declaration of Conscience Correspondence, MCSL.

137. Wilma Thomas to MCS, 6 June 1970, Declaration of Conscience Correspondence, MCSL.

138. Anna Glidden to MCS, 2 June 1970, Declaration of Conscience Correspondence, MCSL.

139. Dan Lane to MCS, 3 June 1970, Declaration of Conscience Correspondence, MCSL.

140. John Wentworth to MCS, 3 June 1970, Declaration of Conscience Correspondence, MCSL.

141. Tristram Coffin to MCS, 2 June 1970, Declaration of Conscience Correspondence, MCSL.

142. "Viet Pullback 'Westy's Idea,'" Vietnam War Press Reports, MCSL.

143. MCS to Holly Gardiner, 29 May 1970, Cambodia Correspondence, MCSL. For more on a Republican dove, see Fredrik Logevall, "A Delicate Balance: John Sherman Cooper and the Republican Opposition to the Vietnam War," in *Vietnam and the American Political Tradition: The Politics of Dissent*, ed. Randall B. Woods (Cambridge: Cambridge University Press, 2003): 237–58.

144. MCS to Ted Moon, 13 October 1971, Cambodia Correspondence, MCSL.

145. Dean, *Imperial Brotherhood*, 239.

146. Small, *Antiwarriors*, 28–29.

147. Cited in "The Army on Trial," Vietnam War Press Reports, MCSL.

148. "The Talk of the Town," The *New Yorker*, Vietnam War Press Reports, MCSL.

149. "Vienam's Veterans They've Come Home to Maine," *Maine Times*, 23 April 1971, Vietnam War Press Reports, MCSL.

150. Charles Knox to MCS, 5 November 1969, Vietnam War Correspondence, MCSL.

151. Stanley Karnov, *Vietnam: A History* (New York: Penguin Books, 1984), 529.

152. Clarence R. Wyatt, *Paper Soldiers: The American Press and the Vietnam War* (New York: W. W. Norton & Company, 1993), 119–20, 122. Also, see Joyce Hoffman, *On Their Own: Women Journalists and the American Experience in Vietnam* (Cambridge, Mass.: Da Capo Press, 2008), 252.

153. Sheehan, *A Bright Shining Lie*, 347.

154. Moyar, *Triumph Forsaken*, xvi, 234, 241. Moyar argues that Diem, "who has been incessantly depicted as an obtuse, tyrannical reactionary by orthodox historians, was in reality a very wise and effective leader" (xiv).

155. Marguerite Higgins, *Our Vietnam Nightmare* (New York: Harper & Row, Publishers, 1965), 5, 14, 63, 68, 105–6, 288. That the Buddhist protest movement did not rise from popular dissatisfaction with Diem, but instead was "a power play by a few Buddhist leaders," see Moyar, *Triumph Forsaken*, xvi.

156. Higgins, *Our Vietnam Nightmare*, 141, 146.

157. Hoffman, *On Their Own*, 125–26.

158. "The Hanoi Papers Reveal a Double Standard," Vietnam War Press Reports, MCSL.

159. "The Great Atrocity Hunt," *National Review*, 16 December 1969, Vietnam War Press Reports, MCSL.

160. Quoted in Fry, *Debating Vietnam*, 95.

161. U. S. Grant Sharp, "We Could Have Won in Vietnam Long Ago," *Reader's Digest* (May 1969), 118–20, Vietnam War Press Reports, MCSL.

162. Deborah Nelson, *The War Behind Me: Vietnam Veterans Confront the Truth about U.S. War Crimes* (New York: Basic Books, 2008), 3.

163. DeGroot, *A Noble Cause?* 297.

164. Main Street Americans were not silent about Vietcong atrocities. One can find examples not only in letters to Smith but also in letters to Dr. Benjamin Spock, the popular family physician. In 1968, one California man wrote: "For us to abandon innocent Vietnamese peasants to the Viet Cong savages would be not only cowardly and immoral, it would be lousy preventive pediatrics." See Foley, ed. *Dear Dr. Spock*, 172.

165. John Grombach to MCS, 10 January 1967, Vietnam War Correspondence, MCSL. According to Richard Nixon, "Diem appointed his top officials without regard to their faith. Of his eighteen cabinet ministers, five were Catholic, five Confucianist, and eight Buddhists, including the vice president and the foreign minister." Furthermore, most critics wrongly attributed the Buddhist suicides to Diem's repression. "Nobody seemed to notice when the number of suicides increased after he was overthrown." See Nixon, *No More Vietnams*, 65, 67.

166. Gordon Batcheller to MCS, 14 June 1970, Vietnam War Correspondence, MCSL.

167. Mary Landin to MCS, 7 February 1970, Vietnam War Correspondence, MCSL.

168. Patty Mulheren to MCS, 13 May 1970, Vietnam War Correspondence, MCSL.

169. Debbie Blanchard to MCS, 26 April 1970, Vietnam War Correspondence, MCSL.

170. For a film portrayal of "demonic" communism played out against American prisoners of war, see *Hanoi Hilton* (USA: 1987). Released by Cannon Films. 130 minutes.

171. "Statement of Armistead I. Selden, Jr. Acting Assistant Secretary of Defense for International Security Affairs," 3 December 1970, Vietnam War Correspondence; Senator Joseph Montoya to His Holiness, the Pope, 22 August 1969, Vietnam War

Correspondence; G. Warren Nutter to MCS, 24 November 1969, Vietnam War Correspondence, MCSL.

172. Armistead I. Selden, Jr. to MCS, 29 December 1971, Vietnam War Correspondence, MCSL.

173. Courtois et al. *The Black Book of Communism*, 4.

174. Quoted in Karnov, *Vietnam*, 169.

175. Quoted in Kaiser, *American Tragedy*, 339.

176. Stanley Hauerwas explains Ramsey's thinking as follows: "The Christian may be obligated to turn their cheek, but they are not to turn their neighbor's cheek." See Paul Ramsey, *The Just War: Force and Political Responsibility* (Lanham, Md.: Rowman & Littlefield Publishers, Inc. 2002), xi.

177. Dennis J. Doolin to MCS, 19 January 1972, Defense Correspondence, MCSL.

178. "Many Political Leaders Aid Hanoi, Sen. Smith Charges in Skowhegan," Vietnam War Press Reports, MCSL.

179. Moyar, *Triumph Forsaken*, xi.

180. DeBenedetti and Chadfield, *An American Ordeal*, 283.

181. DeBenedetti and Chadfield, *An American Ordeal*, 280–81, 284.

182. Mitchell K. Hall, *Because of Their Faith: CALCAV and Religious Opposition to the Vietnam War* (New York: Columbia University Press, 1990), 63, 66, 104.

183. Small, *Antiwarriors*, 3, 24, 36, 41, 67–68, 153, 155. The Soviets were upset over the mining, but they did not cancel the May meeting.

184. Walter LaFeber, *America, Russia, and the Cold War, 1945–1971*, 2nd ed.(New York: John Wiley and Sons, Inc. 1972), 273–74.

185. DeGroot, *A Noble Cause?* 10.

186. On the shift to congressional politics and the people's loss of confidence in the government, see DeBenedetti and Chatfield, *An American Ordeal*, 285, 298.

187. Sherman, *No Place for a Woman*, 274n100.

188. Jay Powell to MCS, 1 June 1970, Vietnam War Correspondence, MCSL. On polarities of tough versus soft in rhetoric, see Frank Costigliola, "Reading for Meaning," in *Explaining the History of American Foreign Relations*, 2nd Ed., ed. Michael J. Hogan and Thomas G. Paterson (Cambridge: Cambridge University Press, 2004), 295.

189. Christian P. Potholm, *This Splendid Game: Maine Campaigns and Elections, 1940–2002* (Lanham, Md.: Lexington Books, 2003), 87. According to Potholm, "Had she briefly aired even one commercial it is likely she would have defeated Bill Hathaway in 1972."

190. Wallace, *Politics of Conscience*, 187–88; Schmidt, *Margaret Chase Smith*, 319–29; and Sherman, *No Place for a Woman*, 214–18.

191. Wyatt, *Paper Soldiers*, 182. The polling was in October 1967.

192. Powers, *Not Without Honor*, 324.

193. Interestingly, Senator J. William Fulbright, the best known Vietnam War "dove," lost his bid for another Senate term in 1974 by a 65 to 35 percent margin.

Conclusion

Senator Margaret Chase Smith won election after election, serving in Congress for over thirty years, proving that a woman even without any college education could succeed in politics. She accomplished many political firsts for a woman, but her emergence as a genuine Cold Warrior was also remarkable. For her, communism was a sinister force focused on the goal of world domination. Her antagonism toward the communist menace was representative of an American stand that viewed communism as a corrupt system that allowed leaders to order the wanton destruction of human lives, often without any accountability for their acts.[1]

Smith and many Americans also appeared to favor the notion of American exceptionalism, a grand narrative that highlighted the freedoms and values of the United States and that offered a better model to other nations throughout the world. Freedom was paramount. For example, in his article "American Foreign Policy and the Blessings of Liberty," published in January 1962 in the *American Historical Review*, historian Samuel Flagg Bemis wrote that America's "Blessings of Liberty" were worth fighting for even if that meant a nuclear showdown with "Red imperialism." He could not accept "defeatism" and allow "Communist revolution and slavery" to destroy the precious freedoms that America stood for since its origins.[2] Such thinking by this professor emeritus of Yale University was surprisingly common among ordinary Americans. The language or specific statements of preventing the communists from dominating the world seemed like "common sense."[3]

Given the value system of mainstream Americans and the potency of Cold War emotions and language, it seems appropriate to argue that crude and distasteful as anticommunist tactics could be anticommunism made sense to Smith and countless Americans. One did not have to side with Joseph McCarthy to be a legitimate anticommunist and clearly it is a mistake to view all forms of anticommunism as McCarthyism. Certainly, contradictions existed when Americans sought to restrict the freedoms of communists, but most anticommunists, including most who opposed McCarthy, did not judge American society as repressive to the level found in radical literature.

Novelist Howard Fast, who was a member of the American Communist Party during the early Cold War period, wrote of the "witch hunt" and the "kind of terror this country had never seen before or since." Simply put, there was a "spreading, creeping terror" that "overtook the country" and people experienced "professional destruction."[4] Even liberal Hollywood, "saturated with fear," turned its back on leftists.[5] In dramatic language, Fast wrote of McCarthy's manner of accusing communists and how "he shrouded each evocation of the devil in such nasty delight that you could fairly smell the smoke." McCarthy gave the era its name, but the whole American establishment spent countless dollars "in a gigantic campaign of anti-Communist hatred and slander."[6] The Truman government created "a framework of hatred and terror" with its loyalty test for government employees; the press poured out countless messages of anticommunism; the House Committee on Un-American Activities was a "hateful" committee that adopted fascism in its "fraudulent, hysterical battle" against the progressive left; J. Edgar Hoover, the director of the Federal Bureau of Investigations, was "a little Hitler" and "shadow dictator of the United States"; and the "terrifying" Communist Control Act of 1954 "legally turned America into a police state."[7] Fast argued that in this "crazy time of hysteria," the United States was the only Western democracy to carry out persecution against the Communist Party. It was "the greatest hate campaign in American history," targeting communists who were "gentle, decent people of total morality."[8] In Fast's eyes, McCarthyism and anticommunism were synonymous.

Fast is an example of a small number of Americans who saw themselves as among the enlightened who understood the benefits of communist ideals. The irony was their ignorance, for many years, of a genuine horror and "reign of terror" which had occurred under the leadership of Joseph Stalin, Mao, and others which resulted in the death of tens of millions of innocent Soviet and Chinese citizens. In his study of the human cost of communism in China (requested by Senator Thomas J. Dodd [D-CT]), Richard L. Walker, Director of the Institute of International Studies at the University of South Carolina, wrote in 1971: "Those who wish to rationalize public assassinations, purges of classes and groups or slave labor as a necessary expedient for China's progress are resorting to the same logic which justified a Hitler and his methods for dealing with economic depression in the Third Reich."[9]

The truth is many Americans who spoke of global terror often warned of the "great threatening and towering evil of Communism."[10]

As for Smith, the strong moral tone of much of her national security views shared common ground with conservative Christian thinking, even though she appeared to have no direct connection with specific conservative Christian individuals or organizations. In addition to her identification with and appreciation of a Christian framework to combat communism, she upheld masculine ideals to prove her worthiness to face the aggressive enemy. Although her rise to political prominence occurred outside the "brotherhood" of privilege and power that was the typical experience of major foreign policymakers,[11] she rarely lost any ground to her male Cold Warrior colleagues. In the mid-1950s, one foreign woman's magazine referred to her as "one of the most balanced and nerveless legislators" in Congress.[12] She hated circumlocution and her direct manner projected strength.

Smith fought McCarthyism at considerable risk to her political career, but her abhorrence of communism was no less than that of McCarthy. In fact, her opposition to communism was probably more serious and genuine, in light of McCarthy's questionable anticommunist motives and strategies. After June 1, 1950, when she confronted McCarthy for his irresponsible methods, she became the darling of those who desired a better way of dealing with communist threats. She made the cover of *Newsweek* and there was talk of her as a potential vice president. Some conservatives were unhappy with her stand against McCarthy and to them she belonged to the eastern and liberal Republican "Me Too" bloc. They were partly wrong. She was a moderate on many domestic issues, yet McCarthyites could not successfully characterize her as a so-called "sissified" eastern establishment figure or "godless" politician who was soft on communism.

Smith's response to the Korean War in her syndicated column "Washington and You" clarified her Cold Warrior credentials. In her no-nonsense manner, she continued to alert Americans that the United States was letting its guard down by forgetting the lessons of history. Warning the people that they could not afford to embrace an unhealthy attitude of overconfidence and complacency, she was a female politician willing to support the use of the atomic bomb against Asian communists. This was a frightening idea to be sure, but her Cold Warrior stand on the Korean conflict reflected the emotions of other Americans who welcomed her support of allowing MacArthur to drop atomic bombs on communist foes. Her analysis of the Korean War and characterization of communist leaders as evil men resonated with many of those who demanded a tougher America to face a growing red menace. The year before he died, McCarthy congratulated Smith for her hard-line stand against giving aid to communist and Yugoslavia leader Josip Broz Tito.[13] This praise and especially her push for legislation to ban the Communist Party in the United States suggest a less than celebratory, right-wing, side of Smith.

There was no mistaking Smith's toughness on the issue of nuclear credibility. She was a champion of "massive retaliation" in the 1950s and her vote against the Nuclear Test Ban Treaty of 1963 clearly demonstrated there was no softening of her stand against communism. In an ABC television interview in August 1963, she stated that an emphasis on military spending did not hurt domestic programs.[14] Again her recognition as a moderate on civil rights and other issues certainly did not apply to national security. By the late sixties, her opposition to the Safeguard anti-ballistic-missile system was not due to any adoption of liberal views. Rather, she took a hawkish stand against any money toward a system that appeared unable to stem communist world domination. Where others saw nuclear arms buildup as insanity, she saw nuclear deterrence as an effective strategy to combat communism.[15]

In her final years in the Senate, she turned more of her attention to the "moral decay" which she believed was evident in American society. Convinced that national security depended on a strong moral society, she spoke out against the forces that challenged her values and sense of morality. She upheld "a high sense of ethics" that recognized sin and the importance of character and responsibility; in her mind, it was tragic that "the end justifies the means" was a creed increasingly adopted by many Americans unwilling to respect traditional values. Smith was unhappy that religious leaders embraced "personalized revisions of theology," and that the new morality modeled by "immoral" celebrities had a strong impact on young people.[16] There was a fear that young people were seeking easy and quick answers from the wrong sources, unwilling to appreciate the good things that America had stood for since its origins. Smith found college radicalism particularly troubling and others were likewise critical of the romanticism of college radicals and their attacks on the military, business, and government. "Having had no experience with such a phenomenon as the Great Depression, and having only the most superficial view of the magnitude of the task of making even gradual changes in the vast economy of a land like ours," one evangelical wrote, "they [campus radicals] mouth endlessly the slogans of 'destroying this rotten order' and of 'cleaning up the mess the older generation has left.' Theirs is a bland assumption that there is a law of Phoenix-regeneration by which new and viable order rises out of chaos."[17]

Campus radicals represented a small minority, but when young people in general flouted authority and traditional values and did their own thing, parents feared that their children would do the same, a sign that the nation was "falling apart." And activist antiwar college students "were disproportionately represented among the children of the establishment at leading colleges and universities." Their parents, who were influential in political, business, and media circles, worried that the war could push their children to become hippies, criminals, drug addicts, or revolutionaries.[18] A common reaction of many such parents was to oppose the war. Smith, not a parent and unsympathetic of the politicization and generational identity of young people, maintained her Cold Warrior stand. Supportive of her, other Americans viewed military action in Southeast Asia as a worthwhile cause, arguing that there was a gap between young people "long in idealism and the desires for immediate accomplishment" and older people who defeated totalitarianism in World War II only to face the communist world that sought "the overthrow of our country and the Democratic or free world."[19]

As more people feared that the nation was tearing apart, Smith wanted to see a forceful military effort. Tormented by the statistical numbers of Americans killed and the chants of antiwar protesters, Lyndon Johnson was one who appreciated the steadfast support she voiced on the Vietnam War. In one of his final letters before he turned the presidency over to Nixon, Johnson wrote to Smith: "I am indeed proud to call you 'my friend'—a good friend, a steadfast friend, a loyal friend. You have helped the load that I have carried as President and you have enriched my life. Thank you, from the bottom of my heart."[20]

Smith received plenty of correspondence that reinforced her hawkish stand. A Texan and World War II veteran thanked her for highlighting the dangers of left extremism and for her support of the soldiers.[21] In January 1968, an Indiana woman, echoing others, told Smith that the Vietnam War represented a fight against "the entire Communist bloc of nations."[22] One soldier about to begin his ninth month in Southeast Asia reported to Smith that "the South Vietnamese really like us and want to please us in every way as best they can and win for the Free World."[23] In antiwar circles such a statement would be viewed as false, but it was these types of letters that bolstered her confidence that she was doing the right thing in supporting American involvement in Southeast Asia. Even as they abhorred the Vietnam War and the tragic loss of lives and fracturing of American society, there were those who continued to see communism as a ruthless monolithic system which destroyed lives in wild abandonment. Responding to a request by Smith to provide additional information for a critic of the war, William B. Macomber, Jr., Assistant Secretary for Congressional Relations, clarified that "no independent country yet in history has willingly and freely elected a Communist government."[24]

Commenting on Tom Dooley's *Deliver Us From Evil: The Story of Viet Nam's Flight to Freedom* (1956), one historian argues that "Dooley may have fabricated or exaggerated the atrocities he claimed to have witnessed in Vietnam."[25] If it is true that there were millions of Americans duped by Dooley's account of communist evil, many embraced a theology of anticommunism which had a much broader foundation than the writings of one popular missionary doctor. There was enough information on communist criminality in general to make Dooley's accounts believable in the sixties and into the seventies. Christian publications were especially serious about reporting the violence of communism. News reports informed Americans that the North Vietnamese were "eradicating Roman Catholicism" and for years the Vatican had virtually no contact with the remaining 300 North Vietnamese priests. Fundamentalist preacher Carl McIntire was one who was relentless in fighting against the "international conspiracy of godless Communism." For example, in early April 1970, he marched with 50,000 others in Washington demanding "We want victory in Viet Nam."[26] Almost three decades after the publication of Dooley's book, an American president singled out the Soviet Union as an "evil empire" and countless ordinary Americans concurred.[27]

A growing number of Americans did not view the communist danger as overwhelming, including Robert McNamara, who concluded that American involvement in Southeast Asia had been "terribly wrong."[28] Even President Johnson, by 1967, was offering a more upbeat account of American relations with the Soviets.[29] In contrast, Smith gave no signs that she recognized the possibility of moderating forces and change stirring in communist regimes. By the early 1970s, many Americans disagreed with her belief that the communists sought to conquer the world and that the United States had a moral responsibility to stop them. This caused her to fear that the violence, militancy, and anarchy in American society gave the Kremlin confidence in conquering the United States without a nuclear attack. She asked, "Why would they want to have the tremendous problem of rehabilitating and reconstructing a nuclear-devastated country when they are growing so confident from trends here that their own advocates among Americans will ultimately deliver this country to them?"[30] A similar message that was simplistic and dangerous in the eyes of antiwar activists was her 1971 letter to the *New York Times*: "Military weakness and national insecurity literally invite diplomatic blackmail and the strategy of terror from the Soviet Union. . . . Let us pray that recognition and action on the frightful truth comes sufficiently in advance to bolster our national security to such strength as to save our nation and people."[31]

In his study of gender and foreign policy, Robert Dean argues that establishment figures, such as John F. Kennedy, were warrior intellectuals who "deployed a rhetoric of polarized opposites against political opponents: manly strength and feminized weakness, youth and age, stoic austerity and debilitating luxury."[32] Even though Smith was old, her rhetoric was far from weak and her anticommunism did not waver as had been the case of some male warrior intellectuals.

Smith showed greater signs of being one-dimensional, having an overarching ideology without analysis of nuance, but her electoral defeat in 1972 was not primarily due to her hawkish views, as some argue.[33] To be sure, the flawed packaging and application of her antiwar message did hurt her some. Her response to antiwar protest lacked wisdom and she had the tendency to write all young people off as irresponsible. She was guilty of overreacting and losing sight of the antiwar concerns and activism that were commendable. Smith saw signs of an erosion of moral values, but she did not see that many of the young people who viewed American participation in the war as immoral were also upholding moral values in their own understanding. She and many antiwar college students were coming at it from opposite angles, but there was the common ground of desiring a return to some moral standards.[34] Unfortunately, in her 1972 memoirs she did not find grace to publicly admit failures and her American stand on the communist threat, which shone brightly throughout the fifties and the early sixties, lost some of its luster. Smith's reactionary tone likely caused a rethinking among some who had been sympathetic and supportive of her efforts in earlier years. However, more significant was the larger backlash of many Americans to the rabble-rousing speeches and violent behavior of a small number of radical protesters who cast a shadow on the credibility and efforts of the many Americans who opposed the war.

Politicians like Smith benefited from the fact that anticommunism persisted in the minds of countless Americans, and, in fact, voting patterns suggested that younger people were more hawkish than those beyond fifty years old.[35] Her position on nuclear arms did not result in much negative publicity because this issue, with the exception of antinuclear protest groups, did not generate consistent emotional intensity, and outside college campuses most of the opposition to the Vietnam War was not due to its immorality, but to its futility.[36] Senator J. William Fulbright, a realist intellectual who according to one biographer failed to give evil its due, complained in 1973: "It is much easier to inflame the emotions of members of Congress—and the public as well—by emphasizing the alleged brutality and intransigencies of any Communist country than it is to sell a restrained and reasonable policy."[37] According to one study on anticommunism, even the labor union movement continued to view communism as a menace. As late as 1974, George Meany, leader of the AFL-CIO, attacked liberal politicians for their tolerance of communism, stating that "we owe the cold warriors an apology."[38] In his work on the contested memory of the Vietnam War, Robert J. McMahon claims that the comments of conservatives "betray a palpable frustration with their failure to erase societal memories of Vietnam as the lost, pointless, morally repugnant war."[39] There is truth to this. However, there are those who are equally guilty of dismissing the commitment of many Americans in fighting communism. Smith was one who viewed the red menace in Southeast Asia and elsewhere as a genuine evil force and opposition to it was not pointless. The images of death and destruction in Vietnam were haunting, but she sincerely thought her unwavering message was the correct one, especially at a time when she sensed with others that a "national consensus on America's role in furthering freedom and opposing tyranny throughout the world is fast evaporating."[40]

Smith had experienced tough economic times in her early years and the burdens of a woman in politics, but her construction of a Cold Warrior image helped make her victorious at the political polls. She fully supported the United States stepping forward after World War II to thwart the red menace. In her Senate years, she heard from thousands of Americans who appeared comfortable sharing their Cold War views with a no-nonsense, reassuring, and in the eyes of some, harsh senator. For others, it made a difference that she was not an ideologue on most political issues. Her story is one of a local girl from small-town America making her way successfully in the corridors of political power dominated by well-educated males. In her final years, some of her assessments were not judicious and she was short on energy and vision, but there was always support from those who accepted the notion that America had a moral duty to confront the sinister ways of communism.

NOTES

1. There was a lack of checks and balances to stop authoritarian leaders from committing criminal acts. In *We Now Know*, Gaddis asks, "[W]ho is to tell the authoritarian in charge that he is about to do something stupid?" (20).

2. Samuel Flagg Beamis, "American Foreign Policy and the Blessings of Liberty," *The American Historical Review* 67, no. 2 (January 1962), 292, 301, 305.

3. Costigliola, "Reading for Meaning," 297, 299.

4. Howard Fast, *Being Red* (Boston: Houghton Mifflin Company 1990), 25, 132, 145, 182.

5. Fast, *Being Red*, 161, 168.

6. Fast, *Being Red*, 1, 27.

7. Fast, *Being Red*, 146–47, 166, 177, 198, 336–37.

8. Fast, *Being Red*, 86, 243, 261, 265.

9. The Human Cost of Communism in China (Washington, D.C.: U.S. Government Printing Office, 1971), xi.

10. "Religion Called Force to Stop Reds," *Los Angeles Times*, 10 July 1950.

11. Dean, *Imperial Brotherhood*, 13.

12. "Margaret Chase Smith," Scrapbook, Vol. 164, 105, MCSL.

13. MCS to Joseph McCarthy, 14 July 1956, Smith-McCarthy Correspondence, MCSL.

14. Senator Margaret Chase Smith Interview, ABC-TV, 13 August 1963, MCSL.

15. As one evangelical wrote in 1967: "The fiftieth anniversary of the Bolshevik revolution should remind free men of the necessity to continue their vigilant opposition to Communism in all its manifestations." See, "The Danger of Christian-Marxist Dialogue," *CT*, 27 October 1967, 26–27.

16. Smith, *Declaration of Conscience*, 422–25.

17. "The Rationale of the Student Left," *CT*, 8 November 1968, 31–32.

18. Small, *Antiwarriors*, 80–81, 162.

19. "Vietnam in Perspective," Vietnam War Press Reports, MCSL.

20. Lyndon Johnson to MCS, 17 January 1969, Correspondence, MCSL.

21. H. Dick Golding to MCS, 8 June 1970, Declaration of Conscience Correspondence, MCSL.

22. Carolyn Brooks to MCS, 19 January 1968, Vietnam War Correspondence, MCSL.

23. Gerald Griffen to MCS, 22 May 1970, Vietnam War Correspondence, MCSL. As a Nixon supporter, it was his opinion that "[t]he only people that want the Communists to win in Vietnam are their student and professor pals back home."

24. William Macomber, Jr. to MCS, 28 April 1967, Vietnam War Correspondence, MCSL.

25. Jacobs, *America's Miracle Man in Vietnam*, 149.

26. "A Theology of Violence?," *CT*, 22 November 1968, 49–50. "North Viet Nam Case Study," *CT*, 22 November 1968, 44. Carl McIntire's Victory: 'In This Sign Conquer,' *CT*, 24 April 1970, 35.

27. Frances Fitzgerald, *Way Out There in the Blue: Reagan, Star Wars and the End of the Cold War* (New York: Touchstone, 2000), 25–26. Especially sensitive to the phrase "evil empire" were many Bible-believing Christians, Fitzgerald writes: "To conservative evangelicals . . . the phrase would trip-wire the whole eschatology of Armageddon."

28. McNamara, *In Retrospect*, xx, 30.

29. John Dumbrell, *President Lyndon Johnson and Soviet Communism* (Manchester: Manchester University Press, 2004), 16.

30. Smith, *Declaration of Conscience*, 402.

31. "Weakness Invites Strategy of Terror," *New York Times*, 20 November 1971; MCS to the *New York Times*, 28 October 1971, Press Relations Correspondence, MCSL.

32. Dean, *Imperial Brotherhood*, 170.

33. For example, see Jeffreys-Jones, *Changing Differences*, 127. Lacking is evidence to support the argument that the "Vietnam War was the critical factor in her defeat."

34. This paragraph draws from a more general discussion of generational conflict in "America's Young People," *CT*, 19 June 1970, 22–23. Also, see "Students on the Rampage," *CT*, 11 October 1968, 25.

35. LaFeber, *America, Russia, and the Cold War, 1945–1971*, 2nd ed, 273–74. On the backlash of Americans to radical activities, see D. Elton Trueblood, "The Protest Mentality," *CT*, 17 July 1970, 14–15.

36. DeGroot, *A Noble Cause?* 307.

37. Woods, *Fulbright*, 642, 692.

38. Powers, *Not Without Honor*, 340.

39. Robert J. McMahon, "SHAFR Presidential Address: Contested Memory: The Vietnam War and American Society, 1975–2001," *Diplomatic History* 26, no. 2 (Spring 2002), 182.

40. "Has America Passed Her Peak?" *CT*, 1 March 1968, 28–29.

Bibliography

PRIMARY SOURCES

Margaret Chase Smith Library
Aiken-Smith Correspondence
Armed Services Committee Correspondence
Cambodia Correspondence
Communism Correspondence
Communism Folder
Declaration of Conscience Correspondence
Declaration of Conscience Folder
Foreign Relations Correspondence
McCarthy, Joseph R. Folder
McCarthyism Correspondence
Korean War Correspondence
Press Relations Correspondence
Religion Correspondence
Scrapbook
Smith-McCarthy Correspondence
Smith-Rhodri Jeffreys-Jones interview, 29 July 1991
Statements and Speeches
Vietnam War Correspondence
Vietnam War Press Reports
Views and Issues Correspondence
"Washington and You"
World Trip Report

FILM

Hanoi Hilton (USA: 1987). Released by Cannon Films. 130 minutes.

OTHER GOVERNMENT DOCUMENTS

The Report of the President's Commission on Campus Unrest, Superintendent of Documents, U.S. Government Printing Office, Washington, D.C. 20402.

NEWSPAPERS AND MAGAZINES
(ADDITIONAL TO MCS SCRAPBOOK)

Chicago Tribune
Christianity Today
Christian Science Monitor
Evening Star (Washington)
Frederick Post (Maryland)
Herald-Tribune (New York)
Houston Chronicle
Lewiston Daily Sun
Lewiston Evening Journal
Los Angeles Herald Examiner
Los Angeles Times
Manchester (N.H.) Union Leader
New York Times
Portland Press Herald
Saturday Evening Post
St. Louis Globe-Democrat
Washington Post

SECONDARY SOURCES

Acheson, Dean. *The Korean War*. New York: W. W. Norton & Company, 1971.
Ambrose, Stephen E. *Nixon: The Triumph of a Politician 1961–1972*. New York: Simon & Schuster, 1989.
Anderson, David. "The Vietnam War." In *A Companion to American Foreign Relations*, edited by Robert D. Schulzinger. Malden, Mass.: Blackwell Publishing, 2003.

Apers, Benjamin L. *Dictators, Democracy, and American Public Culture: Envisioning the Totalitarian Enemy, 1920s–1950s.* Chapel Hill: University of North Carolina Press, 2003.

Applebaum, Anne. *Gulag: A History.* New York: Anchor Books, 2003.

Appy, Christian G. *Patriots: The Vietnam War Remembered from All Sides.* New York: Viking, 2003.

———. *Working-Class War: American Combat Soldiers and Vietnam.* Chapel Hill: University of North Carolina Press, 1993.

Bailey, Thomas A. *The Man in the Street: The Impact of American Public Opinion on Foreign Policy.* New York: The Macmillan Company, 1948.

Baritz, Loren. *Backfire: A History of How American Culture Led Us into Vietnam and Made Us Fight the Way We Did.* New York: Ballantine Books, 1985.

Baron, Michael, and Steven Heller. *Red Scared! The Commie Menace in Propaganda and Popular Culture.* San Francisco: Chronicle Books, 2001.

Beamis, Samuel Flagg. "American Foreign Policy and the Blessings of Liberty." *The American Historical Review* 67, no. 2 (January 1962): 291–305.

Beisner, Robert L. *Dean Acheson: A Life in the Cold War.* Oxford: Oxford University Press, 2006.

———. "SHAFR Presidential Address: The Secretary, the Spy, and the Sage: Dean Acheson, Alger Hiss, and George Kennan." *Diplomatic History* 27, no. 1 (January 2003): 1–14.

Bellah, Robert. "Religion in America." *Dædalus* 96, no. 1 (Winter 1967): 1–21.

Berman, Larry. *No Peace, No Honor: Nixon, Kissinger, and Betrayal in Vietnam.* New York: The Free Press, 2001.

Bernstein, Robert A., and William W. Anthony. "The ABM Issue in the Senate, 1968–1970: The Importance of Ideology." *The American Political Science Review* 68, no. 3 (September 1974): 1198–1206.

Beschloss, Michael R. *The Crisis Years: Kennedy and Khrushchev 1960–1963.* New York: Edward Burlingame Books, 1991.

Black, Conrad. *The Invincible Quest: The Life of Richard Milhous Nixon.* Toronto: McClelland & Stewart, 2008.

Bottome, Egar. *The Balance of Terror: Nuclear Weapons and the Illusion of Security, 1945–1985*, rev. ed. Boston: Beacon Press, 1986.

Bradley, Mark Philip, and Marilyn B. Young, eds. *Making Sense of the Vietnam Wars: Local, National, and Transnational Perspectives.* Oxford: Oxford University Press, 2008.

Brocheux, Pierre. *Ho Chi Minh: A Biography.* Translated by Claire Duiker. Cambridge: Cambridge University Press, 2007.

Brokaw, Tom. *The Greatest Generation.* New York: Random House, 1998.

Buzzanco, Robert. "Where's the Beef? Culture without Power in the Study of U.S. Foreign Relations." *Diplomatic History* 24, no. 4 (Fall 2000): 623–32.

Calhoun, Charles C. *A Small College in Maine: Two Hundred Years of Bowdoin.* Brunswick, Maine: Bowdoin College, 1993.

Casey, Steven. "Selling NSC-68: The Truman Administration, Public Opinion, and the Politics of Mobilization, 1950–1951." *Diplomatic History* 29, no. 4 (September 2005): 655–90.

———. "White House Publicity Operations During the Korean War, June 1950–June 1951." *Presidential Studies Quarterly* 35, no. 4 (December 2005): 691–717.

Caute, David. *The Great Fear: The Anti-Communist Purge under Truman and Eisenhower.* New York: Simon and Schuster, 1977.

Chambers, Whittaker. *Witness.* New York: Random House, 1952.

Chang, Jung. *Wild Swans: Three Daughters of China.* New York: Anchor Books, 1992.

Chatfield, Charles. "At the Hands of Historians: The Antiwar Movement of the Vietnam Era." *Peace and Change* 29, no. 3 and 4 (2004): 483–526.

Clark, Charles E. *Bates Through the Years: An Illustrated History.* Lewiston, Maine: Bates College, 2005.

Condon, Richard H. "Maine Out of the Mainstream, 1945–1965." In *Maine: The Pine Tree State from Prehistory to the Present,* edited by Richard W. Judd, Edwin A. Churchill, and Joel W. Eastman. Orono: University of Maine, 1995.

Costigliola, Frank. "The Creation of Memory and Myth." In *Critical Reflections on the Cold War: Linking Rhetoric and History,* edited by Martin J. Medhurst and H. W. Brands. College Station: Texas A & M University Press, 2000.

———. "Reading for Meaning." In *Explaining the History of American Foreign Relations,* 2nd ed., edited by Michael J. Hogan and Thomas G. Paterson. Cambridge: Cambridge University Press, 2004.

Costigliola, Frank, and Thomas G. Paterson, "Defining and Doing the History of United States Foreign Relations: A Primer," in *Explaining the History of American Foreign Relations.* 2nd ed., edited by Michael J. Hogan and Thomas G. Paterson. Cambridge: Cambridge University Press, 2004.

Courtois, Séphance, et al. *The Black Book of Communism: Crimes, Terror, Repression.* Translated by Jonathan Murphy and Mark Kramer. Cambridge, Mass.: Harvard University Press, 1999.

Cronkite, Walter. *A Reporter's Life.* New York: Ballantine Books, 1996.

Crosby, Donald F. *God, Church, and Flag: Senator Joseph R. McCarthy and the Catholic Church, 1950–1957.* Chapel Hill: University of North Carolina Press, 1978.

Crouse, Eric R., ed. *Dear Senator Smith: Small-Town Maine Writes to Senator Margaret Chase Smith about the Vietnam War, 1967–1971.* Lanham, Md: Lexington Books, 2008.

———. "New Evangelicalism, *Christianity Today,* and U.S. Foreign Policy, 1956–1965." *Canadian Evangelical Review* 30–31 (Fall 2005–Spring 2006): 38–54.

———. "Popular Cold Warriors: Conservative Protestants, Communism, and Culture in Early Cold War America." *Journal of Religion and Popular Culture* II (Fall 2002): 1–16.

———. "Responding to the Reds: Conservative Protestants, Anti-Communism, and the Shaping of American Culture, 1945–1965." *Historical Papers 2002: Canadian Society of Church History Historical Papers,* edited by Bruce Reimer. 97–109.

———. "Senator Margaret Chase Smith Against McCarthyism: The Methodist Influence." *Methodist History* 46, no. 3 (April 2008): 167–78.

Cumings, Bruce. *The Origins of the Korean War, Volume II: The Roaring of the Cataract, 1947–1950.* Princeton, N.J.: Princeton University Press, 1990.

Cuordileone, K. A. "'Politics in an Age of Anxiety': Cold War Political Culture and the Crisis of American Masculinity, 1949–1960." *The Journal of American History* 87, no. 2 (2000): 515–45.

Daugherty, Leo. *The Vietnam War: Day by Day.* Miami: Lewis International, 2002.

Davies, Richard O. *Main Street Blues: The Decline of Small-Town America.* Columbus: Ohio State University Press, 1998.

Dean, Robert D. *Imperial Brotherhood: Gender and the Making of Cold War Foreign Policy.* Amherst: University of Massachusetts Press, 2001.

———. "Masculinity as Ideology: John F. Kennedy and the Domestic Politics of Foreign Policy." *Diplomatic History* 22, no. 1 (1998): 29–62.

DeBenedetti, Charles, and Charles Chatfield (assisting author). *An American Ordeal: The Antiwar Movement of the Vietnam War.* Syracuse, N.Y.: Syracuse University Press, 1990.

DeGroot, Gerald J. *A Noble Cause? America and the Vietnam War.* Essex, U.K.: Longman, 2000.

Divine, Robert A. *Eisenhower and the Cold War.* Oxford: Oxford University Press, 1981.

Dooley, Thomas A. *Deliver Us from Evil: The Story of Viet Nam's Flight to Freedom.* New York: Signet Books, 1962.

Duiker, William J. "Ho Chi Minh and the Strategy of People's War." In *The First Vietnam War: Colonial Conflict and Cold War Crisis*, edited by Mark Atwood Lawrence and Fredrik Logevall. Cambridge, Mass.: Harvard University Press, 2007.

Dumbrell, John. *President Lyndon Johnson and Soviet Communism.* Manchester: Manchester University Press, 2004.

Edelman, Bernard, ed. *Dear America: Letters Home from Vietnam.* New York: Pocket Books, 1986.

Ellsberg, Daniel. *Secrets: A Memoir of Vietnam and the Pentagon Papers.* New York: Viking, 2002.

Erickson, Robert P. "The Role of American Churches in the McCarthy Era." *Kirchliche Zeitgeschichte* 3, no. 1 (1990): 45–58.

Eskridge, Larry. "Billy Graham, the Jesus Generation, and the Idea of an Evangelical Youth Culture." *Church History* 67, no. 1 (March 1998): 83–106.

Farley, Miriam S. "Crisis in Korea." *Far Eastern Survey* 19, no. 14 (16 August 1950): 149–56.

Fast, Howard. *Being Red.* Boston: Houghton Mifflin Company, 1990.

Fitzgerald, Frances. *Fire in the Lake: The Vietnamese and the Americans in Vietnam.* Boston: Little, Brown, 1972.

———. *Way Out There in the Blue: Reagan, Star Wars and the End of the Cold War.* New York: Touchstone, 2000.

Fleming, Alice. *The Senator from Maine: Margaret Chase Smith.* New York: Thomas Y. Crowell Company, 1969.

Flynt, Wayne, and Gerald W. Berkley. *Taking Christianity to China: Alabama Missionaries in the Middle Kingdom, 1850–1950.* Tuscaloosa: The University of Alabama Press, 1997.

Foley, Michael S. *Confronting the War Machine: Draft Resistance During the Vietnam War.* Chapel Hill: The University of North Carolina Press, 2003.

———, ed. *Dear Dr. Spock: Letters about the Vietnam War to America's Favorite Baby Doctor.* New York: New York University Press, 2005.

Fraser, Steve, and Gary Gerstle. *Ruling America: A History of Wealth and Power in a Democracy.* Cambridge, Mass.: Harvard University Press, 2005.

Freeland, Richard M. *The Truman Doctrine and the Origin of McCarthyism: Foreign Policy, Domestic Politics, and Internal Security, 1946–1948.* New York: New York University Press, 1985.

Fried, Richard M. *Nightmare in Red: The McCarthy Era in Perspective.* New York: Oxford University Press, 1990.

Fry, Joseph A. *Debating Vietnam: Fulbright, Stennis, and Their Senate Hearings.* Lanham, Md.: Rowman & Littlefield Publishers, Inc., 2006.

Gaddis, John Foster. *The Long Peace: Inquiries Into the History of the Cold War.* Oxford: Oxford University Press, 1987.

Gaddis, John Lewis. *The Cold War: A New History.* New York: The Penguin Press, 2005.

———. *We Now Know: Rethinking Cold War History.* Oxford: Oxford University Press, 1997.

Gallant, Gregory Peter. "Margaret Chase Smith, McCarthyism and the Drive for Political Purification." PhD dissertation, University of Maine, 1992.

Garfinkle, Adam. *Telltale Hearts: The Origins and Impact of the Vietnam Antiwar Movements.* New York: St. Martin's Press, 1995.

Goldberg, Robert Alan. *Barry Goldwater.* New Haven, Conn.: Yale University Press, 1995.

Goldwater, Barry M. *With No Apologies: The Personal and Political Memoirs of United States Senator Barry M. Goldwater.* New York: Berkley Books, 1980.

Graham, Billy. *I Saw Your Sons at War: The Korean Diary.* Minneapolis: Billy Graham Association, 1953.

———. *World Aflame.* New York: Doubleday & Company, Inc., 1965.

Graham, Frank, Jr. *Margaret Chase Smith: Woman of Courage.* New York: The John Day Company, 1964.

Graham, Katherine. *Personal History.* New York: Vintage Books, 1998.

Graham, Thomas, and Bernard Kramer. "The Polls: ABM and Star Wars: Attitudes Toward Nuclear Defense, 1945–1985." *The Public Opinion Quarterly* 50, no. 1 (Spring 1986): 125–34.

Granastein, J. L., and Norman Hillmer. *For Better or For Worse: Canada and the United States to the 1990s.* Toronto: Copp Clark Pitman Ltd., 1991.

Grose, Peter. *Operation Rollback: America's Secret War Behind the Iron Curtain.* Boston: Houghton Mifflin Company, 2000.

Haas, Steven C. "Reassessing Lessons from the ABM Treaty." *International Affairs* 64, no. 2 (Spring 1988): 233–40.

Halberstam, David. *The Best and the Brightest.* New York: Random House, 1972.

Hall, Mitchell K. *Because of Their Faith: CALCAV and Religious Opposition to the Vietnam War.* New York: Columbia University Press, 1990.

Hamby, Alonzo L. *Man of the People: A Life of Harry S. Truman.* New York: Oxford University Press, 1995.

Harbutt, Fraser J. *The Cold War Era.* Malden, Mass.: Blackwell Publishers Inc., 2002.

Haynes, John Earl, and Harvey Klehr. *In Denial: Historians, Communism & Espionage.* San Francisco: Encounter Books, 2003.

———. *Early Cold War Spies: The Espionage Trials That Shaped American Politics.* Cambridge: Cambridge University Press, 2006.

Heale, M. J. *American Anticommunism: Combating the Enemy Within, 1830–1970.* Baltimore: Johns Hopkins University Press, 1990.

Heineman, Kenneth J. *Campus Wars: The Peace Movement at American State Universities in the Vietnam Era.* New York: New York University Press, 1993.

———. *God is a Conservative: Religion, Politics, and Morality in Contemporary America.* New York: New York University Press, 1998.

Hellman, Lillian. *Scoundrel Time.* New York: Bantam Books, 1977.

Henriksen, Margot A. *Dr. Strangelove's America: Society and Culture in the Atomic Age.* Berkeley: University of California Press, 1997.

Herbst, Susan. *Numbered Voices: How Opinion Polling has Shaped American Politics.* Chicago: The University of Chicago Press, 1993.

Herman, Arthur. *Joseph McCarthy: Reexamining the Life and Legacy of America's Most Hated Senator.* New York: The Free Press, 2000.

Herring, George C. *America's Longest War: The United States and Vietnam, 1950–1975.* 2nd ed. New York: Alfred A. Knopf, 1986.

Hess, Gary R. *Presidential Decisions for War: Korea, Vietnam, and the Persian Gulf.* Baltimore: The Johns Hopkins University Press, 2001.

———. "The Unending Debate: Historians and the Vietnam War." *Diplomatic History* 18, Issue 2 (1994): 239–64.

Higgins, Marguerite. *War in Korea: The Report of a Woman Combat Correspondent.* Garden City, N.Y.: Doubleday & Company, Inc., 1951.

———. *Our Vietnam Nightmare.* New York: Harper & Row, 1965.

Himmelstein, Jerome L. *To the Right: The Transformation of American Conservatism.* Berkeley: University of California Press, 1992.

Hoffman, Joyce. *On Their Own: Women Journalists and the American Experience in Vietnam.* Cambridge, Mass.: Da Capo Press, 2008.

Hogan, Michael J., and Thomas G. Paterson. *Explaining History of American Foreign Relations.* 2nd ed. Cambridge: Cambridge University Press, 2004.

Holifield, E. Brooks, *God's Ambassadors: A History of the Christian Clergy in America.* Grand Rapids, Mich.: William B. Eerdmans Publishing Company, 2007.

The Human Cost of Communism in China. Washington: U.S. Government Printing Office, 1971.

Hunt, Michael H. "Beijing and the Korean Crisis, June 1950–June 1951." *Political Science Quarterly* 107, no. 3 (1992): 453–78.

———. *Lyndon Johnson's War: America's Cold War Crusade in Vietnam, 1945–1968.* New York: Hill and Wang, 1996.

Immerman, Richard. "Psychology." In *Explaining the History of American Foreign Relations*. 2nd ed., edited by Michael J. Hogan and Thomas G. Paterson. Cambridge: Cambridge University Press, 2004.

Inboden, William. *Religion and American Foreign Policy, 1945–1960*. Cambridge: Cambridge University Press, 2008.

Isserman, Maurice, and Michael Kazin. *America Divided: The Civil War of the 1960s*. New York: Oxford University Press, 2000.

Jacobs, Seth. *America's Miracle Man in Vietnam: Ngo Dinh Diem, Religion, Race, and U.S. Intervention in Southeast Asia*. Durham, N.C.: Duke University Press, 2004.

Jeffreys-Jones, Rhodri. *Changing Differences: Women and the Shaping of American Foreign Policy, 1917–1994*. New Brunswick, N.J.: Rutgers University Press, 1997.

Jenkins, Philip. *The Next Christendom: The Coming of Global Christianity*. Oxford: Oxford University Press, 2002.

Johnson, Robert David. *Congress and the Cold War*. Cambridge: Cambridge University Press, 2006.

Kaiser, David. *American Tragedy: Kennedy, Johnson, and the Origins of the Vietnam War*. Cambridge, Mass.: Harvard University Press, 2000.

Kaner, Norman. "I. F. Stone and the Korean War." In *Cold War Critics: Alternatives to American Foreign Policy in the Truman Years*, edited by Thomas G. Paterson. Chicago: Quadrangle Books, 1971.

Karnow, Stanley. *Vietnam: A History*. New York: Penguin Books, 1984.

Kennan, George F. *Memoirs 1925–1950*. Boston: Little, Brown and Company, 1967.

Kimball, Jeffrey. *Nixon's Vietnam War*. Lawrence: University Press of Kansas, 1998.

Klehr, Harvey, John Earl Haynes, and Kyrill M. Anderson. *The Soviet World of American Communism*. New Haven, Conn.: Yale University Press, 1998.

Kolko, Gabriel. *Anatomy of a War: Vietnam, the United States, and the Modern Historical Experience*. New York: Pantheon Books, 1985.

———. *The Roots of American Foreign Policy*. Boston: Beacon Press, 1969.

Kovel, Joel. *Red Hunting in the Promised Land: Anticommunism and the Making of America*. London: Cassell, 1997.

LaFeber, Walter. *America, Russia, and the Cold War, 1945–1971*. 2nd ed. New York: John Wiley and Sons, 1972.

———. *America, Russia, and the Cold War, 1945–1996*, 8th ed. New York: McGraw Hill, 1997.

———. *America, Russia, and the Cold War, 1945–2002*, updated 9th ed. New York: McGraw-Hill 2002.

Lait, Jack, and Lee Mortimer. *U.S.A. Confidential*. New York: Crown Publishers, 1952.

Lakoff, George, and Mark Johnson. *Metaphors We Live By*. Chicago: The University of Chicago Press, 1980.

Landers, James. *The Weekly War: Newsmagazines and Vietnam*. Columbia: University of Missouri Press, 2004.

Leffler, Melvyn P. "The Cold War: What Do 'We Now Know'?" *The American Historical Review* 104, no. 2 (April 1999): 501–24.

———. "National Security." In *Explaining the History of American Foreign Relations*, 2nd ed., edited by Michael J. Hogan and Thomas G. Paterson. Cambridge: Cambridge University Press, 2004.

———. *A Preponderance of Power: National Security, the Truman Administration, and the Cold War*. Stanford: Stanford University Press, 1992.

———. *The Specter of Communism: The United States and the Origins of the Cold War, 1917–1953*. New York: Hill and Wang, 1994.

Levering, Ralph B. *The Public and American Foreign Policy, 1918–1978*. New York: William Morrow and Company, 1978.

Levine, Robert A. "Deterrence and the ABM." *World Policy Journal* 18, no. 3 (Fall 2001): 23–31.

Levy, David W. *The Debate Over Vietnam*. 2nd ed. Baltimore: Johns Hopkins University Press, 1995.

Logevall, Frederik. "Bernath Lecture: A Critique of Containment." *Diplomatic History* 28, no. 4 (September 2004): 473–99.

———. *Choosing War: The Lost Chance for Peace and the Escalation of War in Vietnam*. Berkeley: University of California Press, 1999.

———. "A Delicate Balance: John Sherman Cooper and the Republican Opposition to the Vietnam War." In *Vietnam and the American Political Tradition: The Politics of Dissent*, edited by Randall B. Woods. Cambridge: Cambridge University Press, 2003.

Lorence, James J. *Screening America: United States Through Film Since 1900*. New York: Pearson, 2006.

Lunch, William L., and Peter W. Sperlich. "American Public Opinion and the War in Vietnam." *The Western Political Quarterly* 32, no. 1 (March 1979): 21–44.

Mann, Robert. *A Grand Delusion: America's Descent into Vietnam*. New York: Basic Books, 2001.

Marks, Frederick. "Religiosity and Success in American Foreign Policy." *The SHAFR Newsletter* 30, no. 3 (September 1999): 9–22.

Martin, William. *A Prophet With Honor: The Billy Graham Story*. New York: William Morrow and Company, 1991.

May, Elaine Tyler. *Homeward Bound: American Families in the Cold War Era*, 2nd ed. New York: Basic Books, 2008.

McAuliffe, Mary S. "Liberals and the Communist Control Act of 1954." *The Journal of American History* 63, no. 2 (1976): 351–67.

McEnaney, Laura. *Civil Defense Begins at Home: Militarization Meets Everyday Life in the Fifties*. Princeton, N.J.: Princeton University Press, 2000.

McFarland, Linda. *Cold War Strategist: Stuart Symington and the Search for National Security*. Westport, Conn.: Praeger, 2001.

McMahon, Robert J. "SHAFR Presidential Address: Contested Memory: The Vietnam War and American Society, 1975–2001." *Diplomatic History* 26, no. 2 (Spring 2002): 159–84.

McNamara, Robert S. *In Retrospect: The Tragedy and Lessons of Vietnam*. New York: Vintage Books, 1996.

Meyerowitz, Joanne. "Beyond the Feminine Mystique: A Reassessment of Postwar Mass Culture, 1946–1958." *The Journal of American History* 79, no. 4 (March 1993): 1455–82.

Micklethwait, John, and Adrian Wooldridge. *The Right Nation: Conservative Power in America*. New York: Penguin Press, 2004.

Miller, Glenn T. *Piety and Profession: American Protestant Theological Education, 1870–1970*. Grand Rapids, Mich.: William B. Eerdmans Publishing Company, 2007.

Miller, Nathan. "The Making of a Majority: The Senate and the ABM." *The Washington Monthly* 1, no. 9 (October 1969): 60–72.

Millett, Allan R. "Introduction to the Korean War." *The Journal of Military History* 65, no. 4 (October 2001): 921–36.

Moen, Matthew C., Kenneth T. Palmer, and Richard J. Powell. *Changing Members: The Maine Legislature in the Era of Term Limits*. Lanham, Md.: Lexington Books, 2005.

Morgan, Patrick M. *Deterrence Now*. Cambridge: Cambridge University Press, 2003.

Morgan, Ted. *Reds: McCarthyism in Twentieth-Century America*. New York: Random House, 2003.

Morgenthau, Hans J. *A New Foreign Policy for the United States*. New York: Frederick A. Praeger, Publishers, 1969.

Moyar, Mark. *Triumph Forsaken: The Vietnam War, 1954–1965*. Cambridge: Cambridge University Press, 2006.

Myers, Robert. "Anti-Communist Mob Action: A Case Study." In *Readings in Collective Behavior*. 2nd ed., edited by Robert R. Evans. Chicago: Rand McNally, 1975.

Nafziger, Ralph O., Warren C. Engstrom, and Malcolm S. Maclean, Jr. *The Public Opinion Quarterly* 15, no. 1 (Spring 1951): 105–14.

Nash, George H. *The Conservative Intellectual Movement in America Since 1945*. New York: Basic Books, Inc., 1979.

Nelson, Deborah. *The War Behind Me: Vietnam Veterans Confront the Truth about U.S. War Crimes*. New York: Basic Books, 2008.

Never Underestimate. . . . The Life and Career of Margaret Chase Smith Through the Eyes of the Political Cartoonist. Skowhegan, Maine: Northwood University Margaret Chase Smith Library, 1993.

Nixon, Richard. *The Memoirs of Richard Nixon*. New York: Grosset & Dunlap, 1978.

———. *No More Vietnams*. New York: Arbor House, 1985.

Noble, John. *I Found God in Soviet Russia*. Grand Rapids, Mich.: Zondervan, 1971.

Northcutt, Susan Stoudinger. "Woman and the Bomb: Domestication of the Atomic Bomb in the United States." *International Social Science Review* 74, issue 3/4 (1999): 129–39.

Nutt, Rik. "For Truth and Liberty: Presbyterians and McCarthyism." *Journal of Presbyterian History* 78, no. 1 (Spring 2000): 51–66.

Olsen, James C. *Stuart Symington: A Life*. Columbia: University of Missouri Press, 2003.

Oppenheimer, Mark. *Knocking on Heaven's Door: American Religion in the Age of Counterculture*. New Haven, Conn.: Yale University Press, 2003.

Oshinky, David. *A Conspiracy So Immense: The World of Joe McCarthy*. New York: The Free Press, 1983.

Paterson, Thomas G. "Introduction: American Critics of the Cold War and Their Alternative." In *Cold War Critics: Alternatives to American Foreign Policy in the Truman Years*, edited by Thomas G. Paterson. Chicago: Quadrangle Books, 1971.

———. "Presidential Foreign Policy, Public Opinion, and Congress: The Truman Years." *Diplomatic History* 3, issue 1 (January 1979): 1–18.

Perlstein, Rick. *Before the Storm: Barry Goldwater and the Unmaking of the American Consensus*. New York: Hill and Wang, 2001.

Pierpaoli, Paul G., Jr. *Truman and Korea: The Political Culture of the Early Cold War* Columbia: University of Missouri Press, 1999.

Potholm, Christian P. *This Splendid Game: Maine Campaign's and Elections, 1940–2002*. Lanham, Md.: Lexington Books, 2003.

Powaski, Ronald. *Return to Armageddon: The United States and the Nuclear Arms Race, 1981–1999*. New York: Oxford University Press, 2000.

Powers, Richard Gid. *Not Without Honor: The History of American Anticommunism*. New York: The Free Press, 1995.

Preble, Christopher A. "'Who Ever Believed in the 'Missile Gap'?': John F. Kennedy and the Politics of National Security." *Presidential Studies Quarterly* 33, no. 4 (December 2003): 801–26.

Prendergast, William B. "State Legislatures and Communism: The Current Scene." *American Political Science Review* XLIV, no. 3 (September 1950): 556–74.

Preston, Andrew. "Bridging the Gap between the Sacred and the Secular in the History of American Foreign Relations." *Diplomatic History* 30, no. 5 (November 2006): 783–812.

Radosh, Ronald, and Joyce Milton. *The Rosenberg File: A Search for the Truth*. 2nd ed.. New Haven, Conn.: Yale University Press, 1997.

Ramsey, Paul. *The Just War: Force and Political Responsibility*. Lanham, Md.: Rowman & Littlefield Publishers, Inc., 2002.

Reeves, Thomas C. *The Life and Times of Joe McCarthy*. New York: Stein and Day, 1982.

Reinhard, David W. *The Republican Right since 1945*. Lexington: University Press of Kentucky, 1983.

Ribuffo, Leo P. "Moral Judgments and the Cold War: Reflections on Reinhold Niebuhr, William Appleman Williams, and John Lewis Gaddis." In *Cold War Triumphalism: The Misuse of History After the Fall of Communism*, edited by Ellen Schrecker (New York: The New Press, 2004)

———. "Why Is There So Much Conservatism in the United States and Why Do So Few Historians Know Anything about it?" *The American Historical Review* 99, no. 2 (April 1994), 438–49.

Riesman, David. *The Lonely Crowd*. Garden City, N.Y.: Doubleday & Company, Inc., 1953.

Riley, John W., Jr., Wilbur Schramm, and Frederick W. Williams. "Flight from Communism: A Report on Korean Refugees." *The Public Opinion Quarterly* 15, no. 2 (Summer 1951): 274–86.

Rose, Lisle A. *The Cold War Comes to Main Street: America in 1950.* Lawrence: University Press of Kansas, 1999.

Rotter, Andrew J. "Chronicle of a War Foretold: The United States and Vietnam, 1945–1954." In *The First Vietnam War: Colonial Conflict and Cold War Crisis,* edited by Mark Atwood Lawrence and Fredrik Logevall. Cambridge, Mass.: Harvard University Press, 2007.

Rovere, Richard H. *Senator Joe McCarthy.* New York: Harper Torchbooks, 1959.

Russo, David J. *American Towns: An Interpretive History.* Chicago: Ivan R. Dee, 2001.

Safire, William. *Before the Fall: An Inside View of the Pre-Watergate White House.* New York: Da Capo Press, 1975.

Sandler, Stanley, ed., *The Korean War: An Encyclopedia.* New York: Garland Publishing, Inc., 1995.

———. *The Korean War: No Victors, No Vanquished.* Lexington: University Press of Kentucky, 1999.

Schlesinger, Arthur M., Jr. *The Cycles of American History.* Boston: Houghton Mifflin, 1986.

———. *Robert Kennedy and His Times.* Boston: Houghton Mifflin Company, 1978.

———. *The Vital Center: The Politics of Freedom.* Boston: Houghton Mifflin Company, 1962.

Schmidt, Patricia L.. *Margaret Chase Smith: Beyond Convention.* Orono: University of Maine Press, 1996.

Schrecker, Ellen, ed. *Cold War Triumphalism: The Misuse of History After the Fall of Communism.* New York: The New Press, 2004.

———. "McCarthyism: Political Repression and the Fear of Communism." *Social Research* 71, no. 4 (Winter 2004): 1041–86.

Settje, David. "'Sinister' Communists and Vietnam Quarrels: The *Christian Century* and *Christianity Today* Respond to the Cold and Vietnam Wars." *Fides et Historia* 32, no. 1 (2000): 81–97.

Shaw, John M. *The Cambodian Campaign: The 1970 Offensive and America's Vietnam War.* Lawrence: University Press of Kansas, 2005.

Sheehan, Neil. *A Bright Shining Lie: John Paul Vann and America in Vietnam.* New York: Random House, 1988.

Sherman, Janann. *No Place for a Woman: A Life of Senator Margaret Chase Smith.* New Brunswick, N.J.: Rutgers University Press, 2000.

———. "'They Either Need These Women or They Do Not': Margaret Chase Smith and the Fight for Regular Status for Women in the Military." *The Journal of Military History* 54, no. 1 (1990): 47–78.

Sibley, Katherine A. S. *Red Spies in America: Stolen Secrets and the Dawn of the Cold War.* Lawrence: University Press of Kansas, 2004.

Small, Melvin. *Antiwarriors: The Vietnam War and the Battle for America's Hearts and Minds.* Wilmington, Del.: SR Books, 2002.

———. *Covering Dissent: The Media and the Anti–Vietnam War Movement.* New Brunswick, N.J.: Rutgers University Press, 1994.

———. *Democracy & Diplomacy: The Impact of Domestic Politics on U.S. Foreign Policy, 1789–1994.* Baltimore: The Johns Hopkins University Press, 1996.

———. *Johnson, Nixon, and the Doves*. New Brunswick, NJ: Rutgers University Press, 1988.

———. "Public Opinion." In *Explaining the History of American Foreign Relations*, edited by Michael J. Hogan and Thomas Paterson. Cambridge: Cambridge University Press 1991.

Smith, David C. *The First Century: A History of the University of Maine, 1865–1965*. Orono: The University of Maine Press, 1979.

Smith, Earl H. *Mayflower Hill: A History of Colby College*. Hanover, N.H.: University Press of New England, 2006.

Smith, Geoffrey S. "National Security and Personal Isolation: Sex, Gender, and Disease in the Cold-War United States." *The International History Review* XIV, no. 2 (May 1992): 307–37.

Smith, Margaret Chase. *Declaration of Conscience*, edited by William C. Lewis, Jr. Garden City, N.Y.: Doubleday & Company, Inc., 1972.

Sobel, Richard. *The Impact of Public Opinion on U.S. Foreign Policy Since Vietnam: Constraining the Colossus*. New York: Oxford University Press, 2001.

Spalding, Elizabeth Edwards. *The First Cold Warrior: Harry Truman, Containment, and the Remaking of Liberal Internationalism*. Lexington: The University Press of Kentucky, 2006.

Stouffer, Samuel A. *Communism, Conformity, and Civil Liberties: A Cross-section of the Nation Speaks Its Mind*. Garden City, N.Y.: Doubleday & Company, Inc., 1955.

Stuckey, Mary E. *Defining Americans: The Presidency and National Security*. Lawrence: University Press of Kansas, 2004.

Stueck, William. *The Korean War: An International History*. Princeton, N.J.: Princeton University Press, 1995.

Taylor, Mark. *The Vietnam War in History, Literature and Film*. Tuscaloosa: The University of Alabama Press, 2003.

Tucker, Spencer C., ed. *Encyclopedia of the Vietnam War: A Political, Social, and Military History*. Oxford: Oxford University Press, 1998.

Ungar, Sheldon. "Moral Panics, the Military-Industrial Complex, and the Arms Race." *The Sociological Quarterly* 31, no. 2 (Summer 1990): 165–86.

Vinz, Warren L. "Protestant Fundamentalism and McCarthy." *Continuum* 6, no. 3 (Autumn 1968): 314–25.

———. *Pulpit Politics: Faces of American Protestant Nationalism in the Twentieth Century*. Albany: State University of New York Press, 1997.

Wald, Kenneth D. "The Religious Dimension of American Anti-Communism." *Journal of Church and State* 36, no. 3 (1994): 483–506.

Wallace, Patricia Ward. *Politics of Conscience: A Biography of Margaret Chase Smith*. Westport, Conn.: Praeger Publishers, 1995.

Warford, Pamela Neal, ed. *Margaret Chase Smith: In Her Own Words*. Skowhegan, Maine: Northwood University, 2001.

Weathersby, Kathryn. "The Soviet Role in the Korean War." In *The Korean War in World History*, edited by William Stueck. Lexington: The University Press of Kentucky, 2004.

Weintraub, Stanley. *MacArthur's War: Korea and the Undoing of an American Hero.* New York: The Free Press, 2000.

Wells, Tom. *The War Within: America's Battle over Vietnam.* Berkeley: University of California Press, 1994.

White, G. Edward. *Alger Hiss's Looking-Glass Wars: The Covert Life of a Soviet Spy.* Oxford: Oxford University Press, 2004.

Whitfield, Stephen J. *The Culture of the Cold War.* 2nd ed. Baltimore: The Johns Hopkins University Press, 1996.

Whyte, William W. *The Organization Man.* Garden City, N.Y.: Doubleday & Company, Inc., 1956.

Wills, Garry. *John Wayne's America: The Politics of Celebrity.* New York: Simon & Schuster, 1997.

Witze, Claude. "The ABM Showdown: Rationality Wins by a Single Vote." *Air Force/ Space Digest* (September 1969): 46–50.

Woods, Randall Bennett. *Fulbright: A Biography.* Cambridge: Cambridge University Press, 1995.

———, ed. *Vietnam and the American Political Tradition: The Politics of Dissent.* Cambridge: Cambridge University Press, 2003.

Wyatt, Clarence R. *Paper Soldiers: The American Press and the Vietnam War.* New York: W.W. Norton & Company, 1993.

Zarlengo, Kristina. "Civilian Threat, the Suburban Citadel, and Atomic Age American Women." *Journal of Women in Culture and Society* 24, no. 4 (1999): 925–58.

Index

About the Author

Eric R. Crouse is associate professor of history at Tyndale University College, Toronto, where he teaches modern American history. His areas of research are: the Cold War, U.S.-Israel relations, and fundamentalism. He is the author of *Revival in the City: The Impact of American Evangelists in Canada, 1884–1914* (McGill-Queen's University Press 2005) and *Dear Senator Smith: Small-town Maine Writes to Senator Margaret Chase Smith about the Vietnam War, 1967–1971* (Lexington Books, 2008).

Made in the USA
Middletown, DE
11 December 2021

55205678R00123